C0-CDY-494

The eyes of the world are turning today to the once forgotten continent of Africa —a continent in which the South African black–white racial problem is assuming a position of increasing interest. For the Union of South Africa, and indeed, for the whole African continent, it is a problem of immense importance. A problem in which opinions abound but in which facts are few. Relatively little is known about the one and a half million urbanised Africans who form South Africa's black middle class. Yet these people—the more educated, sophisticated and vociferous element, are the crux of the South African racial problem.

This is a study of these people—their make-up personality, their motivations, their frustrations, their ambitions, and their inherent limitations. Written with scientific accuracy, not only into the problems of the urban African himself, but also into the social, economic and political realities of the environment in which he lives, it gives an unbiased account of the black townsman of South Africa. The urban African of South Africa is one of the most industrialised and socially advanced members of the African community south of the Sahara.

E AUTHOR

Ridder, studied at Rand uth Africa, where in 1957 s Ph.D. He is at present earch on African leadertive training methods and licable to present needs in

THE PERSONALITY OF
THE URBAN AFRICAN
IN SOUTH AFRICA

INTERNATIONAL LIBRARY OF SOCIOLOGY AND SOCIAL RECONSTRUCTION

Founded by Karl Mannheim
Editor: W. J. H. Sprott

A Catalogue of the books available in the INTERNATIONAL LIBRARY OF SOCIOLOGY AND SOCIAL RECONSTRUCTION and new books in preparation for the Library will be found at the end of this volume.

THE PERSONALITY OF THE URBAN AFRICAN IN SOUTH AFRICA

A Thematic Apperception
Test Study

by

J. C. DE RIDDER

M-03414

LONDON
ROUTLEDGE & KEGAN PAUL

First published 1961
by Routledge & Kegan Paul Limited
Broadway House, 68–74 Carter Lane
London, E.C.4

Printed in Great Britain by
Butler & Tanner Limited
Frome and London

© J. C. de Ridder 1961

No part of this book may be reproduced
in any form without permission from
the publisher, except for the quotation
of brief passages in criticism

To My Parents
D. D. de R. and J. de R.

CONTENTS

'You can find us in the mealie fields and in the mines; you can find us in the shebeens quaffing "Macbeth" brews to the jazz and jive of the cities, or outside the grass huts of our fathers, telling tales with the old women. You can see us gaffing each other or breaking suddenly into song and dance; into swear-words, fighting and tears. We are here in the robes of our grand-fathers and the tight-trousered dress of the big towns. All this is us.'

From Daniel Canadoce Thembas's preface to *Darkness and Light—An Anthology of African Writing* by Peggy Rutherford.

PREFACE

THE South African racial problem has assumed a position of increasing international interest during recent years. The discussion of the social, economic and political aspects of African life in the Union has become a hardy annual in the debating halls of the United Nations. The world press is giving more and more prominence to the 'African problem'; politicians, professional and otherwise, South African and foreign, spend a great deal of their time expounding on this topic. It has become an 'election platform' for the major political parties in South Africa, it has motivated the boycott abroad of Union produce, it has formed an ideal rallying-point for members of the Afro-Asian block at UNO.

Unfortunately, however, as so often happens with such social problems, their discussion tends to generate more heat than light. Opinions abound, facts are few. This text, which presents the results of some six years' research into the urban African personality as it has evolved in the major industrial area of the Union of South Africa, is an attempt to bridge this gap between opinions and facts.

Research of this nature is naturally a social undertaking during the course of which one becomes indebted to many persons. I wish to express my gratitude to the management of PUTCO OPERATING AND TECHNICAL SERVICES for the opportunity and the time allowed me to complete this text, and to the SHELL COMPANY OF SOUTH AFRICA for their financial assistance in the form of a research grant, a portion of which has been used in the compilation and presentation of this study.

I am especially indebted to Lyn Shaw, Manager of the Aptitude Test Centre, who read the complete manuscript of this work, for her suggestions, her help and advice. My thanks also to my colleagues, Shirley Cochrane and Don Strauss, who assisted in the processing of the data.

I wish to acknowledge the help received from Raymond Mtembu and John Masilela, who in addition to helping me with my spelling of African words were in charge of the filing systems of test protocols and assessments.

I am indebted furthermore to Mr. Paul Irwin, Editor-in-Chief of

ix

Preface

The World, for permission to reproduce copies of this newspaper in this study; to Mr. H. Schrader, City Engineer of Johannesburg, who supplied me with detailed maps of the South-Western African townships: to Mr. D. Klapka, Manager of the Welfare Branch of the Johannesburg Non-European Affairs Department, and to Mr. Frans Cronje, Administrative Officer of the Bantu Affairs Department, in Johannesburg, both of whom were always willing to discuss with me the many problems which arose during the course of this work.

My thanks go also to the great many unnamed Africans who have assisted me with their 'contacts', their information and their advice.

My thanks finally to Mrs. B. Godfrey, who typed the successive versions and revisions of the original draft, and to Mrs. Hazel G. Simms, who prepared and collated the final manuscript.

J. C. DE RIDDER

Aptitude Test Centre,
Putco Operating and Technical Services Limited,
Johannesburg.
December, 1960.

INTRODUCTION

THE City of Johannesburg, situated almost in the centre of the eighty-mile-long curve of the Witwatersrand goldbearing 'reef', is the focal point of the greatest gold-mining industry on earth. Radiating outwards from the central city is a vast urban complex—a kaleidoscopic variety of élite 'garden' suburbs, European sub-economic housing schemes, model African townships, and squalid, shanty-town slums. Within this economic diversity live a heterogeneous community of Whites, Coloureds, Africans and Asians —a conglomeration of races, differing in colour, creed, cultural traditions, economic wealth and status, and standards of civilized advance.

The Africans form what is the largest single non-White unit within this diversified community. A group drawn basically from the five ethnological divisions of the Bantu people, they live in and about the main city in vast, sprawling locations and townships. They constitute a group known collectively as 'urban Africans'—although as individuals they differ greatly amongst themselves in educational standards, intelligence, and adaptability, tribalism and urbanization.

Much has been written about urban social problems, yet few detailed surveys exist on the urban African as an individual, and virtually no systematic research has been undertaken into the communal personality components, characteristic of the urban Africans as a group.

It has been truly said by Ruth Benedict that 'the white man knows little of any ways of life but his own', a statement which is applicable not only to the Western world but to the majority of White South Africans who, while working in such close contact with the urban Africans as they do, are still, nevertheless, remarkably ignorant of the ways of life of these people, and of the general patterns of personality emerging from urban African society.

The urban Africans are undoubtedly the most vocal of the African populations, and they are increasingly providing the leadership for their people. A study of the general personality components characteristic of one of the largest and oldest established urban African communities in the African continent, the Bantu of the Johannesburg urban areas, is therefore long overdue.

The present text will deal with the study of such personality components. While variations and exceptions which disprove most rules are present in all human societies, we are here interested in communal personality traits characteristic of the group, rather than in the individual variations within the group.

Our subject is the personality of the urban African. However, because of the intimate relationship between culture and personality, we have sought firstly to portray the essentials of the culture of the urban African—or rather the essentials of the cultures of the urban African—that is, his tribal past and his urban present. As Carothers has expressed it: 'No cultures are quite static; they could not be so and survive. But, unlike modern Western cultures, all preliterate cultures are relatively static, and their survival depends on gradualness of change.'

The 'raw' African one meets is, nine times out of ten, not really in his aboriginal state, but is an 'African in transition'. But here the transition is a slow one.

In the urban areas this transition is taking place far more rapidly and, as a result, behavioural forms foreign to the original culture are already apparent. Such phenomena are characteristic of most sudden social changes. Faris, in discussing behavioural disorders in the industrial cities of America, says:

> Such movements break up the social systems that control and integrate the behaviour of persons, so that new, unconventional and abnormal types of behaviour appear. These abnormalities are not essentially aspects of city life or civilized society, but rather of the populations which are changing from one system to another.

In order to fully appreciate the significance of such 'unconventional' behavioural patterns, it is necessary to firstly observe the social systems which such people in transition are straddling. The social systems which the African in the city is straddling are the systems of tribal society and urban society.

The term 'urban African', when used to indicate detribalization, is consequently, at this stage of African development, a little premature. It should be considered as denoting the direction of the social change taking place, rather than as presupposing that the social change has already occurred. The distance any individual African has travelled in the 'urban direction' will depend upon the individual factors within his personality and not simply on his length of stay in the urban areas. As populations are made up of individuals, it is not possible to demarcate with any degree of certainty the stage at which a tribal people become an urban people.

The criteria of differentiation used in this study, while purely arbitrary, are as definite as possible under the circumstances.

Introduction

For the purposes of this study, which deals exclusively with males, urban Africans are considered as a people who are members of any Bantu group, or who are the offspring of the union of members of any two different Bantu groups, who are resident in the urban areas of Johannesburg, who have adopted European dress, who are literate, and can read and write and speak English or Afrikaans, who are over eighteen years old, and who have the permission of the local authority to seek work in the urban areas of Johannesburg.

The sample population under review consists of some 2,500 urban Africans. It includes men from every township and location with the Johannesburg urban complex: men from Alexandra Township, from Western Native Township, from Eastern Native Township and from the South-Western Bantu Areas.

The personality conclusions represent the results of six years of study, of designing, modifying and validating an African personality test, of analysing results and comparing, recording, indexing, reviewing and filing personality data. The personality test used is a modification for urban Africans of the Thematic Apperception Test originally devised by Morgan and Murray of the Harvard Psychological Clinic. The Thematic Apperception Test or T.A.T. and its modifications are technically classified under the broad heading of projective tests. These are tests which require the individual to respond to particular stimuli, such as, in this case, a series of pictures showing various social situations to which stories are told, thereby creating a situation into which the individual can project his feelings, needs, wishes, and desires. These response patterns are then analysed to assess the personality of the storyteller.

From the point of view of the T.A.T., perception is considered a key site for the study of personality. Translated into psychoanalytic terminology, the act of perceiving brings the personality (the ego) in touch with the outer world (reality); the reaction of the personality to the world by its response to a given perception will be in terms of its mode of meeting the world (its ego-controls). The organism continually strives to maintain a balance between its inner needs (id impulses) and the demands of reality. In this task the ego puts perception to use—the personal style of the ego (its perceptual attitude) being determined by the demands of the id impulses on the one hand and the demands of reality on the other. The perceptual stimulus is adapted by the ego in terms of its particular ego-control or defence mechanism.

Physiologically visual perception depends upon light and upon its receptor, the eye. The visual processes enable us to perceive form, colour, brightness and motion. It has been estimated that 80 per cent of our knowledge comes to us by way of the eye.

Introduction

The light-sensitive part of the eye is generally conceded to be an extension of the brain, and its neural network is considered almost as complex in structure as that of the brain itself. Before the visual impression is attained, light energy must set off a chain of chemical, neural and mental processes. The impressions transmitted through the eyes are carried to the visual centres of the brain for integration, evaluation, and interpretation. In this integrative, evaluative and interpretative process the light energy of the reality perception is adapted and modified by the ego-controls of the personality. In other words, because the organism is always to some extent prepared by its ego-controls and is never randomly set, it not only perceives but, more important, it apperceives.

Apperception, from the Latin 'ad' meaning 'plus' and 'percipere' meaning 'to perceive', is defined as: 'The process by which new experience is assimilated to and transformed by the residuum of past experience of any individual to form a new whole. The residuum of past experience is called the apperceptive mass' (C. P. Herbart).

Apperception is consequently an organism's dynamically meaningful interpretation of a perception. It follows, therefore, that apperceptive distortions of perceptual impressions are indicative of the underlying nature of the ego-control mechanisms, in other words, of the personality.

The African T.A.T. is consequently a personality test, a test that was originally designed to meet an immediate practical need—the need to overcome problems in connection with the selection of potential African bus-drivers for a transport company.

The initial selection procedures consisted of a series of aptitude and intelligence tests and a number of psychomotor tests; tests which measure the candidate's ability to co-ordinate his hand movements, his speed of reaction and his ability to distribute his attention.

It was found that, while drivers selected on such tests all proved to be very good trainees compared with their non-tested predecessors (the training pass-rate on the Johannesburg municipal driving test rose immediately with the institution of aptitude tests from 40 per cent to 70 per cent and later to 90 per cent, where it has since remained), the accident record of this group, once they went on to the roads, was worse than their less-intelligent predecessors.

Subsequent research into this problem revealed the importance of personality and temperament functions in driving, and indicated the need for some sort of personality assessment device. The African T.A.T. was designed to fill this need.

Before employing the test for the assessment of new intake, however, a thorough validation study was undertaken on the new African T.A.T. The test was applied to 163 of the company's existing drivers, and the test material was then subjected to a blind analysis. Only after predictions had been made, purely on the basis of the test, was any attempt made to compare prediction with fact; that is, to compare what sort of an employee and accident risk the test said each man would be with what his actual record showed him to be.

The factors against which a test is measured are known statistically as criteria. In order to establish the employee criterion, the disciplinary record of each of the 163 was analysed and rated and a disciplinary criterion of each man's employee liability was made.

For the establishment of the accident criterion the services of a consulting statistician were utilized. Dr. H. S. Sichel, of the Operational Research Bureau, undertook a two-year research project which involved the analysis of the accident records of some 980 of the Company's drivers, both past and present. He established mathematically that among these drivers accident proneness definitely did exist and that each driver had an individual accident pattern and an individual level of accident liability. By using a new method based on the time intervals between each driver's accidents, he also found a way of giving a relative value to that level and a method of classifying the drivers into various grades of accident liability. This factual, stable criterion was the criterion against which the African T.A.T. was measured as a predictor of accident liability.

The validation of the T.A.T. against the disciplinary and accident criteria, though carried out when the test was still in its development stage, gave very gratifying results.

Of the men considered on the basis of the test to be satisfactory accident risks, comparison with the accident criterion showed that 98 per cent of them did in fact have satisfactory records.

Of the men considered on the basis of the test to be satisfactory disciplinary risks, 78 per cent had satisfactory disciplinary records.

And of the men who, on the basis of the test, could be considered satisfactory all round risks, 87 per cent were in fact a success on the combined disciplinary and accident criteria.

The results of the validation proved very definitely that the test had considerable potential as a predictor of accident proneness and employee behaviour. It was therefore put into operation as part of the selection procedure for all new driver intake.

The T.A.T. has subsequently been used for selection in other job grades within the Company, as well as being used in the consultative selection services undertaken by the Aptitude Test Centre for the selection of various grades of African staff for other organizations.

The following T.A.T. study represents the results of six years of work undertaken at the Putco Operating and Technical Services'

Introduction

Aptitude Test Centre by a team of six African and European re-
searchers. It represents the results of the co-operation of some 2,500
unnamed urban African subjects who underwent the test. It represents the results of the help and assistance of innumerable individual
African members of the Putco staff—men who acted as our 'contacts
with the people', men who knew and lived in the urban locations
and townships, men who brought in their friends and associates for
discussions at the Test Centre, men who induced the 'tsotsis' or
young African criminals to come for interview, men who introduced
us to the township herbalists, and witchdoctors, men who were always ready to discuss, to criticize, to suggest new lines of approach
and to attempt to answer the hundred-and-one questions and problems which cropped up during the course of this study.

The major portion of this text will be devoted to the analysis of
various aspects of the urban African personality as they appear in
the test. Such personality functions will be illustrated by extracts
from the subjects' actual test responses or stories. The association
between the personality characteristics isolated and the cultural influences to which the urban African is subjected will also be discussed and analysed in some detail. Separate chapters will furthermore be devoted to the personality of the African nationalist and a
detailed study will be presented on the personality analysis of a
known African nationalist. A number of complete case studies will
be included to show both the type of response and the clarity with
which recurrent themes appear in the various stories of urban subjects.

The year 1960 is generally considered as 'Africa's year'. A review
of the major personality components emerging from a study of one
of the most highly educated and industralized African populations
in the continent of Africa—the African of the Johannesburg urban
areas—is both timely and pertinent.

I

PERSONALITY STUDY

THERE are a number of ways to study man psychologically. Yet, to appreciate him most fully he must be considered as an individual. The outstanding feature of man is his individuality. It is the supreme characteristic of human nature.

The term individuality, as expressed in this context, signifies more than the mere separateness and uniqueness of each human being. Psychologically the term individuality embraces that complex organization within each individual, comprising his distinctive modes of thought and expression, his unique attitudes, traits and interests, and his own peculiar philosophy of life. It is this 'total manifold psycho-physical individuality, commonly referred to as personality, that engages the attention of the psychologist' (Allport, G. W.).

The approaches to the study of personality are numerous and varied. Over the years personality predictions have been made in terms as diverse as the influence of totem animals, the creases on the palms of individual hands and the position of the stars on the night of one's birth. It is obvious, from the diversity of approaches to the problem, that the term personality has many meanings. Scarcely any word is more versatile and consequently, unless explained, more vague and useless for scientific discussion. Explanation is, however, more meaningful and better appreciated when embodied in a theory. The presentation of any one theory, however, in no way implies the rejection of all other theories within the particular field. As Kluckhohn and Mowrer have pointed out, the history of science permits two inductions:

(a) that it is useful to behave experimentally with respect to conceptual schemes without necessarily claiming 'truth' for one to the exclusion of all others; and

(b) that a conceptual scheme may well be appropriate for analysing one group of problems, but most inappropriate for treating the same data in the light of a different group of equally legitimate questions.

1

The presentation of such a conceptual scheme can most conveniently be approached from two angles:

(*a*) the presentation of the determinants and components of the problem; and

(*b*) the presentation of a body of theory within which to study the problem.

Determinants and Components of Personality

Clark Hull has stated: 'In the beginning there is (*a*) the organism and (*b*) the environment'—an over-simplification which, although intrinsically correct, is nevertheless misleading unless amplified and explained. Accepted on its face value it is immediately reducible to the old problem of heredity versus environment; whereas the pertinent question is: 'Which of the various genetic potentialities will be actualized as a consequence of a particular series of life events in a given physical, social and cultural environment?' (Kluckhohn and Mowrer). However, the problem is further complicated by the dynamicism inherent in each of these functions. Individual genetic potentialities vary in time; the physical environment changes within limits, societies are not static phenomena, and cultural influences fluctuate, become modified and alter. Such personality determinants are consequently not only actualizing but also dynamic in nature—a fact that must always be borne in mind when discussing them. The social order, the biological potentialities and the physical and cultural environments form 'a web of inter-weaving, shifting, and constantly changing situations and relationships within which, to be sure, all is not chaos, but nevertheless, not fixity and unchangeableness' (Kreuger and Reckless). Personality determinants are essentially dynamic entities.

Biologically, man is an animal of distinctive physical appearance. All men are bound to face certain problems by virtue of their biological make-up: they are all normally born with two hands, two feet and two eyes, they must all breathe air, eat, drink and excrete; they have sexual and other needs and they all grow, all age and all ultimately die.

Human beings must adjust these biological determinants within the framework of their particular societies. Biological factors may consequently influence personality formation directly—by endocrine balance, for example—or indirectly, in their social definition and expression.

The human infant must travel a long way before it acquires all the physical and intellectual skills, the biological modifications of expression, the social requirements and culturally determined reactions

2

expected of every full-fledged member of a human group. 'The long years of interplay between the formative influences of society and the native endowment of the growing person are, in the terminology of the social sciences, referred to as the process of socialization' (Bram). Growing-up is a long-drawn-out process in our species, a process of basic socialization and acculturation which consumes roughly one-third of a human lifetime.

Social living, as Ralph Linton puts it, 'is as characteristic of homo sapiens as his mixed dentition or opposable thumb'. The human species realized long ago that the battle for survival was better fought in organized groups rather than as separate individuals. And while this concept of organized group living is also practised by man's sub-human relatives, the difference between human society and sub-human society is enormous.

The society developed in an ant hill would, for instance, appear to closely resemble the human situation. However, whereas these social insects, the ants, have evolved into living automatons with a minimum of individuality, existing in fixed environments as standardized units, in man the evolutionary process tends towards increasing differentiation, specialization and individualization. The consequence is, that insects have developed their instincts at the expense of their learning ability, whereas man, in his individuality, has advanced to the stage of literally being able to 'think for himself'. Thus every man develops his own patterns of behaviour. These patterns of behaviour must, however, be viewed against the background of his own particular group culture. His individualism is the result of his deviations from the cultural pattern of this group.

> In this fact lies the great importance of cultural studies for personality psychology. Until the psychologist knows what the norms of behaviour imposed by a particular society are and can discount them as indicators of personality he will be unable to penetrate behind the façade of social conformity and cultural uniformity to reach the authentic individual (Linton).

A penetrating knowledge and a depth of understanding of 'the norms of behaviour imposed by a particular society' are essential prerequisites in any personological study. To appreciate the individual, the assessment of him must be made against his cultural setting.

It is culture, then, rather than social institutions, that distinguishes man from the rest of the biological world. A stress on culture rather than on society tends to emphasize the specifically human aspects and elements of man's behaviour.

> Culture is the way of living which any society develops to meet its fundamental needs for survival, perpetuation of species, and the

3

ordering of social experience. It is the accumulation of material objects, patterns of social organisation, learned modes of behaviour, knowledge, beliefs, and all the other activities which are developed in human association (Roucek and Warren).

Culture is the storehouse of ready-made solutions to problems. It is the accumulation of knowledge and tradition gathered over generations.

Culture studies involve surveys, not only of the institutions that mould man's reactions to his society but also such extra-institutional aspects as the relationship between personality and culture. Volumes have been written on the influence of cultural practices upon personality formation, indicating the manner in which the individual personality reflects the culture of the community. However, as Du Bois remarks:

> It is important to stress that a single discipline of childhood or a single traumatic experience is rarely sufficient in itself to set cultural personality types. Repeated experiences in different behavioural, value and institutional contexts alone will create personality constellations . . . of force and consistency . . .

An excellent example of such cultural personality patterning is given by Margaret Mead in her *Researches in Bali*. She says:

> The mother teases and flirts with the child until she produces either a state of hysterical delight or of violent weeping, and then, refusing to become involved herself, she turns casually to something else. By the time the Balinese child is three or four years old, it learns not to respond to this one-sided situation; it withdraws more and more into itself; and the basis is formed for the insulated type of personality which is typically Balinese and which fails to enter into close emotional relationship with anyone, relying instead upon ritual and art as a means of emotional expression.

The influence of such cultural personality patterning has an almost direct carryover into the political and economic spheres of life—a factor that is becoming increasingly apparent in Africa as a result of the cultural diversity within the rapidly emerging African states.

> Thus, in Kenya the Kikuyu were so eager to adopt European ways that, when frustrated in their desires, many resorted to the violence of Mau Mau. The Masai, Pakot, and other Nilotic peoples in the same country have followed the opposite course, remaining aloof and proudly indifferent to European influence; except for minor details, they have withstood the efforts to change their ways. Between these extremes, the Ganda of neighbouring Uganda, with a cultural background, which includes a highly organized political system, have adapted to European culture with less resistance than the Nilotics but with less enthusiasm than the Kikuyu.

These differences in reaction to European contact cannot be explained solely, as is so often implied, in terms of variations in colonial policy or of duration and intensity of contact. Equally, if not more important are the pre-established patterns of African culture. The tendency to neglect the factor of traditional modes of behaviour and systems of belief has had far reaching practical consequences where the framing of programmes for economic or political development has been involved (Herskovitz and Bascom).

Certain cultures, like the culture of the Nilotic peoples, have manifested a greater stability and resistance to external cultural influences than other African cultures. And the peoples of such Nilotic cultures have largely maintained their 'traditional cultural personalities'. Not only have they largely retained their traditional outlook, but their conservatism and pastoral outlook have influenced many Europeans living in their country. So much so that these 'personality converts' are spoken of as suffering from 'Masaiitis'.

As the name suggests, it was first manifested among the officials assigned to the Masai (a Nilotic people) who sometimes became so enamoured of Masai ways that they lost their effectiveness as administrators and had to be transferred (Schneider).

In the relationship between culture and personality, language plays an important liaison function. Dorothy Lee, who studied the people of the Trobriand Islands within this frame of reference, found that the Trobrianders who value 'static states of being, unanchored in time and space' above the 'preoccupation with self-advancement' have a language with no tenses. As Dunlop says:

In studying the structure of the language of a people, we are studying the forms and methods of their thinking. In studying their vocabulary, we are finding their types of discrimination. The description of a language as the crystallized thought of a people is far from wrong.

This crystallization of thought in language mirrors both the cultural and environmental influences which a particular people are subjected to. For example, the camel because it is ideally suited to a desert environment has become of extreme importance to Arab culture—an importance which is reflected in the Arabic language, some six thousand names being connected in some way with this beast, names which differentiate between riding camels, marriage camels, slaughter camels, and milk camels, names of breeds and of lineage. There are as many as fifty words for pregnant camels, states of pregnancy, the stage at which foetal movement is first felt, for mothers who suckle and for mothers who don't. Similarly the Eskimo words for 'snow' and 'ice'—both major features of their environment—

5

include names for: soft snow, falling snow, drifting snow, hard snow, ground snow, etc., and they have different names for salt-water ice, fresh-water ice, broken ice and cracking ice.

As cultures change, so ideals, beliefs and attitudes change, and so the languages associated with such cultural modifications and alterations change also. The African 'tsotsi' [1] of the Johannesburg urban areas—an almost completely detribalized, often illegitimate, usually teenage criminal delinquent, who neither understands nor respects the tribal customs and culture of his forefathers—has developed a language called 'Witty' or 'Wittisha' (from the English word 'wit')—a 'tsotsi' slang, which is fully understandable only to gang members. This language serves not only to identify gang members or to convey secret messages in public but it mirrors the ego-ideals of the 'tsotsi', namely, the American gangster and his way of life. As Laura Longmore has stated:

> African tsotsis live in a kind of fantasy-world of American gangster films, for the tsotsi is a cinema addict and models his life and deeds on the actions of characters portrayed on the screen . . . The terminology of tsotsism is largely derived from films.

The gang leader is known as the 'big shot' or 'the boss', their women are (amongst other terms) called 'molls' and money is referred to as 'smackers'.

Bram maintains that 'The phonetical endowment of the human infant is that of a potential polyglot. Regardless of his race or nationality, every baby spontaneously produces a rich collection of sounds.' This vocal versatility is channelized by cultural pressures through members of the particular society, according to their system of communication or language. The existence of culture signifies the existence of language. A culture is simply a configuration of learned behaviour, and language is one of the major aspects learnt in this process of acculturation.

Between man and his natural environment is always interposed a human environment, a society. In this section we have attempted to briefly indicate the comparison between the cultural content of a society and the personality content of its members. As Linton has pointed out 'it is the individual's interaction with these, which is responsible for the formation of most of his behaviour patterns, even his deep-seated emotional responses'.

Considered within this frame of reference, the urban African personality is a development which has evolved as the result of the intermingling of the cultural patterns of three societies: the tribal society,

[1] 'Tsotsi'—Sesotho for 'something small', denoting the 12-inch-bottomed stovepipe trousers originally characteristic of the dress of these criminal delinquents.

Personality Study

the urban township or location society, and Western European society. To restate Linton's concept: it is the individual African's interaction with each of these cultures which is responsible for the formation of the urban African personality.

Contrary to popular belief, Western European culture, while it has modified the African's traditional tribal culture, has by no means completely submerged and shattered it. Were this the case, then urban township or location society would have evolved into being merely a black Western European culture—and this has definitely not been the case.

Before we can approach an analysis of the urban African's personality we must therefore detour via a study of his tribal past and his urban present.

The following two chapters will, therefore, be devoted to an analysis of the Tribal Environment on the one hand, and the Urban African Environment on the other.

II

THE TRIBAL ENVIRONMENT

In present-day Africa we see the results of centuries of migration, inter-marriage and conquests; and it is also evident that, except in the least accessible regions (such as parts of Ethiopia, the Kalahari waste, or the Nile swamps), the geographical features of Africa have themselves facilitated the fusion of stocks rather than their segregation. It is inevitable, therefore, that existing classifications should be based on language or culture rather than on physical characteristics (Hailey).

SELIGMAN'S African racial classification—the grouping most generally acceptable to authorities—differentiates five great African racial groups: Bantu, Negroes, Hamites, Bushmen, and Hottentots. And although various criteria are cited in his book *Races of Africa*, the main determining factor is language. A fact which Seligman readily admits when he says:

. . . the study of the races in Africa has been so largely determined by the interest in speech, and it is so much easier to acquire a working knowledge of a language than of any other part of man's cultural make-up, that names based upon linguistic criteria are constantly applied to large groups of mankind and, indeed, if intelligently used, often fit quite well.

Of these racial groups, the Bantu (which includes roughly all peoples in whose language the root -ntu, with its appropriate prefix, means 'man') number some 60 million. The Bantu constitute the predominant population of Africa south of the so-called 'Bantu-line' —an imaginary line which runs irregularly from the mouth of the Rio del Ray in western Africa to the Juba River in the East.

West Africa, from the mouth of the Senegal River to the eastern frontier of Nigeria, is inhabited by the Negro group who number about 45 million.

The languages of the next group, the Hamites, are found in north-east Africa, the main areas being Somaliland, Ethiopia and Eritrea. The Nilo-Hamites, a sub-group of the above, are made up of the 3 million inhabitants of the upper Nile basin, the pastoral tribes of northern Kenya and Uganda and the Masai of the Kenya highlands and eastern Tanganyika—who total about 1½ million people.

Seligman's two final groups, Bushmen and Hottentots, are numerically insignificant. The few remaining Bushmen are found in the Kalahari wastes, and the surviving Hottentots in South-West Africa north of the Orange River.

However, despite the diversity of communities in Africa, there are a number of common characteristics in their cultures which differentiate them from those associated with Western European civilization.

The great majority of Africa's indigenous peoples are characteristically peasants or herdsmen, producing for subsistence rather than for the market. The disparity in individual wealth is usually not marked, and the standard of wealth is not as much a mark of status as it is in Western cultures. The possession of wealth is nevertheless, in certain cultures, often associated with authority. As Hailey says:

> The possession of wealth, however, is often a source of authority, and where centralized political institutions exist and are maintained partly by the right of the Chief to levy tribute, custom prescribes that he should distribute wealth in various forms of largesse.

The kinship system is fundamentally important in traditional African systems. Kinship bonds link together those who claim common descent from an ancestor—either patrilineally or matrilineally. As a consequence of this kinship system, individual land ownership is unknown in traditional societies. Individuals work a piece of land by virtue of hereditary rights, rather than by the right of individual ownership. While marriage within such a system 'is seen as a system for securing legitimate descendants for lineage rather than for regulating sex relations, and is held to create binding obligations not only between partners but between the kin of each of them' (Phillips, *Survey of African Marriage and Family Life*), an essential requirement in traditional customary unions is the payment in terms of goods or services by the bridegroom and his kinsmen to the kinsmen of the bride. In traditional systems as far as marriage is concerned, polygamy is the social ideal.

Belief in witchcraft is almost universal. Deaths, illnesses and disasters are attributable to evil spirits rather than to natural causes. Various forms of magic are employed to protect people and placate annoyed ancestral spirits, or vanquish undesirable evil spirits. Age in traditional systems carries a special respect and prestige—the old men of the tribe are those in closest contact with the spirit world of tribal ancestors.

Ceremony and ritual are fundamental to such systems. They mark the seasons, the stages of life, and important tribal events. The

9

duties of males and females are clearly defined and differentiated, the sexes have set patterns of behaviour to which they must adhere and exclusive ceremonies which they must attend.

Such broad cultural aspects are inherent in all traditional African systems and help to differentiate them all from Western European culture. There are, however, cultural practices which are specific to certain African racial groupings—the Bushmen, for example, produced a unique form of art, a type of pictorial representation found in none of the other racial groups of indigenous African peoples. Cultural differences also exist between the various racial groupings of the indigenous races of Africa.

Our primary interest in this study is centred upon the traditional cultural practices of the Bantu group—the group from which the Johannesburg urban township or location dwellers are drawn, the group from which the urban personality has evolved.

Seligman's main ethnic groupings are by no means absolutely intra-culturally homogeneous. The Bantu group is reducible to five main tribal groups, on the basis of geographical, linguistic, historical and cultural criteria—each of these having sub-groups within itself.

We will deal firstly with the group similarities within the Bantu group as a whole, and then with the practices of the five main tribes who constitute the Bantu peoples.

COMMON BANTU CHARACTERISTICS
THE TRIBE

The most characteristic grouping amongst the Bantu is the tribe. These tribes vary in number from a few hundred members to the size of important Tswana tribes averaging between ten and twenty thousand people.

The tribe is basically composed of a body of kinsmen who traditionally trace their descent from a common ancestor, the tribal chief claiming the most direct descent. In reality, however, tribal membership is determined more by allegiance to a particular chief than by birth, tribal unity being fundamentally dependent on the common loyalty of the tribesmen to their chief. Depending on a chief's popularity, so the tribe may become increased or decreased in size.

THE HOUSEHOLD

Within the tribe, the outstanding social unit is the household, a group consisting typically of a man with his wife or wives and dependent children, together with any other relatives or unrelated dependants who may be attached to him, but composed frequently also of other combinations of close relatives (Hoernle).

The polygamous household, in turn, is comprised of individual family units of the mother and her children—a group apart living in their own home. These wives vary in social status and importance, and so do their children. As van Warmelo points out, 'Bantu social structure knows no equals . . . The first-born of the same parents is always the superior of those born after him.'

As groups of individual families comprise a household—which may vary from one husband and one wife to one husband and a number of wives and families—so do groups of households comprise a kraal or settlement. Such kraals are scattered over tribal territory a small distance apart from one another.

THE SUB-DISTRICT AND DISTRICT

A grouping of kraals forms a social unit definable as a sub-district, under the administrative and judicial direction of a headman. A number of sub-districts grouped together fall into a district, which falls under the jurisdiction of the tribal chief.

THE KIN

1. Relatives by Blood

Kinship bonds play a part of paramount importance in the lives of the people. None of the tribes has any great degree of economic division of labour. Each household is to a very great extent a replica of every other, so that economic interdependence is not one of the main principles of linking different households together. Instead, kinship bonds, bonds of common descent, ramify through the country and link together those, wherever they may be, who claim common descent from an ancestor, be that on the paternal or maternal side (Hoernle).

The kinship group plays a most important formative rôle in the development of the behaviour patterns of the children of the group— the chief control over the children belongs by custom and in law to the father and his kin. As head of the family, the father has complete authority over all of his children for as long as they remain in his household, and even to a lesser extent after they have left. As head of the household he controls the economic duties and legal affiliations of those under his protection, he has direct control over land and animals, he is the disciplining force over his household, he is responsible for all actions of members of his household, he is the intermediary between them and the ancestral spirits. His children, and even his wives, treat him with deference and respect amounting almost to awe.

On the other hand, the deepest emotional bonds of affection and

11

mutual understanding grow up between the mother and her children. The individual family unit, within the household, is bound together by the love of the mother for her children.

Within the immediate family, as within the families comprising the household group, a strict hierarchical structure prevails. Among children within a family, age and sex are the basic differentiating factors. Boys usually take precedence over girls, older boys over their juniors and older girls over their younger sisters. The wives also have their order of precedence within the broader household.

Outside the immediate family group or even the household, the principles of kinship determine the children's life to a very great extent. So the father's brothers are grouped under a kinship in which they are 'fathers' to their brothers' children and the children learn to behave towards them as they do towards their real father.

Another important kinship relationship exists between the children and their father's sister, and between the children and their mother's brother. Concerning these relations, Hoernle says:

> The behaviour to a father's sister is definitely controlled by her membership of the same family as the father. If he is 'father', she is 'female father', with the same background and traditions as he. She knows the peculiar ways and traditions of the paternal home far better than the mother is thought to do, so that on important occasions she may be called in to see that family ways are maintained . . .
>
> A maternal uncle similarly plays his part in the lives of his sister's children, on the basis of the behaviour controlling his relation to his sister. If she is 'mother', he is 'male mother' in most tribes, a relative of the mother's family of the same generation as she, and sharing in the whole gentle protective attitude of the mother to her children . . .

And Hoernle concludes:

> Looking out of the world from his own home, the Bantu child knows where he may seek hospitality and succour of every kind; where, also, he may of right be called upon to render assistance in case of need. The barriers of reserve shutting off human beings from one another are largely down so far as these classes of relatives are concerned, so that for economic assistance, for friendly counsel, in time of sorrow and in time of joy, these are the natural categories of people to turn to, the core of people with whom one is close-knit from birth in a web of reciprocal rights and duties.

2. Relatives by Marriage

Traditional marriage is as much a contract between two families as it is between the man and woman concerned. By marriage the behaviour of a large group of people is changed towards one another.

A whole new series of formal, custom-prescribed relationships is brought into being, relationships which determine the man's behaviour towards his mother-in-law and the woman's relation towards her father-in-law, his brothers and kinsmen. The behaviour of relatives by marriage is usually formal, restrained and strictly regulated.

The tribe, the household, the family, the kraal; the organization of sub-districts and the grouping of districts; the influence of blood relatives, and the relationships with relatives by marriage; these are the main areas determining the similarity existing within Bantu culture as a whole. Bantu life, behaviour and customs are clearly prescribed by these well-defined mores. They regulate behaviour, determine personal status and organize group relationships. They form a systematic pattern of living, a predetermined organization of social contacts, a behavioural frame of reference, for all Bantu.

Such are the main institutions of social organization within Bantu culture.

Individual development within this social framework is determined by group associations, child-rearing practices, practical education, tribal rites and requirements.

The child in a traditional culture lives through a number of 'ages', each having an important formative influence. We will now briefly sketch the main developmental stages, indicating their importance on the individual personality. In so doing we will quote extensively from an excellent article on Bantu, 'Individual Development', by Eileen Krige.

> In Bantu society, where the status of a man is measured largely by the size of his kraal and that of a woman by the number of children she has borne, the birth of a child is hailed with great joy as an event of importance to the whole village.

The Bantu baby is regarded as being particularly prone to injury by evil spirits and its birth is usually heralded by numerous magical ceremonies to ward off such malicious influences. As Junod has pointed out, the Bantu look upon babyhood as a period of ill health ended by weaning.

The Bantu child is weaned at the age of two or three years old. Pregnancy by the mother during this period is severely censured and considered to directly affect the feeding child, making it thin or paralysing it.

The child is given its birth-name, usually when it is taken out of the hut for the first time.

> After weaning, the child becomes one of a group of many mischievous toddlers to be seen about every Bantu village. It is never lonely nor does it lack playmates . . . Toddlers are looked after by their mothers and

13

elder sisters, who take great pride in teaching tham the correct way of greeting their elders, of receiving gifts, of dancing to the clapping of hands, and countless other things. When naughty they are frightened by tales of monsters who in Bantu folklore carry off disobedient children. Their greatest danger is that of falling into the open fires that burn in the huts; but for the rest they live a carefree life, with no clothes to keep clean, and few of the dangerous instruments of civilization that take their toll of child life.

At an early age the children are taught the basics of good manners and to respect age; they are taught not to speak to elders until spoken to, not to interrupt the conversation of an adult, they learn not to sit and eat in the company of their elders, and they learn not to receive anything from an elder with one hand, but to proffer both hands in a submissive, grateful attitude. They spend most of their time with those of their own age-group and they are recognized by the tribal elders as a group—a group from which collective responsibility in herding and other occupations is expected.

At the age of about six, boys and girls start the traditional education for their respective sex rôles within the tribe. The girls learn the basics of homecraft and housework, the boys start by herding goats and progress, with age, to cattle-herding.

While herding all day, the boys acquire a wealth of veldlore. They learn to know the names of all the edible birds and plants, they learn to make traps and to organise their own hunts and fights, becoming adept at killing birds on the wing by hurling knobkerries at them . . . Many of the boys' games, such as stabbing at a tuber rolled down a slope, give them an excellent training in exactness of aim, which will stand them in good stead later on when they hunt . . .

Education for the Bantu child is education by imitation and practice, conscious teaching or formal education being given only in the initiation schools. The boy learns from other older boys and by watching his father, the girl by imitation of what the older girls do, and by assisting her mother.

Traditional tribal education has certain very definite aims, aims which are very different from those inherent in the European approach to teaching.

European education is conceived largely as the handing down to the next generation of a system of knowledge, essential for overcoming the difficulties and solving the problems of adult life. In Bantu society success and welfare are not bound up with knowledge alone, and difficulties are overcome not so much by the application of science, as by the use of magic and appeal to ancestors. For the natural forces to work, for rain to fall and crops to mature, it is essential that correct ritual be observed, taboos remain unbroken, and customs be faithfully adhered

14

to. What a man knows therefore is less important than what he does, how he lives and behaves; success and welfare are closely related to morality and any change from traditional ways is looked upon with suspicion.

Individual development in Bantu society is seen as a progression from one life stage to another. Transition from one stage to the next calls for ceremonial ritual, to ask for ancestral guidance and blessing and to instruct the initiate in the duties of his next progression. Various types of initiation schools inculcate into the tribal member the demands required of him in each stage.

The Puberty Ceremonies mark the transition between childhood and adult life. These ceremonies are intended to impress the transition between childhood and adulthood on to the initiates, to teach them the tribe's secrets and to initiate them into sex practices. Boys are trained in courage and endurance; they are subjected to various hardships; they are made to suffer various forms of torture without flinching. The methods employed vary and the length of training differs amongst the various tribes. Much of the instruction is given in learning tribal songs and special dances, in learning set tribal formulae and by imitating the actions of the school elders. The ceremonies are kept highly secret and include feasts and dancing. Much of the instruction is given in archaic language not readily intelligible. But, as Malinowski has pointed out, the importance of such ceremonies lies in the atmosphere created in order to dramatize the entry into adult life with its responsibilities.

The initiation schools lay down the rules of behaviour for both sexes, they regulate the trainee's system of living, and they transfer to him the tribal sex mores and customs, the marriage practices and the tribal concepts of social behaviour and individual responsibility. The initiation schools prepare the young men and women for the next important stage in their lives, namely, marriage and family responsibility.

Marriage for the tribal Bantu carries none of the sentiments of romantic love associated with European unions, it is primarily an affair between groups rather than individuals. Family connections outweigh personal predispositions; the social and economic aspects are basic; personal likes and desires, while appreciated, are of secondary importance. The choice of partners is also largely defined by tribal custom, there being in different tribes certain people who may not marry one another.

The universal marriage custom amongst the Bantu is the payment of 'lobola', usually in cattle, goats and sheep, by the man and his kinsmen to the household of the woman. 'Lobola' has many aspects. Only through 'lobola' can a man claim the children of a woman,

15

and in some ways, by acting as compensation to the group that has lost a member, it serves as a means of restoring a disturbed equilibrium.

With marriage the individual is recognized as a full member of the society.

As the years go by, his status grows even greater in this society in which respect for age is so marked a characteristic. Mature age is the Bantu ideal: the old man is honoured for his wisdom and experience while the old woman enjoys respect and freedom from many taboos of her younger days.

FIVE MAIN TRIBES

Having considered the common elements of Bantu society and presented the main formative aspects of individual development within this social organization, we will now consider the important cultural features of the main tribal groups which comprise the Bantu.

The three major Bantu groups will be reviewed here: the Nguni, the Sotho, and the Shangana-Tonga groups. These are the largest of the groupings, the vast majority of the urban dwellers being drawn from their ranks. The Venda and Lemba groupings, although ethnologically of interest, are not considered numerically significant enough to exert any appreciable influence in the urban areas. They will consequently not be dealt with.

NGUNI GROUP

1. History and Ethnic Composition

With a few exceptions, the Nguni tribes live between the escarpment of the Drakensberg and the sea, in a belt extending from Swaziland, through Natal into the Cape Province.

A 'cattle-people', their languages are characterized by the presence of 'click' sounds, attributed by authorities to their early contact with the pastoral Hottentots.

The most important recordable event in the history of the Nguni group is, without a doubt, the tribal turmoil caused by the rise of the Zulu military empire under the greatest of all Zulu Chiefs, Shaka. As van Warmelo puts it:

. . . we should note that, had the events of the past century, due to Shaka's founding of the 'Zulu' empire, not taken place, practically the whole Nguni group would have borne a different appearance. One entire sub-group, for instance, that of the 'Fingo and others', owes its existence to the tremendous happenings which accompanied the birth of that empire; and several other most important Nguni offshoots, like

16

the Rhodesian Ndebele, also came into existence in the same fashion. In the storm centre, where these disturbances took their rise, things of course took such a turn that research largely consists of the fitting together of fragments.

Cape Nguni

The Nguni of the South, these tribes are mainly centred in the Transkeian and Ciskeian territories. The most important of the Cape Nguni are: *the Xhosa*, represented by sub-tribes, like the Gcaleka, the Ngquika, the Dushane and the Ndlambe; *the Thembu*, represented by sub-tribes like the Qwathi, the Mpondomise, the Hala and the Jumba; and *the Mpondo*, represented by sub-tribes like the Nci, the Kwetshube, the Kwalo, the Ngntyana and the Bhala.

Fingo Immigrants

During the Zulu upheavals under Shaka, the Fingo (Mfengu) fled to Xhosaland, and many subsequently settled in the Western Transkei, where today many thousands of them live. A little-known and less-studied group, we can say little of their present customs and culture.

Natal Nguni

The tribes of this area have all been influenced by the military power of the relatively small Zulu tribe under Shaka. This mighty Chief completely subjected larger tribes, annihilated others, and caused yet others to flee the country. He disrupted the tribal set-up of the whole of the Natal area. As van Warmelo says:

> In consequence, the only grouping now practicable is to include all the Natal tribes into one common category. Before 1815 one would have classified them into separate groups: (*a*) the true Nguni or Ntungwa, with perhaps a subdivision for (*b*) the Mbo; and (*c*) the Lala tribes. But today this is impossible, for the rule of the Zulu kings not only introduced their own Zulu culture everywhere, but also promoted the growth of standard language and custom. This accounts for the large measure of uniformity found throughout Natal today. Variations in cultural detail do still exist, but they cannot be defined except in extremes, and they form such an intricate pattern that dividing lines cannot be drawn . . . We must therefore consider the Natal Nguni as a whole.

Swazi

Under Sobhuza I the Swazi gradually came into being as a nation, and through the conquests of Chief Mswati, a descendant of

Sobhuza, the Swazi drove out the original Sotho inhabitants of the area we know today as Swaziland and established themselves there. As Hilda Kuper has pointed out in her study, *The Swazi*:

> The name most commonly used for the people themselves is 'ebantfu bakangwane' (People of Ngwane), 'Ngwane' being considered as the founder . . . The name Swazi was popularised by whites who arrived in the reign of Mswati.

Transvaal Ndebele

This Nguni tribal group falls into two sections, the Northern Ndebele and the Southern Ndebele.

The Southern group comprises a single tribe, the Manala; they trace their descent from Chief Msi, who long ago settled near Pretoria, where the tribe is still centred.

The Northern group is composed mainly of the Langa Ndebele living in the Potgietersrus district.

2. Social Organization

In discussing the social organization of the Nguni tribes, we will describe the main elements of their social system within the frame of reference presented by Hoernle in her chapter in *The Bantu-Speaking Tribes of South Africa* (Editor, I. Schapera).

The Nguni group, especially during the reign of Shaka, underwent considerable change, but all the tribes of this group have retained one universal and, from the point of view of their social structure, one highly important common feature: they all prohibit marriage or sexual relations between all people related through any of the four grandparents.

Shaka's military exploits amongst the Northern Nguni caused a considerable disruption of their social organization, and these Zululand tribes have evolved certain new ways, whereas the Southern Nguni tribes have, despite many wars with the Europeans and with other Bantu, preserved their social system in a less altered form.

We will consequently deal with the more culturally traditional system first (that of the Southern Nguni) and thereby indicate by contrast the Northern Nguni modifications, with which we will then deal.

Southern Nguni

The Household. The household or 'umzi' of the Southern Nguni is ideally polygamist, revealing a complex status grouping of wives and their children. The central focus of such a settlement is the cattle kraal, with the principal hut of the household facing the kraal entrance. A large household is characterized by a series of family huts (of the various mothers and their children), usually in circular formation. The two most important wives are the principal wife—the one first married—and the 'right-hand' wife ('umfazi wasekunene'). Any other wives married are subordinate to these two.

Should the principal wife prove to be barren, then a 'seed-bearer' may be married. She, unlike all other wives, has no independent property; even the children she bears are regarded as the offspring of the principal wife.

Each household has its own name and each important family unit within the household has its name. The principal son has the right to use the household or 'umzi' name.

Such traditional social units have evolved social security systems for all classes of members. Among the Xhosa, for example, widows of a man usually remain at the deceased's 'umzi', others establish their own 'umzis' with their grown children, and yet others return to their childhood home to join the 'dikazi'—the husbandless women who have borne children. In the Mpondo tribe, where the custom of 'ukungena' prevails, a widow is taken over by the male next-of-kin of her late husband; children from this union are regarded as children of the first husband.

A custom peculiar to new subordinate wives is that of 'hlonipha'. This requires that the wife must as far as possible avoid the male members of the household during the course of her daily duties. She must not mention the personal names of her husband or his elder relatives, not even to the extent of uttering words containing the principal syllables of their names. This 'hlonipha' custom has caused a considerable extension of language, so that common objects have a variety of different names to assist the woman in 'hlonipha'. The 'hlonipha' custom remains with the woman until she is head of her own family unit or 'indlu'.

Within this close-knit society of the 'umzis' there is a strong co-operative spirit, and within the smaller unit of the 'indlu', the family of mother and her children, the young members get all the sympathy and affection they need.

Household Groupings. As the 'indlu' is the family unit and the 'umzi' is the household unit, so the 'ikundla' is the district unit. The 'ikundla' is a grouping of households. These 'ikundla', in turn, are grouped together to form larger districts known as 'ibandla'. At the head of the whole hierarchy comes the grouping of 'ibandlas' into the Paramount Chief's 'amabandla'.

This hierarchical grouping has considerable significance on social occasions, for legal obligations and in the Nguni army organization. Amongst the Mpondo, for instance, the army was formed on the 'ibandla' basis. Each petty headman collected his 'ikundla' and made his way to his district headman, who in turn led his 'ibandla' to his superior, each 'ibandla' constituting a division of the army, the 'amabandla' of the Paramount Chief, which gathered at the tribal headquarters.

The Clan. A kinship grouping, the clan consists of a group of people claiming descent from a common ancestor in the male line. As the 'ibandla' grouping is the fundamental grouping within the Mpondo army, so the clan grouping is the basic unit within the Xhosa army. And because of the association with a common ancestor in the male line, clan groupings necessarily transcend and spread over 'ibandla' or district groupings. The 'ibandla' is a territorial grouping, the clan a grouping by intermarriage.

Such clans have a stated order of precedence, the clan of the Paramount Chief being most directly descended from the common ancestor of the tribal nucleus.

Age Groupings. Within the 'umzi' strict precedence is given to seniority, a precedence which is carried over into the 'ibandla' unit as well. Such age groupings are, however, of most importance within the 'umzi' and are subordinate to both the clan or territorial groupings.

Sex forms a natural grouping within the age groups and, while important from a social point of view, the Southern Nguni tribes appear to have no formal sex hierarchy.

Northern Nguni

As Krige has pointed out in her book, *The Social System of the Zulus*, these people, the Zulu, were, prior to the rise of Shaka, the Black Napoleon, one of the many hundreds of insignificant coastal tribes of South-East Africa. However, as a result of their history of conquest and incorporation under Shaka, and to a certain extent under his brother Dingane, the Zulus of today are a considerable mixture of most of the Nguni clans of Natal. The name Zulu has spread so that today almost all of the Natal Bantu call themselves Zulus.

The Household. Like the Southern Nguni, the Northern tribes consider the household as the primary territorial unit. The individual 'indlu', or family group of the mother and her children, is exactly similar in significance and importance to that of the Southern Nguni.

The hut grouping of the Northern Nguni is different from that of

20

the Southern tribes, but the same general principles of kinship, seniority, 'ibandla' groupings and 'hlonipha' customs prevail.

Household Groupings. The hierarchical groupings of 'umzis' into 'ikundlas', which in turn are grouped into 'ibandlas', which are combined into the 'amabandla' of the tribal Paramount Chief, are exactly similar to those of the Southern Nguni.

The kinship system is also the same.

Age Groupings: Age groupings in the Northern tribes are, however, more organized than further south.

> In the large 'umzi' of a polygamous man, the children of similar age will constantly be found together and form, together with their age mates of the little sub-district around their home, the 'intanga', the age set the members of which spend so much of their childhood days together (Hoernle).

Although the system of military kraals is gone today, the 18–20-year-olds are still grouped into 'amabutho' or regiments. They undertake group projects of a developmental nature required by the tribe. In the old days they formed themselves into fighting regiments, today their energies are mostly turned to social activities of a less violent nature, although every so often 'ibutho' of opposing tribes engage in faction fights.

Nguni Offshoots. The fundamentals of the Nguni social structure have been preserved by these offshoots who have spread as far afield as the Southern Transvaal Ndebele, the Swazi, the Rhodesian Ndebele, and the Ngoni of Nyasaland and Tanganyika.

Slight modifications have naturally enough occurred, and these groups have attempted to maintain the purity of the blood. But certain foreign influences have penetrated; the South Transvaal Ndebele, for example, have adopted the Sotho custom of totem animals. While the Rhodesian Ndebele have a ranking system based on blood purity, there are three recognized social grades: the pure Ndeble; a middle rank with Ndebele fathers and Shona mothers; and finally the commoners, the Shona, who have merged tribally with the Rhodesian Ndebele.

SOTHO GROUP

1. History and Ethnic Composition

The Sotho group differs in certain important respects from the Nguni peoples, especially with regard to social organization and language. The group is basically differentiable into the Southern Sotho, the Tswana or Western Sotho, and the Eastern Sotho.

21

The Tribal Environment

The Southern Sotho

This group consists of the people of Basutoland and the adjoining territories. As Ashton has stated in his work: *The Basuto*:

> The first Bantu to enter Basutoland were three Nguni groups, who crossed the Drakensberg from the east in three waves and settled south of the Caledon River. They were the Phetla, the Polane and the Phuthi. Some years later they were joined by the 'First Basuto', who were the Peli, Phuthing, Sia and Tlokoa.

These tribes lived for the most in peace with one another, a peace which was, however, shattered early in the nineteenth century as a result of the military exploits of the Zulu Shaka. Tribes fleeing before the might of the Zulu 'impi' burst over the Drakensberg with the Zulu regiments in pursuit, ravaging and plundering. The relative peace of the region was suddenly broken, fighting became general, the Tloka who bore the brunt of the first invasion broke and fled to the south. Famine and cannibalism resulted, whole tribes were broken; the land was devastated.

It was then that one Moshesh appeared on the scene.

> Moshesh was one of the most brilliant native statesmen of Africa, he gathered round him the remnants of former tribes at Butha Buthe . . . and moulded these remnants into a fighting unit and slowly beat back the invaders (Ashton).

A born diplomat, exceptionally intelligent, with an extraordinary foresight, Moshesh is indeed the father of the Basuto Nation.

> With great political wisdom he accepted all stray people who came to him for protection, warded off the attacks of Mzilikazi's Ndebele and built up a great tribe. At one time probably all the southern Sotho were under his control. This ceased when the boundaries of Basutoland were defined (van Warmelo).

With the entry of the Boers into his territory, Moshesh asked for protective support from the British. He experienced heartbreaking setbacks, but in 1868 Basutoland was declared British territory and the Basuto proclaimed British subjects.

This extraordinary man died in 1870, after having moulded the scattered, defeated groups of hunger-stricken people of the many different tribes and sub-tribes of the Basutoland area into one mighty nation. All this within one lifetime—truly a remarkable achievement.

The Western Sotho

The history of the tribes constituting this division is scant and imperfectly recorded. The Tswana, from whom the bulk of this sub-group is descended, migrated southwards many centuries ago, moving along the edge of the Kalahari. They merged with the Bushmen of that area, the present-day maSarwa being the descendants of the intermingling. The Tswana proper are still living along the Kalahari edge. They comprise the Thlaro, the Rolong, and the Huruthse tribes. Further north there are the powerful Kwena, Ngwaketse and Ngwato tribes of Bechuanaland.

Eastern Sotho

The bulk of this group consists of the so-called Pedi tribes in the Sekukuniland and Pakwani districts—so called because apart from the Pedi tribe proper there are a number of tribes speaking the Pedi language which have been under Pedi control and influence for some time, tribes such as the Tau, Kwena, Ntwane and Koni, for example, who have collectively been classified as Pedi.

These Pedi tribes appear to have a common history, a history, however, which has only just been touched upon, and, like so many Bantu migrations, has been inadequately investigated.

2. Social Organization

All Sotho groups follow basically the same social organization. The Southern Sotho of Basutoland, however, as the most homogeneous political group, include the concept of nationhood in their social set-up.

> The nation is essentially a political group and is composed of all who acknowledge the authority of the Paramount Chief. It includes everyone living in Basutoland, for such domicile automatically implies political adherence, as well as Basuto living outside the territory who pay Basutoland taxes (Ashton).

The nation is, however, not an ethnic group, for not all Basuto are nationals, nor are all nationals Basuto. Political dependence to the Paramount Chief is the determining factor. Many Basuto while they speak the same language and have the same common culture, are, on account of their political independence, not regarded as belonging to the nation. Apart from this political grouping, the social organization of the Southern Sotho is identical to that of the other two main Sotho groupings.

The Sotho tribes all allow certain types of kin to marry. As with the Nguni, there is the same basic type of kin classification into kin relatives on the father's side and relatives on the mother's side. The system of behaviour within the household, because of familiarity with kin, is less strained and formal than the Nguni system.

23

When the bride comes to her husband's home, not as a stranger, a non-relative, but as a close kinswoman, known probably from childhood at least to the parents of the husband, if not to the husband himself, there is bound to be a less strained system of behaviour within the household (Hoernle).

The rigidly enforced 'hlonipha' system of the Nguni is considerably modified in the less formal atmosphere of the Sotho family.

The Village. In the Sotho system we find a true village in place of the Nguni 'umzi' or household system, the village itself being divided into households. In Basutoland these villages are small, the inhabitants being mostly relatives chiefly in the paternal line. The unity of the village is revealed by the common 'khotla' or gathering-place in the centre of the various household dwellings.

Most households have two kinds of hut, one large and the other small. The latter (mokhoro), of which there may be more than one, is used as a storeroom and kitchen, and as a dormitory for bachelors and herd-boys . . . the larger is where the parents and young children sleep. Older girls sleep with a grandmother or aunt . . . (Ashton).

The Ward. Among the Tswana, people are divided into wards consisting of a number of families united under the leadership of a headman. The ward is essentially a localized administrative unit. Local business is dealt with by the headman assisted by the more important heads of families.

A ward among the Tswana may constitute either a separate village or part of a village, unlike the Southern and Eastern Sotho where the village and the ward are one.

The Totem Group. All Sotho tribes are divided into clans. These are primarily social groupings or affiliations distinguishable by name and also by totem and other cultural features.

Most clans have their own emblems, commonly called totems. This totem grouping cuts across the limits of tribes. 'These emblems— whether metals, trees, animals or insects—symbolize a mysterious being, a god, all the more to be feared because he is a "molino", that is an invisible being' (Ellenberger and MacGregor).

Totems are regarded as sacred.

Their stock bear its mark as a sign of protection. They put it on their shields . . . they swear by these animals, and by them they conjure evil spirits. If anyone ate such an animal during famine he was looked upon as sacrilegious and worthy of punishment by the gods (*Journal des Missions*, 1844).

The status of various clans differs. Clanship being of prime importance to the higher, more important families, they should not marry beneath their clan. While the Koena clan of the Paramount Chief is ordinarily given pride of place, the clan position with regard to status is very confused and no list of clan seniority would meet with the general approval of all.

SHANGANA-TONGA GROUP

1. History and Ethnic Composition

From the evidence of Shangana-Tonga culture and language one obtains little insight into their early history. All that can be said is that they probably supplanted an earlier and different people, of which the Chopi and Tonga are a survival.

Geographically, the original Shangana-Tonga group is settled in Portuguese East Africa. However, like other groups, the Shangana-Tonga peoples suffered as a result of Shaka's military expansionism. With the rise of Zulu power many Nguni tribes sought refuge in Shangana-Tonga territory. First came Soshangane with his Zulu-speaking tribesmen. He established himself in Gasaland and extended his rule over the Tonga tribes. From the first days of Soshangane's invasion the country was plunged into a period of continual fighting. The result was that many of the peaceful Shangana-Tonga sought safety elsewhere and they began to trickle over the Lebombo Hills to the dry low, unpopulated Eastern Transvaal. From here they spread slowly, both to the north and to the south.

2. Social Organization

These people follow the general social organization of the Nguni, with one great difference, namely, that the mother's family plays a much greater part in the lives of her children than is the case amongst the Nguni, or for that matter amongst the Sotho.

This group, in their social organization, are very closely allied to the Nguni system, they have the same underlying kinship structure, the same hierarchy of age and the same dominance of one lineage in their political structure. Like the Nguni, too, they have no totemic groupings.

They follow the same system of family and household groupings, of district organizations and of kinship structures, as the Nguni group. Their age transitions are celebrated by similar-type ceremonies, and their age-groupings follow the same general developmental trends.

25

III

THE URBAN ENVIRONMENT

IN the preceding section we discussed the African's tribal roots. We turn now to a consideration of his urban environment. Bearing in mind the important influences exerted by a society in determining the behavioural patterns of its members, we must review not only the society from which the urban African stems—the tribe—but we must consider the society in which he is now living—the township society. A thorough grasp of the social and cultural influences of both these environments to which the urban Africans have been exposed, either directly, as in the case of the township environment, and sometimes directly or indirectly in the case of the tribe, will allow for a more balanced assessment of their resulting personality formations.

The strength of the influence of the personality-culture interactions of the various Bantu ethnic groups living in the urban areas of Johannesburg is virtually impossible to estimate. One faces amongst other things the problem of inter-tribal marriages, of illegitimacy, of urbanization and education, of migrant labour, plus the influences of the estimated 340,000 foreign-born Africans employed in the Union of South Africa. The best one can do is to give the numerical distribution of the various ethnic groups that comprise the Union's estimated 9·5 million Bantu (1957):

Xhosa	2·8 million
Zulu	2·5 ,,
Southern Sotho	1·0 ,,
Northern Sotho	1·0 ,,
Tswana	0·8 ,,
Tonga	0·4 ,,
Swazi	0·3 ,,
Venda	0·2 ,,
Ndebele	0·2 ,,
Others	0·3 ,,
	9·5 million

The general consensus of opinion is that the Nguni group (Xhosa, Zulu and Swazi) and the Sotho group (Southern Sotho and Northern Sotho) form the most influential cultural blocks in the urban areas, with the Shangana-Tonga group (Tswana and Tonga) following in importance and influence. We have dealt with the basic cultural forms of each of these main groupings in the last section. In the present chapter, however, the urban Africans will be discussed as a group, rather than tribally.

The Johannesburg African areas may best be described as a city within a city. Like all cities, there are marked differences in the residential areas: there is both poverty and luxury, there are both hovels and good houses, there is both filth and cleanliness.

The urban Africans are starting now to sort themselves out into social status groups. The history of this process, the evolution of this social change, began with the discovery of gold on the 'Reef', when the first influx of Africans into the urban areas took place. Its recorded history, however, begins with the establishment of the Johannesburg Municipality's Non-European Affairs Department in 1927. The Johannesburg urban African population at that time was estimated at 136,000 persons. In 1936, nine years later, the first official census for which records are available, placed the African population at 229,122. By the 1946 census, with the tremendous influx of labour to the 'war industries', the number had risen to 395,231. An unofficial estimate by the Non-European Affairs Department for the same year, however, put the African total at 400,847. The reason for the discrepancy between the 'official' census and the 'unofficial' Departmental estimate is attributed by Mr. W. J. P. Carr, the present manager of the Department, to the 'rooted objection of many urban Natives to being "counted" because of a fear that persons found to be in excess of the officially ordained labour requirements would be sent back to the reserves or the farms' (*Optima*, December 1959).

By 1953 the official census recorded 400,500 Africans in the Johannesburg urban areas, the unofficial estimate being 516,620. The census of 1957 placed the urban African total at 432,900, while an unofficial estimate by the Non-European Affairs Department, some two and a half years later in July 1959, placed the figure at 555,000 persons.

These, then, are the impersonal statistics of the growth of the urban African population; they show its progression over a period of thirty-two years. The planning and organization of social amenities, of townships and of housing facilities, however, did not progress in anything like a similar fashion. It took some time before the authorities realized the urgency of the problem and, no doubt startled by its growing immensity, were jolted into action. 'Reading through one can nicely break it up into successive phases—indifference, vague realization that something should be done, suddenly developing crises threatening to become near-panic—and then action' (*The Star*, February 26, 1960).

The most noticeable result of this action has been the development of what is officially known as the South-Western Bantu Areas. From the shanty-towns and squatter camps, where thousands upon thousands of immigrant families lived in dirt and misery in their corrugated-iron, grass and mud hovels, in a crazy maze of misshapen rusted-tin encampments sprawled over the bare Transvaal highveld, a start was made to develop and plan the South-Western Bantu Areas.

In 1939 the City Council of Johannesburg had built one house for every estimated twenty-eight Africans living in the city. The rest of the African population were living in shacks and squatter camps, without water or sanitation. Housing progress was limited: all building was undertaken by European artisans: costs were high: small cottages were costing up to seven hundred pounds each.

By 1951 there was an estimated backlog of 30,000 houses. Then, in that year, the Native Building Workers Act was passed: Africans were trained on the job for building construction work: costs tumbled: the pace of building increased. In 1952 the Native Services Levy Act was passed and this increased the rate of progress still further. This act requires that all employers pay three shillings a week to the city for every African employed but not housed on their premises. Part of the levy is used to pay off the capital costs of transport services: the rest goes to providing water, sanitation, roads and street lighting for the growing African townships. This levy provides £600,000 a year for the Johannesburg African areas.

Since 1951, some 50,000 families have been re-housed, and more than 200,000 Africans now live in vast townships where only nine years ago there was nothing but bare veld. An African commercial class has sprung up: general dealers (410), butchers (225), greengrocers (165), merchants (118) and herbalists (104). Private enterprise has developed: restaurants (78), fish shops (69), dairies (53), and tailors (52) heading the list. There are an estimated 2,000 men making lively incomes in trade.

The South-Western Bantu Areas, which stretch for over twenty-six miles of undulating veld, are separated from the European areas by a buffer strip of gold-mining land. Their distance from the industrial and commercial concerns in the city requires that a great many African workers have to travel between 12 and 20 miles to their work. Nearly all travel by train, the rail fares being subsidized by the government.

The majority of the houses at present being built in the areas administered by the Johannesburg City Council and the Natives'

Resettlement Board have three rooms plus a kitchen. Provision has been made in these areas for the payment of sub-economic rentals where a family's income is below £15 per month.

This is the history and these are the basic statistics of the South-Western Bantu Areas—a vast area with townships already planned to spread over some thirty square miles, an area in which it is estimated that the present 300,000 strong population will double itself within a decade, an area in which such new townships as Dube, Mofolo, Meadowlands, and Jabulani have sprung up; an area which houses a great many of the estimated 230,000 African males who work in Johannesburg.

There are other areas; there are other townships. There is Alexandra Township—an odd square mile housing an estimated 100,000 people, the headquarters of the dreaded Msomi Gang, officially broken but unofficially dormant, a cesspool of vice, a breeding-ground of crime, the home of the old Thutha Ranch Gang and the happy hunting-ground of the Blue Nine gambling boys, the present-day crime school of the Frog Town 'tsotsis'.

A landlord's paradise, with its 2,500-odd stands housing its estimated 100,000 inhabitants, there are as many as 90 people to a plot 80 by 140 feet in extent. It is a tight-packed bundle of brick and iron houses and shanties, a seething mass of black humanity cramped over the Wynberg veld, a town planner's nightmare. This is 'Alex, the dark township', where street lighting was installed only a year ago. This is Alex, the shebeen-queens' playground—the home of the 'one part gin, one part tonic, two parts carbide, cocktail'. This is Alex, situated some nine miles from the centre of the city of Johannesburg. The last remaining freehold township, its houses and shacks are slowly being whittled away, its inhabitants being transported, lock, stock and barrel, to the vast Meadowlands housing scheme.

Another mass removal, and Johannesburg's great urban African community will be both the richer and the poorer for it. For such townships as Alex, while they breed misery and suffering for many thousands of black men, women and children, and while they promote vice, and crime, and disease, have an atmosphere of individualism, of variety, of difference, about them—albeit a difference which is sometimes most depressing. It is something which one notices immediately as lacking in the regimented cleanliness and organized symmetry and uniformity of the mass-produced new townships to the south-west of Johannesburg.

An eyesore, and filthy as it may be, Alex has contributed a great deal to the urban way of life: it has added many elements to the developing urban African culture. And while one may look amazed at its squalor, and wonder how such a 'hell-hole' could possibly contribute to the culture of a people, one must remember that Alex has, for almost sixty years now, been 'home' to countless thousands of urban Africans. It has influenced their lives, and, in turn, the lives of their children and their grandchildren.

There are relatively quiet places too, like Eastern Native Township. This is a small location, snugly secure behind its stout encirclement of high iron railings and wire fencing, the superintendent's brick offices to the left of the main gate, the uniformed Departmental police standing beside it, the African official selling packets of raisins and groundnuts to the inhabitants and carefully weighing out quantities under the shade of a tin veranda, the view down the main street of the small red-brick houses. It is a sleepy place this, not one of Johannesburg's trouble spots, and it has the distinction of being the only African township in the Johannesburg area where electricity is provided in all houses.

African townships, like their inhabitants, are varied and different in character. Yet we have not truly described their character, we have not in this broad survey tapped the urban township pulse. We have presented certain statistics and population estimates and reviewed certain historical developments. Were this a socio-economic survey, we could continue with this introduction by presenting a series of trend tables and discussing the significance of population curves. But we are dealing essentially with those aspects of the environment which influence personality: we are studying human beings and we need more, much more, than statistics to get a 'feel' of the atmosphere in which the urban African lives.

Tribal society is relatively static and we can describe in fair detail the fundamentals of its social system, a system in which the individual forms an integral segment: it is a tradition-determined society, its social changes are gradual, its cultural movements slow.

Urban society, however, differs. It is constantly changing, adapting, readjusting, modifying, regressing and advancing. It is not possible to find a system amidst such sociological and cultural diversity. To understand and appreciate the full complexity of urban township life one must live in the townships—not in one, but a number—for townships differ.

In order to obtain a truer picture of life in the townships, trained African research workers were approached and each was asked to undertake a broad survey of the township area in which he resided.

The different township settings, their atmosphere and the life of their peoples, is excellently portrayed in the following survey reports. Completely unaltered, they give the 'feel' of the African urban areas, their variety and their difference.

Before presenting the first survey on Alexandra Township we

will briefly review the main aspects of the township's history and development.

This African urban area was originally opened up by the South African Township Board for European settlement, but because of its distance from the city of Johannesburg, Europeans were unwilling to settle there.

It was then proclaimed an African freehold township in 1905—the deed of transfer limiting settlement to Africans and Coloured people only.

There were originally 2,521 stands, which were later subdivided to increase the number to almost 2,600. The original size of the stands was 80 by 140 Cape feet. A corner stand could be purchased for £40 —£2 deposit and £1 per month; middle stands cost £35, at the same terms. These prices remained in force up to the year 1930: since then individual estimates vary considerably as to their value.

From around 1915 the township population grew very quickly, and in 1916 the first Health Committee was formed, mainly to organize night-soil removal and to see to the upkeep of the township roads.

The original transport to the city was by horse-drawn bus, later improved to steam-bus, the fare being 1*s*. 6*d*. single or 3*s*. return. Then followed an era of independent bus and taxi services until the transport was taken over by Public Utility Transport Corporation early in 1945.

Well known for its crime record, Alexandra Township has for long been the Chicago of the urban African areas. The first gang, the Blue Nines—a gambling racket—started up in 1929 and lasted to around 1937. The scene was then taken over by the Thutha Ranch Boys—a gang of youngsters who specialized in robberies. During this time the tribal gang, the Amaliyitas (from the Zulu 'to strike a match' because they used to specialize in striking people), came into being. They were composed of mainly Bavenda and Pedi tribesmen, who had to enter Alexandra for their transport connection to their places of work at Modderfontein. They disappeared with the introduction of a bus service which detoured Alexandra Township. 'The Berliners' followed in 1945. They were made up mainly of young boys who carried on gang warfare within the township with a group known as the Frog Town Boys who lived near the river which borders the area. Their fights were mainly over women, but naturally enough township inhabitants also got hurt. Then in 1950, as a direct result of the film *The Mark of Zorro*, Zorro's Gang came into being. Run by an expert knife-thrower and street-fighter, a young Shangaan who named himself Zorro, this gang ran a woman-protection racket, and their 'girls' all bore the mark of Zorro on the inside of their right thighs. They also undertook 'small-time' robberies. This gang, however, broke up

31

in 1952 when Zorro was sentenced to 11 years' imprisonment for rape and assault.

In 1953 the Spoiler Gang came into being. This was the first real 'big-time' gang. They organized large-scale 'protection rackets' on shop-owners and taxi services, and ran 'bank-jobs' and large robberies. They were organized into two groups, the younger set who specialized in the township where they served an apprenticeship, as it were, and the group who had graduated to the senior ranks, who undertook payroll robberies, bank and shop robberies in Johannesburg and its districts.

The Spoilers terrorized the township inhabitants to such an extent that the latter formed themselves into a 'home guard' to clear the area of these gangsters. With the co-operation of the local Wynberg Police Depot they started cleaning up the area and did it so successfully that they slowly merged into a gang themselves and the Msomi Gang (named after Elphas Msomi, a dreaded axe-killer) was born. This gang in turn started their own protection rackets and terrorized the law-abiding citizens as well as carrying on sporadic fights with the remnants of the Spoiler Gang. The Msomi Gang was officially broken in 1959 when the police intensified their efforts and captured the leaders, many of whom were hanged. Unofficially the gang framework is still in existence and the members have gone 'underground' for the time being.

The estimated population of the township today is 100,000 people although the township area is still only about one square mile in extent.

The African point of view of Alexandra Township is presented in the following general report of the area and its inhabitants. It has been written by a university graduate—an African school teacher with years of experience in the township.

ALEXANDRA TOWNSHIP

As I see it Alex is just another Reef township—only more so. By this I mean that one can find in the township all the things that one finds in any other Reef township, except that one must always expect a more liberal supply: crime, cruelty, sporting achievement, business, delinquency, sexual laxity, the lot. There is, in my opinion, only one point in which Alex beats all other townships hands down, and that is housing— or should I say poor housing conditions.

The Alexandra housing situation appears to me to be one of the greatest single causes of the sociological chaos existing in the township today. The rent is so high that most families can afford only one room to accommodate father, mother, young adult son, teenage daughter, and younger children. This hypothetical family is clearly too big for a one-roomed house, especially when one has regard to the normal sex

32

life of the parents. Imagine the frustration of the parents who have continually to wait until they think the children are asleep before they can take advantage of the privileges bestowed upon them by matrimony. Imagine also the effect on the young adult son and teenage daughter should the parents mistake them to be asleep when in fact they are not.

It does not require much imagination to see that sooner or later a pathological attitude must be developed towards sex. Alexandra is not what is normally called a 'housing scheme'. People hire rooms of their own and after that the landlord usually keeps his counsel. This means that the tenant has sole control of the room and that he can do in it what he wishes, as long as he or she pays the rent. This attitude necessarily leads to much independence and freedom which these young people usually mistake for licentiousness and sexual looseness. A youth who has hired a room considers it his castle, and he brings in any amount of women, sometimes changing them faster than he changes underpants. This beginning usually leads to drinking sessions, and it is not unusual to find up to four or five couples spread on the floor of one small dingy room. What happens after the drinking session is nobody's business. Disease is transmitted this way and, of course, many of these girls conceive—the result, illegitimate brats.

The teenage girl in our hypothetical family gets tired of being hemmed in by parents and what parental control there may be; she decides to go it alone and hires a room for herself in the same township. If she happens to be a good looker it does not take her long before she has regular male visitors. Sooner or later she finds the rent a little steep, and at this stage she is usually ready to accept the advances of the most persistent of her suitors. He moves in with her—pays the rent, which automatically entitles him to all 'conjugal rights'. This loose family grows, and if they are happy and want to marry, lobola usually stops them from marrying, but they cohabit all the same. Sometimes, they get tired of each other and separate, to repeat the process elsewhere. If there have been any children in this union, the girl or her parents has to worry about them. These children may grow up not knowing their fathers; indeed, the girl herself may be unable to say for certain who the father is.

A type of exploitation of males is also rife in Alex. A girl usually has a number of boy friends. Of these the most decent is introduced to her parents and he will usually be responsible for whatever happens. He is usually referred to as the 'Rent' boy friend. For some queer reason he will not be her most popular boy friend, usually because he will invariably be fairly careful of how he throws about his money, and will also fight shy of booze parties and other forms of debauchery. He will usually be less exciting, but more of a security than any of the 'wise guys'. He is usually the 'universal ass' who holds the baby when all the fun is over.

Another aspect of the housing problem is the passing on of room keys to school-boy or school-girl friends, who use these rooms during the day for their own filthy ends. I for one am willing to bet that very much less than 10% of the girls at the Secondary School where I teach are virgin. The percentage will be much higher among the boys, and this for another reason which is rather baffling. The girls in our secondary schools will have nothing to do with schoolboys if they can help it. They are tempted and fall victim to the presentation of such material presents as money, clothing, expensive outings, hard drinks, etc. No schoolboy can afford these, hence the fact that boys remain chaste for a longer time than girls.

One must admit that the teenage girl is a much better looking packet than her hard-drinking, fast-living older sister and physically more attractive to working men. However, the association is very seldom a serious one and is usually purely physical. It is not uncommon to hear young and not-so-young working men talk about their school-girl conquests and how different they found them to the regular girl friends. The poor schoolgirls are looked upon as trophies to be won by hook or by crook, and they are usually referred to as 'wee-bits' and 'veal'. Unfortunately some of the teachers also fall victim to the wiles and physical attraction of their young charges. Don't let any teacher tell you that he doesn't ever get tempted. We all do, but most of us brush the temptation aside. In this association it is not the teacher who is wholly to blame. Many of the girls make it their business to arouse the younger teachers sexually. I have had occasion to speak to a few of them and I have verified this statement. Various tricks are resorted to, for example, sitting carelessly in class, smearing fat or oil on the legs, wearing too short uniforms and even bodily pressure. One girl told me how she avoids punishment by a certain teacher who usually requires pupils to bring their books to the table one by one and then he corrects the books seated. This girl, who has been generously endowed with breasts and is also quite a looker, moves up and takes a position behind the teacher. She then leans forward when the teacher talks to her about the work and presses her ample bosom on his right shoulder. She says this method is very successful with this particular teacher, but that with some it doesn't work.

What I am trying to point out is that the Alex surroundings are conducive to sexual awareness being aroused at a very early stage in the children of the township, particularly among the girls who are also the greatest and most pitiful victims of this social phenomenon. Much more can be said about the influence of the housing situation on the development of character and personality, but I think that the most important points have been mentioned.

From the home to the school: The average Alex adolescent pupils, surprisingly, are not nearly as wild and disorderly as one would expect. The problem pupil is the boy rather than the girl, and I think this is largely due to the fact that the boy is more or less the equal of his teachers, where pure physical strength is concerned, and also because some of the wilder boys do not hesitate to use knives, guns, and half-bricks, if these are available. This year alone (1959) two of our boys have been involved in cases of possession of firearms, while the possession of other dangerous weapons is common cause of arrest among others. The teachers are aware of this state of affairs, as well as of the outside connections of certain boys, and are, as a result, naturally rather cautious when it comes to disciplining these pupils. The teachers try hard to hide their caution from these boys, but sometimes I have a feeling that at least some of the boys are aware of their special position in the school. Discipline suffers to a certain extent, but I must say not very much. The female of the species is not necessarily free from blame in this connection, and I have heard some threatening to put their brothers and boy-friends on to certain teachers. I must admit that such rebelliousness is shown only when the pupils think that they are being unfairly punished. I for one have yet to meet a pupil who has refused to accept punishment after he has been shown his fault and made to admit it.

Do Alex schools need a special type of teacher? Maybe yes, and maybe no. It does help if the teacher is a product of Alexandra, because then he usually has access to more or less the same connections as the pupils. I have heard teachers telling pupils not to take them for fools, as they (the teachers) have themselves grown up in the township. I once heard a girl seriously threatening to organize her uncle or some relative against one of the teachers; the teacher at once told the girl to tell the person in question (he had been named) that she had been punished by 'ou ... ... from ... Avenue'. It turned out that the teacher and the chap who was to do the organizing had grown up together and were quite good friends, although the other party had gone 'wrong' after leaving school. On the other hand, a firm and just handling of a class is usually enough, and, as I said, surprisingly effective.

Most parents seem to have lost control of their children, which is not surprising when one considers how they live, the lack of privacy, selling of liquor in houses with its attendant spectacles and dirty talk, and also the parents having to quarrel, etc., in the same one room where the children also sleep. Imagine a couple who have had a few too many quarrelling about the male partner's unfaithfulness with a third party and not caring a hoot whether junior is listening. Where else can they have their family quarrels—unless they want to have them in the street. I think the Alexandra parent has a tough job on his or her hands. Those who talk of lack of parental control just haven't lived in Alex. How do you keep effective control over a girl you, the parent, use to make and sell liquor to a stream of male visitors in order to make both ends meet. The mother may be away some of the time and the patrons being men will naturally make advances. The strongest of the girls must succumb to the temptation sooner or later—all because you asked her to sell liquor, an unavoidable necessity.

What about studying? How can a teenager burn the midnight oil when everyone else is sleeping? How can the liquor-selling girl concentrate on her studies when she has to be serving liquor all night, possibly retiring only after midnight, if at all! I know of a number of cases of this nature. One gives homework and the following day one

35

checks to see whether the work has been done. One sets out on this task knowing full well that So-and-so and So-and-so have not done it, because they just didn't have the time. Does one punish them??? The rest of the class will want to know why not if one doesn't. So one punishes them, knowing deep down that one is doing something morally wrong. Yet, surprisingly, one finds some real good ones from the poorest families.

As if the teacher hasn't got enough to put up with, the inspector comes around with remarks like: 'You're wasting time writing notes on the blackboard.' The teacher answers: 'Very few of them have text-books, sir.' 'Then they shouldn't be here,' rings the voice of Pretoria. He turns to the class and growls: 'All of you must have text-books by Monday.' They all answer: 'Yes, sir.' Inspector then turns to teacher and says, 'All you have to do is tell them.' Teacher says, 'Yes, sir.' Monday comes and teacher still has to write notes on the blackboard.

The same thing happens about school fees. Inspector says, 'They mustn't be allowed to sit for the exam. if they haven't paid.' Teacher knows better, so he allows them to sit and then faces the music. Not very easy living for the teachers. Parents lose control over delinquent children and then shout: 'I don't know what they teach them at school.' Children fail—bad teachers; children pass—clever pupils! Most of the school buildings in the township are in a fairly good state of repair. The Secondary School, however, has to be seen to be believed. Uninspiring is the mildest word I can find to describe it. Many of the pupils at school are illegitimate children maintained at school by the mother or the mother's family. It takes quite a bit of tact not to embarrass these pupils when certain official data are required and have to be asked for in open class. Many of these children can also be detected when they have to address envelopes in which their results are to be posted. It is a common occurrence to find the results of say John Dube addressed to *Miss* Dube, instead of to Mrs. Dube. At the beginning of 1959 I witnessed a major contribution towards delinquency when over 50 pupils were turned away from school because there wasn't enough accommodation at the Secondary School for all the pupils who passed Std. 6 at the end of 1958. The 50 in question had unfortunately passed Std. 6 in the third class. I had the opportunity to see some of them during the year; they were a sorry sight—too young to be employed, too dull to be at Secondary School. The inevitable decline had set in, and in many cases the devil found work for idle hands.

Some of the people of this township just haven't heard of public health and sanitation. Their lavatories are of the bucket-system type, and just why there haven't been many outbreaks of diarrhoea or typhoid beats me. Very few of the lavatories in Alex are ever washed or scrubbed. Some stand-holders do hire people to look after their lavatories, but the stands are usually so over-populated that the lavatories are over-flowing in no time, especially so on weekends when most of the residents are in.

It is common to see a number of small children lined up along the street in the morning, defaecating. No one thinks of teaching them better.

Alexandra latrines are cleared during the daytime. One group goes ahead delivering empty buckets at the gates of various stands. This delivery is usually done by means of throwing off a bucket—somewhere near the gate—from a moving vehicle. The next group comes along, picks up the buckets, carries them into the yards, where they exchange them for full buckets. The full buckets are placed at the gate awaiting the arrival of the sewerage lorry. Until the lorry arrives the street is lined on both sides with buckets full—sometimes overflowing—with human excrement. In the meantime people move up and down the streets and life goes on as usual. This sort of thing happens in the morning and late afternoon. Sometimes I walk down 12th Avenue about 7.30 a.m.; there are students ahead, alongside, and behind me. The road is lined with buckets stinking no end, and all of us walk quietly but briskly ahead, as though to get clear of Alex and its cruelty and filth. Sometimes a naughty boy makes some untoward remark, and I conveniently refuse to hear him. On these occasions Alexandra literally stinks. Alexandra roads are not the best in the world, but cars do manage to move along, sometimes at awe-inspiring speeds. The dirt roads can be quite trying on dry, dusty days. Selbourne Road is quite a good road, and as a result usually overcrowded by the most undesirable kind of driver who is a danger to life and limb. There are other amenities like a public bar, tennis courts, creches, football field, softball pitches, among others. These are on the whole satisfactory and well used. A few more such amenities could make a world of difference to the social life of Alexandra.

Alexandra is notorious for its crime, and one finds that even regular city dwellers from other townships on the Reef refuse point-blank to visit Alexandra. Some will venture to get there during the day, but very few, if any, will visit Alex at night. The crime record of Alex is well-known and has been splashed all over the pages of the popular press. It is true that Alex is by no means rid of all its criminals, but it does seem as though the heavy sentences passed on members of the Msomi gang have acted as a powerful deterrent—at least temporarily. There are still the small-timers who still cannot find work or do not want it, and who still have to eat, dress, and pay rent. These people will continue to stand on street corners with guns, knives, sharpened screwdrivers and bicycle spokes, half-bricks and hammers. They will be there for as long as Alex is there. Many of them are typical examples of the old sociological problem of the unemployed becoming unemployable. Fortunately they are not usually organized and so are a danger to individuals, rather than the all-embracing danger of organized gangs.

There is no doubt that we breed criminals in Alexandra through the lack of schooling facilities for all, the loose sex relations resulting in illegitimate and unwanted and neglected children, the administrative difficulties put in the way of some decent youths who want to earn their living honestly. The sex life of Alexandra is inextricably bound up with the housing situation. The Alex housing position seems to have been handpicked for the most licentious sex life I have ever come across. Let us take old Orlando Township and make a brief comparison with Alex. Orlando houses families where some parental control is made possible by the fact that parents and children do not have to live and sleep and do all sorts of things in the same room. It is not easy for unmarried people, much less for school children, to ask a respectable family man to accommodate them for the night or to lend them his keys while he and his wife are at work. Since unmarried youths do not have their own places in Orlando, sexual looseness is much less than at Alex. It is possible, however, that the number of illegitimate children per thousand of the population is more in Orlando than in Alex. After all, people exposed to an ill for a long time do develop some sort of method of avoiding the undesired results of the evil.

There are no brothels in Alex. There are houses where women are used as an additional enticement to attract and hold those liquor patrons who have money to throw about. A mother will often have her daughter sell the liquor because she is more attractive and can hold the customers for a longer time. Then there are homes frequented by a loose type of woman who will do anything for a drink. These women frequent certain shebeens and expertly cling on to the victim of their choice. The moment the woman in question accepts your drinks she is taken to have agreed to be yours for the night. I have heard people quarrel over this and have seen women beaten. The usual argument is that she has taken my liquor and now she will not play ball. Usually nobody interferes after this explanation has been given. I have seen the same stunt used by trouble-seekers. They approach a girl and say 'this is the woman who drank my money last weekend and then ran away'. The innocent girl will then find herself helpless to deal with the situation. The same system is also used to make trouble for male victims. A tsotsi will demand money allegedly borrowed by the victim some time before to trigger off an assault. Alexandra's sex life is as dirty as its streets and lavatories are, but I haven't heard of a brothel in the true sense of the word, perhaps because there is no need for one, as each little room and shebeen serves the purpose.

Then there are the animals of Alexandra. There are people in Alex who own dogs and other domestic animals when they themselves do not have enough food to eat. The result is that these animals are invariably the worse off for wear, and in spite of the efforts of the S.P.C.A., I have seen dogs, and cats, and cows, that shouldn't be alive. For the first time in my life I have seen dogs eating human excrement and dead dogs, for want of anything better. The animals of the township seem to have adapted themselves well to the existing state of affairs. Dogs upset rubbish bins regularly looking for pieces of food. Cows can be seen moving up a street turning over rubbish bins which have been put onto the streets for collection by the Refuse Disposal Squad. Cats steal into any one's room and are quite capable of leaving with the weekend meat supply. In spite of all this, there seem to be some people who have somehow managed to get their heads above the depressing state of affairs in the township. Educationally, Alex has produced just about every category of academically qualified person, from medical practitioners, lawyers, teachers, Health Inspectors downwards. In the sporting field Alex has produced South African champions in boxing and tennis, and the present Alex soccer team is the strongest on the Reef, i.e. on 1959 records. Alex has produced the best African golfers in the country.

This survey has presented something of the atmosphere and the life of Alexandra Township, a way of life shared by some 100,000 of its inhabitants.

What of the life in other townships? How do the many thousands of urban dwellers in other townships and locations live?

Let us now consider a number of other African townships. Let us firstly consider Sophiatown.

Sophiatown as such was bought in 1897 by H. Tobiansky, who leased it to the Government of the late South African Republic in 1899 for 'a Coloured Location'. In 1903 the lease was cancelled and the land reverted to Tobiansky, who then planned it as a private leasehold township, no portion of which could be sold or leased to a non-white person. Such restrictions were subsequently amended until the position was reached in 1949 when Sophiatown was proclaimed 'as an area predominantly occupied by natives'.

The area known as Sophiatown covered roughtly 113 morgen, and was laid out in 1,694 stands. No provision was made for parks or public buildings.

The houses varied from well-built four-roomed brick buildings housing one or more families, to dilapidated tin shacks occupied by several people. The average stand housed 8·3 families, living in clusters of rooms and shacks. Shared room rents ranged from 10*s*. to 19*s*. per month. Unshared rooms were rented out from between 30*s*. to 40*s*. per month. In 1950 the population of Sophiatown numbered 39,200. The general atmosphere and conditions of the township, in its heyday, are excellently presented in a survey of the area undertaken in 1930 by the Johannesburg Non-European Affairs Department. The survey report summed up the position as follows:

> The residents appeared to live orderly lives, although very few persons venture out at night, and many residents express wonder at the investigator's temerity in visiting at night.
> Drinking and brewing is very prevalent—the latter is done quite openly. Police raids in this connection are taken philosophically and new brews made almost immediately after the departure of the police. There were instances where residents of a whole stand had been arrested for brewing. The selling appears to start at about twelve noon. Drunkenness, however, was not evident during week-days, but at night time and

from Friday afternoons onwards drunken residents hampered investigators as they were unable to give sensible information.

There were large numbers of adolescents loafing at street corners, but at no time did they make any trouble for the investigators, apart from shouting insulting remarks. According to the information received from parents, the majority of these boys were either reported to be working or still in school. It was not possible to check this information owing to lack of time, but the mere presence of these boys in the streets belied the information given by the parents. The residents appear to fear these boys at night time, which might lead one to believe that their numbers are swelled at that time by boys who are actually working during the day.

Several cases of polygamy were found, but no detailed information was taken in this connection; the same applies to mixed marriages (between members of different races), of which there were a fair number.

Old Sophiatown was a complex place. It housed Indians, Coloureds, Chinese and African families. Some in squalor, some in wealth, a few in freehold tenure, the majority on leasehold bonds. There were few owners, and many tenants and sub-tenants. It was a heterogeneous human mass, a complex of different cultures, and yet a group of people united by a feeling of ownership. A feeling which for the vast majority was, however, more an imagined rather than an actual reality. Yet, a feeling which nevertheless engendered resentment and antagonism amongst many of its people, when they were eventually forced to leave the area and were rehoused in the vast townships to the south-west of Johannesburg.

Sophiatown has now almost disappeared; bulldozers have razed great areas to the ground. Yet the influence of this colourful township is indelibly impressed on many thousands of urban Africans, people who were born there and who grew up there, people who knew its system of streets and its maze of alleys like the palms of their own hands. People who remembered the individuality of its houses and the crazy design of its tin shacks, who visited its shebeens and who mixed with its gangsters.

The following survey of Sophiatown, written by an African who was born and brought up there, portrays something of this feeling.

SOPHIATOWN

There will never be another place like Sophiatown. In Sophiatown everything was different. Sophiatown was clean, though it had slums. The streets of Sophiatown were never deserted, they were always full, there was always life, people always going up and down like ants. Sophiatown had variety. Sophiatown had difference. Sophiatown was unlike any of the new municipal townships. The people of Sophiatown enjoyed themselves, there were few regulations, people didn't care about staying in one room, as long as they were free to live and to sleep and wake as they liked. The township was a hotch-potch of people. One got the educated, the semi-educated and the uneducated all living together. Yet with this difference of education and with this difference of background, the people of different groups mixed freely. The educated man mixed with the tsotsi, they mixed basically because their lives were similar, their hopes and their fears were the same, and above all they spoke the same language—a kind of lingua franca, a corruption of Afrikaans with dribs and drabs of most African languages and a dash of English.

The Shebeen was the converging point. Here, with a glass of beer or a glass of whisky and a buxom lady near, the scene was set for complete and absolute social intercourse. Old Sophiatown had a number of shebeens: there was, for instance, The Church, so called because it was just next door to the Church of Christ the King. Then there was The 39 Steps, although there was not a single step at the entrance to the club. And then there was the well-known Back of the Moon, an old-time Sophiatown shebeen. In such places one could sit until the following day just as long as one bought liquor. The shebeens were one of the main forms of social entertainment. In old Sophiatown the shebeens were not simply made up of a gathering of drunkards. People came to the shebeens to discuss matters, to talk about things, their daily worries, their political ideas, their fears, and their hopes. There were various kinds of people who frequented the shebeens. But probably the most interesting and the most dangerous types were the politicians. Such people have always tried to influence others and get them to conform to their way of thinking, and if one disagreed he immediately became suspect and classed as an informer. For, in the old Sophiatown shebeens the police often planted spies and if one had a different point of view to that of the politician one automatically became branded.

As with the shebeens of other townships, in Sophiatown the shebeens were mostly run by women. The owner may have been a man, but he always got a woman to run it. Such men knew that the customers would buy more when a woman served them. The liquor drunk in the shebeens was bought mainly from European hoboes, who worked on a commission basis. There were other women in these shebeens too, mainly loose women, but not prostitutes in the true sense of the word. They were women who may best be described as prepared to do anything for a drink. Such were the Sophiatown shebeens, dirty, dark little rooms, hidden away in some back alley, or smart posh joints furnished with contemporary Swedish furniture. The shebeens of old Sophiatown were an excellent means of escaping from the realities of the world about. In a haze of whisky one could easily forget the rising cost of living, the embarrassing rentals, and the problem of feeding a family on an inadequate salary.

With regard to the problem of illegitimacy, Sophiatown was little different from most of the other townships. Amongst urban Africans contraceptive methods are not at all popular. And in the townships there is a saying that 'it is better done flesh to flesh'. The pregnancy of the woman doesn't matter much because damages can be paid. The normal amount of damages is assessed at about 3 cattle, that is, about £15. Another major cause of illegitimacy is that the African looks down upon the woman who has not borne children. She is considered as barren. So, as a result, no man is prepared to marry a girl he loves before they have had a child. However, after the birth the actual marriage may be delayed, by trying to evade the African custom of lobola, and more often than not the man finds himself unable to pay the required price. The woman is then left with the child. Such children are usually brought up not by the mother but by her parents. The attitude of the fathers of such children is best expressed by the African saying, 'Even if I die tomorrow, I have left my picture in the world.'

And the witchdoctors did good business in Sophiatown. Fortune-telling was their main business. People who believed that someone was bewitching them always consulted the witchdoctor. The fee for such consultation was normally 5/-.

The tsotsis, too, did good business in Sophiatown. They usually were most active on Fridays, the pay-day. They would attack the unsuspecting workman, and if they did not get any money off them, the likelihood was they would stab him. Money in the townships is, in fact, in a sense a protection. For if you have money you will probably just get a crack or a lash with a sjambok and told to run away. If you had no money you would, more often than not, be stabbed. When you came to enjoyment, in old Sophiatown, first and foremost was the enjoyment of music and dancing. The different tribal groups had their own particular forms of amusement. The Basuto people had their 'famu' dance. The Zulus their war dances. The Pedi their fighting circles, in which two opponents would clash in a brutal fight while surrounded by a circle of cheering onlookers. Then there was the more modern enjoyment of jiving. In Sophiatown there was a wedding almost every weekend. At such weddings people ate freely. Everybody was invited, there was free food and free drinks. Sophiatown knew how to enjoy itself. Such was old Sophiatown. A township quite different from all others. There will never be another place like Sophiatown.

From Old Sophiatown we will now turn to consider two townships of the vast South-Western Bantu Areas. As the history and development of this enormous project was discussed in some detail at the beginning of this chapter, only the survey reports, written by the African field workers living in these townships, will be presented here.

The two areas which have been selected are:

1. Dube Village.
2. Orlando East.

DUBE VILLAGE

This model village derives its name from the famous Dr. J. Dube (popularly known as Mafukuzela) of Ohlange Institution. The late

Dr. Dube was a popular figure and it is fitting that his name should be associated with this village.

The first portion of Dube (near Westcliffe Orlando) is known as the B.E.S.L. (British Empire Service League) Section. This ex-soldiers' association did all the spade work to have this particular area established. The idea was to help ex-servicemen to settle in civilian life. This association helped with the planning and also advanced members the money to deposit on their houses. The conditions are lease-hold over 30 years. This also applies to the other sections of Dube and Mofolo.

The B.E.S.L. Section has mostly four-roomed concrete pre-fab houses. There were also sites for owner-builders, and these were lapped up by the land-hungry people in a very short time. The City Council then built houses for sale in 1957. These could be bought for £250, the conditions being £25 deposit and the rest payable over 30 years. The snag is, however, that the interest is calculated on the balance (after a certain date, the 7th of every month) and in reality these houses cost something nearer £700 each in the end.

Population

Unlike other new townships, Dube has no ethnic grouping. The authorities did not worry the people with this annoying requirement. You can find many racial groups in this area, and the people speak to you in the language in which you address them.

Transport

Transport is provided by the railways, and the area is served by both Phefeni and Dube stations; there are also buses passing from Zola to Baragwanath Hospital. The Dube trains, however, are so congested that it is almost impossible for people to get seats in them. To overcome this some people travel via Meadowlands to Western Native Township and then to town. The fares are 1s. 4d. for a single journey. Many of them can ill afford this, but they say that the trains are killers because of the discomfort involved.

Social Amenities

Although Dube is one of the posh townships it lacks most of the social amenities of other townships. There are no street lights. There is no clinic. The nearest clinic is at the Orlando shelters. Most sick people have to go to Baragwanath (a 6d. journey) by bus. Churches have just been built although the place is more than 6 years old. Schools were only opened this year. Shops are very few and some residents have to travel some distance to buy groceries. The better-built homes have electricity but they must pay to have it connected, because the Council has not started a scheme. It is surprising to find that such recognized churches as the Anglican and Methodist church have no buildings in this area. The Dutch Reformed Church, however, put up one of the very first church buildings in the area. There is also a club house which is used as a boys' club. It is very small and its main advantage is the fact that it is electrically lit.

Crime

There is little or no crime in Dube. This may be because the place is occupied by families of a certain age group, whose children are still young. It may also be attributed to the fact that most families in this area are of the highest paid professional group. There are teachers, clerks, doctors, drivers, police sergeants and factory workers. An unusual sight in Dube especially at night is to see women walking around unescorted. They even greet you when you speak to them. One does not often see such a thing in the African townships.

The relationship between the sexes, however, is rather unsatisfactory in Dube. There are more divorces in Dube than other places. I once asked a reporter about this, and he disagreed with me, saying that most people in Dube are well known, so that whatever they do is news (which helps to keep my reporter friend employed). He may be right. But if I were asked for an opinion I would say that my people are at the moment in a very delicate stage of their development and progress. We as a people regard women as our inferiors, and the women in Dube, because they work and contribute towards the comforts of the home, feel that they are no longer junior partners—hence the trouble.

Joints (Shebeens)

Most Dube residents (because of the wages they earn) have permits and are therefore not in dire need of liquor. We, however, have our own joints in this place. There are a number of rather well-known shebeens. The most famous is probably 'Fallen Leaves'; this place gives all the others a start and a beating. All the smart set meet there and the place has real atmosphere. It is comfortable, well-furnished and well laid out. One thing about these joints in Dube is the fact that we have no trouble at all from them. The patrons are real ladies and gentlemen (who just enjoy themselves) and are never interested in causing trouble. As I have said, in Dube all the tribes live together. There has been no race trouble between the different tribes.

Most Sophiatown people (with means) now live in Dube. They availed themselves of the privilege of selecting sites and building houses, some of which could give dignity even to the famous European suburb of Houghton.

Sports

There are some football grounds in the area, but because they have only been in use for a very short time they are still not popular. Most of the senior football clubs are still playing in places like the Bantu Sports Ground and the Wemmer Stadium. It will take quite some time to convince them that football is football even if it is played in Dube. There are some softball clubs, but as this is a new venture with the residents, it is difficult to determine the results of its popularity.

Witchdoctors

As in all African communities, the witchdoctors are part and parcel of the place. And Dube is no exception on that score. However, they do not practise their trade in this area. I know only one who is fairly near to my own home. He will not admit that he is a witchdoctor but says that he is a herbalist. This is regarded by all as in keeping with the modern trend. He compares his trade with that of the European chemist.

Religious Sects

There are few religious sects in Dube. And those that there are do not have their prayer meetings in this area, they prefer to travel to other places like Zondi, Jabulani, Zola and Mdeni. They go to these areas to beat their drums.

Conclusion

Dube is definitely a high-class township, the people are of a better class and the houses definitely have character. It is a peaceful community.

ORLANDO EAST

1. The township which I have confined myself to is known as Orlando East. It covers about four square miles. Population: between 25,000 and 30,000. Houses 5,000. Rents, Sub-Economic: 17/4d. for two-roomed and £1. 1. 8. for three-roomed. Economic rents: £2. 5. for two-roomed and £2. 15. 0. for three-roomed. Transport: Trains, Buses, Taxis and private cars. Fares: Trains, 11d. return 3rd Class to Johannesburg. 2/- Second Class. Buses none; except those leaving from Noordgesig at 9d. a single trip. Taxis, from 1/- to 2/6d. single—30/- special trips; private cars: it depends on the owner.

2. Roads: Bad and eroded. The pavements are overgrown with grass and weeds. Yard poles on pavement have fallen down due to footpaths being made through the fences and water washing away the soil. Disused cars are often left, taking up part of the road and pavement, thus obstructing the traffic.

Lights are available but due to poor maintenance the lanes and stormwater drains have become criminal hide-outs. Amenities: Communal bathrooms exist but are insufficient. There is no supervision. There are no bathrooms in houses.

Shops are better planned for than churches, i.e. most churches are on the outskirts. A library which could have been of great service, if it had been built more to the centre of the township, has been put on the main road too far away for the people who would like to use it after a hard day's work and could relax after supper by reading.

3. The general standard of living is poor. The people live mainly on bread, tea, milk and porridge, with meat once a day at the most. The occupations of the inhabitants are mainly of a manual and clerical nature. Their salaries average £3 per week.

4. The crime rate is high. Robbery and assault are rife, especially at weekends.

The very writer was once attacked and curry-powder was thrown in his eyes. He had the sum of £13 and a few shillings in his pocket. But the attacker failed to rob him of the money. He reported at the clinic and was taken by ambulance to Baragwanath Hospital where he was treated. The following week he was stabbed in the back four times and robbed of his driving licence and other documents. This time he carried no money with him.

There is one police station in the area. It is staffed mainly by Africans. And from the looks of things the police are inadequate. There are no street patrols and no flying squads, the police being mainly interested in pass and liquor raids, rather than on concentrating on criminals. The police also tend to be very open to bribery and take advantage of the lack of legal knowledge of most of the residents. This attitude leads to many false arrests. For example: the 21st of April I was assaulted by a shop owner and arrested for fighting. When I questioned the constable why I was arrested alone and with whom was I fighting? I was not given an answer. When charged at the police station, I was charged under the pass laws. (Charge Slip D.3 . . .) I reported to the officer in charge and showed him the marks of assault and tried to prove the wrong of the charge. He in turn shrugged his shoulders and gave no opinion. I subsequently got my discharge at the Commissioner's Court, Braamfontein, after having spent a night in the cells.

5. Concerning the husband-wife relation in this township, one finds that the husband has lost much of his controlling powers as head of the home. The reason being that his wife has to work and supplement his meagre salary, and feels independent. Furthermore, working wives at times become a target for unscrupulous men. Often too, a strained relationship between husband and wife occurs due to lack of common interest.

6. Regarding the general morals of the township, illegitimacy is on the increase. The reason being that children are left too much to themselves without parental control. Boys have the tendency to bully girls.

No school feeding schemes operate in the township and many children leave for school without breakfast. They usually have no school uniforms, and because of their cost they are usually unable to procure all the prescribed books. Children are often sent back home because they have not paid their school fees and many are unable to partake in sporting activities because of the club contributions required.

Because both parents are more often than not out working all day, the children of the township have little parental control and are open to many temptations. Children are tempted to steal because of hunger and lack of pocket money, tempted to lie to obtain money and tempted to organized crime to obtain what they want.

Like the children, the animals of the township are neglected and underfed. They roam around knocking over dustbins, breaking down fences and causing damage to gardens. They are usually thin, starved and dirty.

7. If it were possible for most mothers to stay at home and for fathers to earn enough to support their families adequately, crime would lessen. If children were well fed and kept busy with sports and under parental control, better results in schools could be achieved. If rent worries and the fear of the police were blotted out, the people would be better citizens. If houses were provided with sufficient rooms and bathrooms and streets with good lights, the people would be much happier.

In this chapter we have endeavoured to present insights into urban African life in a number of townships and locations. Let us now consider township life from another angle, from the African newspaper reporter's point of view. For township news is revealing of township society. The African Press is an aspect of urban African life which mirrors the joys and the fears, the trials and the tribulations of the township dwellers, from the point of view of their news value.

A comparatively recent development, the growth of African tabloids and newspapers, is indicative of the increasing literacy rate amongst the urban population. It has been estimated that one in every eight Africans in the Johannesburg area reads a newspaper.

The World, which is the most widely read African newspaper in the Johannesburg area, has a circulation of some 39,000, while the Natal paper, *Ilanga Lase Natal*, tops the list with a readership of some 48,000.

The English Press in South Africa also has a large African readership—a fact which has influenced the editorial policy of a number of African newspapers. They have striven not to repeat the news contained in English papers and have stressed news items of particular interest to the urban dweller, namely, township news. An example of such a paper is *The World*, a paper which has striven to portray the urban African world, the world of the vast majority of its readers, a world which is graphically portrayed by a study of its news headlines.

To illustrate what constitutes township news, a series of front pages from *The World* are reproduced here; front pages which tap the pulse of the Johannesburg urban townships; headlines which illustrate the urban African world of violence, gang warfare, juvenile

47

delinquency and crime; news items which show both what is happening in the urban townships, as well as what has news value for the Johannesburg urban African.

The following series of African front-page news items gives a vivid portrayal of the urban African contemporary scene in the Johannesburg area.

Such are the urban African townships. Huge housing projects and tumble-down squatter camps, each with its own characteristics, each with its own peculiar individuality.

It is in such townships, scattered in and around the Johannesburg area, that the urban African personality is evolving.

The following chapters will be devoted to the study of this personality and the test designed to assess it.

BRIDGE
COAL STOVE SPECIALISTS
JEWEL ENAMEL STOVE
CORONET ENAMEL STOVE
in Grey, White, Blue.
Deposit £5.10.0 Monthly £2.6.6
133 Jeppe St., off Harrison St.

Price 3d.

The World

Midweek Edition

SOUTH AFRICA'S LEADING AFRICAN NEWSPAPER
JOHANNESBURG, WEDNESDAY, MAY 25, 1960

BRIDGE
COAL STOVE SPECIALISTS
GLENWOOD ENAMEL STOVE
Deposit £5.10.0 Month: £3.5.0
all "DEFY" Models in Stock
133 Jeppe St., off Harrison St.

BLACK AGAINST MAROON IN REEF TERROR REIGN

BERET GANGS AT WAR

Death roll now ten in bitter feud

BOARDMEN HAVE ASKED THE BENONI POLICE TO TAKE ACTION AGAINST TWO RIVAL ARMED GANGS WHICH ARE MENACING THE PEACE AT WATTVILLE AND BENONI LOCATION.

Both gangs wear berets. The Wattville gangsters wear black berets. The Benoni Location gang wear maroon berets.

Her last farewell

Riot boys say why they made protest

THIS much complaint of the boys expelled from Bodibeng High School, Maseru, is that the scanty and goodness of the food has been cutting down, while school fees are going up.

The boys have found it convenient, mostly dealing with food as reason for their going on strike and rioting.

There is no longer any sort of morale, they say, and the need to buy and of poor quality. The facilities and soap obtainable at the storeroom of the Maseru and they are not happy with the preferential given to store of Europeans than to some of the blacks.

Nkrumah sails

DR. KWAME NKRUMAH, Prime Minister of Ghana, sailed from Takoradi, London, on Sunday on his way home to attend the Prime Ministers Conference in England.

RENTS SHOCK

RENTS in Pretoria's locations will rise by 7s per year for some much-housed.

And people living in government mortgage houses will pay 10s per cent more than when new rates gazetted by the Springs Municipality become effective on July 1.

The increase is being made in spite of the fact that the Pretoria Advisory Board rejected a recommendation from the Council that people earning £50 a month to more should pay "economic" rents.

The new rates have come as a bombshell, said Mr. F.D. Lagadi, who has been a member of the board for 17 years.

There are £25 worth in Pretoria, on which people have built their own homes. Rents on these were 10s a month. It is proposed to raise the rent to 15/6d. a month.

Rents for three-roomed municipal houses will rise from £1.3s. a month to £2.7s. There are 180 such houses.

Four-roomed houses where greater rents pay 15s. to £2.10s will now be raised to £2.9s. £2.8s.3d. and £2.19. respectively.

KNIFEMEN ROB PASSENGERS

A GANG of youths carrying long knives robbed passengers on a crowded train between Florida and Krugersdorp on Saturday night.

They threw pepper in their victims' eyes and menaced them with the knives.

Grim find after jive party
DEAD MAN IN EMPTY HOUSE

AFTER a big jiving party had been held in an empty house in Daveyton, the body of an unknown man was found lying on the floor.

The party began last Friday when a number injured house and carried in a radio and records.

Soon a big jiving party was in progress in the house, which has been unoccupied from the beginning of the month.

The music was power and hot. Then in the night a squabble broke out.

... then silence?

The music stopped. The dancing crowd hurried away. And all was silent.

Over the weekend the Daveyton police found the dead man. He had been stabbed.

When reporters visited the

empty house, they saw blood on the floor of two rooms.

There was a paper bag lying near a pool of blood and an overcoat was thrown on top of it.

Spots of blood

Outside the building there were spots of blood.

Daveyton police said that the South African C.I.D. had been called in and were investigating.

It is understood that detectives questioned a woman about the dead man.

Members of the local advisory board said they knew nothing about the party.

Nobody else is allowed to wear berets with these colours. It proves a man to the gang because 'their berets are taken once at once.

Both old women have been stopped and told to take off their berets.

Boardmen told the Benoni Commandant of Police that there is a gang headquarters somewhere near the police station in Benoni Location.

The gangsters carry pangas, tomahawks, knives and Tom —

There are about 200 men and men in the two gangs. Some of the thugs are still going to school.

When a scuffling gangster is spotted for a "rob" a gang car carrying a knife or a panga will simply walk straight into a classroom and keep him out.

Teachers helpless

Teachers are helpless against this sort of thing. They have asked the police to protect the schools.

The teeth have been killed in fights between the gangs over the past few months.

Two youths were stabbed during last weekend. Both are now lying in the Benoni-Boksburg Hospital.

Boardmen say that people may not go between the two locations. Dave is a district "key" against crossing over, and the peace-movers is death.

Even the girls of the location may not go between the girls in the other.

The streets are not safe at night.

Boardmen are to have talks with council officials. They will ask for pangas to be supplied from the locations if they harbour children who are gangsters.

BLAUPUNKT

... if you look for

QUALITY

4-SPEED
DRY CELL RADIOGRAMS

LEADER DISPLAY
£64/15/-

FULLY BATTERY-OPERATED
POWERFUL ALL-WAVE RECEPTION
DOUBLE-SIDED DISPLAY-MIRROR BACKS.
EASY TERMS

BROADCAST RADIO CO.

COMPLETE HOME FURNISHERS
70a PRITCHARD ST.   PHONE: 23-2531
SOLE S.A. DISTRIBUTORS
Television and Elec. Distributors (Pty) Ltd. Box 10011
JOHANNESBURG.

Sobukwe appeals against sentences on PAC leaders

ROBERT MANGALISO SOBUKWE, president of the PAC, has appealed against his conviction for incitement against the Pass Laws. He has also appealed against the conviction of 18 PAC men who were sentenced with him in the Johannesburg Regional Court.

The sentences ranged from 18 months to three years in the case of Sobukwe.

The 18 other PAC men who were sentenced to three years each by the Johannesburg Regional Commissioner appeared against the severity of the sentences. Their appeal was noted three weeks ago.

It is understood that when Mr. Sobukwe was still in the Fort awaiting trial, he sent an attorney Mr. N.S.A. Sobukwe.

He instructed Mr. Sobukwe to appeal in the event of a conviction.

1. The judgment is bad in law because the magistrate should have found the accused not guilty, to that the Crown failed to discharge the onus which rested upon it.

2. The judgment is against the evidence and weight of evidence.

3. The sentence was excessive.

In the event of conviction, Mr. Sobukwe appeals that —

1. The other reasons of appeal are forthcoming.

Relatives of the 140 other men who were convicted for the Benin Commissioner held person of attorney from the men.

In terms of these grounds they appealed three weeks ago against the severity of the three years imprisonment each.

To do not tell Mr. Sobukwe whether he would conduct his own defence in the Supreme Court, or whether he would engage an advocate.

If they stood by the PAC principle of "Not out, to fine, no defence," then the PAC men will defend themselves.

The grounds of appeal were filed with the Clerk of the Court in Johannesburg last Friday.

RAID ON PARTY

SPECIAL Branch police raided a party given up the Mantsville Party to a Johwa's home on Sunday. They searched all the house but made no arrests.

According to a leaflet, the three-day party was given by the women of Jehwa to raise money for the legal defence of Mr. Peter Lengene, secretary of the now banned PAC, and Mrs. Elizabeth Mofokelo and other Jehwa women.

A small boy, one slung over one shoulder, peeps into the unoccupied house in Daveyton where the body of an unidentified man was found lying in a pool of blood. The grim discovery was made after a jive party had been held in the house over the weekend. The police detectives are now investigating.

BRIDGE
COAL STOVE SPECIALISTS
JEWEL ENAMEL STOVE
CORONET ENAMEL STOVE
In Green, White, Blue.
Deposit £5.15.0 Monthly £2.6.6
133 Jeppe St., off Harrison St.

BRIDGE
COAL STOVE SPECIALISTS
GLENWOOD ENAMEL STOVE
Deposit £3.10.9 Monthly £1.5.9
all "DEFY" Models in Stock
133 Jeppe St., off Harrison St.

GANGSTERS AGAIN ACTIVE ON THE REEF

400 CRIME VICTIMS

Swoop on pay packets

MORE than 400 victims of assaults were taken to Reef hospitals over the week-end.

And as crime swept through the townships, nine and ten men told grim stories of attacks made on husband over their weekends and pay-packets.

Most workers make their end-of-the month wages. Others were taking home their weekly pay packets.

They were easy targets for the thugs who lurked at the street corners or systematically waited at from hide-outs near railway stations.

Some of the assault statistics were worked out in detail last week-end in the crime news.

Alexandra Township, which was a trouble-free spot after the police cordoned some months ago, came right back into the crime news.

Topping the list

A quick round-up of Reef hospitals show that Alexandra topped the list of casualties with 140 people beaten-up or stabbed.

Residents of the south-western areas of Johannesburg found it hard to get help.

Here's the reason: The "vic" between townships and "private" flared up again.

Orlando murder

Amos Tladi (48) was murdered in his home in Orlando West, Johannesburg, on Sunday.

Two unknown Bantu night watchmen were shot in the heads and battered to death in Springs.

One of the men died on his way to ambulance to the Far East Rand Non-European Hospital.

His left wrist had been handcuffed to his wrist belt by the gangsters who attacked him.

This is the first picture of Basutoland's experience Mr. R., the man who and he fled from South Africa, but whom the political refugees support to a million per Mr. R. told something glamoris to the refugees. The South African police have found that a detective is in any of the territories, Mr. R. is unknown to any of the South African politicians who escaped from the Union after he made contact with...

THOSE "EMERGENCY EXITS"

S.A. bid to close over-the-border escape routes

POLITICAL refugees from South Africa may soon find the Protectorates closed to them as escape routes. And all-out effort to close down the "emergency exists" is being made by the Union Government.

The Nationalist Government is reported to be suggesting with the British Government in an effort to bar Bechuanaland, Swaziland and Basutoland as escape routes to those who fear arrest in the Union.

The South African Government, it is believed, started negotiations following the large number of people who fled into the Protectorates after the March disturbances.

Petrol attack: man arrested

A RHODESIAN police have arrested an African in connection with the death of Mr. Lilian Burton, the White woman who died after a mob had attacked her and burnt her car with petrol.

During the past few days scores of refugees have swarm flown out of Bechuanaland to Ghana, where, it is reported, their escape was easier.

More flights out of the Protectorates will take place this week.

Political observers are doubtful whether the Government's attempt to seal off the Protectorates will succeed.

May not agree

They say that Britain is unlikely to agree to a step which it would bring proper on its head from the rest of the world.

Among those who left the organisations during the weekend and who are now in Ghana are Mr. Arnold Selby, a banned trade union leader; Mr. J. Hazvinei, a banned Congressist, and Mr. and Mrs. P. Anrezume and their three young sons.

MR. LENGENE: AN APOLOGY

MR. Peter Lengene, leader of the Maniniki Party in Jansong, was wrongly described in the May 25 edition of the Mid-Week World as secretary of the now-banned PAC. We regret this unfortunate error and apologise to Mr. Lengene for the mistake.

Leng known as the Maniniki Party chief, he is not connected with the PAC.

The PAC secretary, now jailed for imrisonment, is Mr. Peter Letholo.

DIMBA'S PEACE CALL

Peace must be upheld no matter how people talk about the Government's policies, Bishop W. Dimba said in his Presidential address to the annual conference of the Federation of Bantu Churches.

Preferred above faith and ranging hymns outside the Orlando Hall, where the bishop was addressing members of the seven-member Bantu Churches.

Some members of this church, which is headed by Bishop S.S. Zulu, a relative of the Zulu Paramount Chief, came home from far the meeting.

In the picture on the right is the new-head nominee of the federation, chairing the conference.

In front is Bishop Dimba, who was re-elected president. On the extreme right, him are (left to right) Bishop W. Manana, of Soweto; Rev. M. Ngcabo, a Durban...

White taxi-driver and woman cleared of morals charge

A WHITE TAXI DRIVER was said to have told an African woman found with him by the police in his car at 1 a.m.: "Get out of my car you filthy thing. What do you want in my car?"

Leslie Eaton, 50, and the woman, Maria Thokozile, 32, were acquitted in the Johannesburg Regional Court of a charge under the Immorality Act.

Two policemen who gave evidence differed on a material point.

The magistrate said Eaton "Your story is untrue. No person knowing the provisions of the Immorality Act would give a lift to an African woman in that time of the night for the sake of the kindness of his heart."

Sergeant B. D. Kruger said he was travelling with a constable in a squad car in Benkulen Valley about 1 a.m. on January 23.

Their attention was attracted by a car parked on the side of the street.

They stopped and jumped towards it. Maria, he said, was lying on her back on the front seat. Eaton was close by.

Eaton told Maria to get off his car and "asked he to give a chance."

Eaton, in his defence, said he was driving to Jeppe to charge the battery after finishing work.

He saw Maria at a corner and she asked him for a lift. He picked her up.

He car stalled before they reached the place where he had to drop her.

He was trading under the darkness to see if the light was alright. The headlights were where she had asked.

He denied that he intended to Womrad or indecent act, which breaks out.

afterwards who was absent to treasurer, and during S.S. Mustyana, of Charlestown.

Behind them is Mr. M. Mrs Sibiya, a Johannesburg social worker, who is the secretary.

Motiva Dimba said in his address that, however bad our members visited her Government's policies, it was their duty for the Bantu nation to uphold peace no matter how it expressed its views in South Africa.

He said that the federation had been moved by Dr. Verwoerd's broadcast that he saw no malice in the men who supported in him his duty.

The federation passed a motion of sympathy to the Prime Minister.

The federation desired to ask the Government to be allowed in the way the federation administers its bishops to the Minister of Bantu Administration and Development, Mr. Daan Nel.

On Sunday the conference moved to Benoni, where a new church was named by Bishop Dimba.

TRADERS HIT BY RAIDS

POLICE raids in the South Western Townships have had many African businessmen worried.

According to one trader, the police were making a blitz on peaceful dies who were given work without being inspected.

Many said berries were stopped and the men working on their terms were taken away for questioning. Coal deliveries almost came to a standstill.

Another trader with his store to empty about eighteen bags of coal in a magistrate court.

Africans businessmen did not seem to worry about registration, though some men said they were prosecuted for their contraven to disregard of the new regulations, he added.

They may be prosecuted if their business is damaged if the shortage, he said.

CONGO RIOTS NOW LIKELY

MORE trouble in the Belgian Congo when it becomes independent at the end of June appeared likely and Rhodesian police in the weekend that Rhodesian police have never taken only for the Congo Federation border on June 30 in the case the Congo may strike which breaks out.

BLAUPUNKT
...if you look for QUALITY

4-SPEED DRY CELL RADIOGRAMS

LEADER DISPLAY £64/15/-

FULLY BATTERY-OPERATED POWERFUL ALL-WAVE RECEPTION DOUBLESIDED DISPLAY-MIRROR BACKS

EASY TERMS

BROADCAST RADIO CO.

COMPLETE HOME FURNISHERS

70a PRITCHARD ST. PHONE: 23-2531

SOLE E.A. DISTRIBUTORS

Television and Hire Distribution (Pty.) Ltd. Box 9855
JOHANNESBURG

Basutoland Council move

THE Basutoland Legislative Council is meeting consideration of the Commonwealth Parliamentary Association.

The decision to meet a Parliamentary Association branch in Basutoland was made in the Council in the form of an opposition motion introduced by Mr. B. Bereni, the chairman.

THE Basutoland Legislature next Secretary.

The leader of the Opposition, Mr. B. Hlobshibe, supported the motion.

Basutoland will be eligible to be a subsidiary branch in cause of it's status as a colony. Only self-governing Commonwealth countries can become full members.

TROPHY FOR BEST NURSE

A N eye specialist attached to the St. John Eye Hospital, near Sunnyworth Hospital, has donated a trophy for the best nurse of the year at the Eye Hospital.

It will be presented annual.

The work of the nurses at the hospital is already being warmly studied from year on-the one of the year, when the nurses and her students will select the nurse who has done outstanding work this year.

The trophy will be awarded to the nurse who has done good work in a magnetic efficiency, good behaviour and willingness to cooperate with the hospital authorities.

The specialist has also invented factory and the nurses will receive a cash award.

Nellie Mabe, fourth year nurse, was interviewed at the nurses and receiving hard work, with a view to becoming the first to win it.

Ntsele bids for Madi's crown

Levy Madi, Sophiatown lightweight Transvaal feather-weight champion, defends his title against Eric Ntsele at the Uncle Tom's Hall, Orlando West, on Friday, July 1.

ROBINSON'S
TWO WAY TABLETS

YOUR BLOOD - KIDNEY AND BLAD-
DER - STOMACH - BACKACHE -
CONSTIPATION - BUSINESS -
EXHAUSTION - HEADACHES -
STOMACH ACHE - PILES

2/-
PER PACKET

Price 4d.

The World

SOUTH AFRICA'S LEADING AFRICAN NEWSPAPER

WEEK ENDING, SATURDAY, JUNE 4, 1960

Weekend Edition

ROBINSON'S
SEJESO ITHLISO

5/-

MURDER HUNT AFTER MAN FOUND DYING IN VELD

NEW PANGA TERROR ROCKS THE TOWNSHIPS

ZOLA TOWNSHIP'S MYSTERY PANGA SLASHER HAS STRUCK AGAIN. HE MURDERED AND ROBBED A YOUNG MAN LAST WEEK IN AN OPEN FIELD NEAR THE SUPERINTENDENT'S OFFICE.

The victim, Milton Ngwaye, was attacked while on his way home from work. His head and body were severely slashed by a panga.

He was found dying on the veld. But before he died on his way to hospital, he was able to give a brief description of his killer.

The panga man, according to Milton and other victims, is tall and wears blue overalls.

He works alone in the dark when few people are about. Most of his victims have been attacked from behind.

The panga terror has also spread to the neighbouring Jabulani township.

Many young women assaulted

Mr. James Ndebin, of the Jabulani Vigilance Association, told the "World" that several young women had been assaulted and raped during the past few weeks.

"These attacks take place early in the morning, usually at some lonely place, while the women are on their way to work."

The panga slasher is also thought to be responsible for attacks in the thick woods between Dube South and Mofolo.

A few weeks ago a pretty, young woman was assaulted and raped in the woods.

Jumped out of the woods

She said afterwards that her attacker had suddenly jumped out of the woods and caught her. He stabbed her several times and then raped her.

The woman said that the man was elderly. Because of severe shock, she could not give a clearer description. After assaulting her, the man ran away.

Two other panga victims who were attacked two weeks ago are still being treated daily for their wounds at Baragwanath Hospital.

They are Between Zata, of Zola, who was slashed on the left shoulder and left arm, and Jeremiah Kevani, of Jabulani, who was slashed three times in the arm.

They are slowly recovering from their injuries.

THE MAN THEY CANNOT KILL

Beaten with axe and shot 9 times

WILLIAM MQOWAGWA is one of the luckiest men alive. During the past two months he has been shot nine times and survived a vicious attack with an axe.

Mqowagwa was alone twice in the day when fighting flared up in Krugersdorp in March.

Two months later he was shot seven times in pitch-dark range in Randfontein.

He is a Crown witness in a case arising out of the Randfontein shooting and in the subsequent march against a man charged in the Randfontein Magistrate's Court in connection with seven murders.

BEAUTY QUEEN SAVED FROM KIDNAP GANG

A RAND beauty queen was saved from being kidnapped by thugs in Bursutuland last week. The girl, Maud Lephanane, "Miss Krugersdorp 1957"—was on holiday at Bartha-Butha when she was attacked by four men.

Miss Lephanane was sitting at a table at an inn when a drunk walked up to her and suggested they should go out together.

She told the drunk that she wanted nothing to do with him. The man then left.

A few minutes later he returned — with three henchmen.

They grabbed Miss Lepha-nane and were manhandling her when the "World's" Bartha-Butha reporter, Leonard Bo-matsana, walked into the inn.

Accounts racket

MEN with an almost uncanny knowledge of keeping accounts are keeping a tidy penny in the Johannesburg Southern Township. They pose as qualified bookkeepers and accountants.

Mr. Thomas Kusa, a local shopkeeper, said that clergymen pose as bookkeepers by these bright conversationalists.

Stroomd man

Bamatsana ran up to the men and pulled them away from Miss Lephanane.

Although educated up to one, he told Miss Lephanane "if you go with this girl we will settle accounts." TO call the police.

Without waiting to arrest Bamatsana, the four men slipped out of the inn and ran into the night.

This is Mr. K

Do you know this man? He is the mysterious Mr. K. who is associated by political refugees in Basutoland to be a Beverley Browne detective. Mr. K has told many different stories which started off as (a) a refugee who was a member of the PAC (b) as an member of the ANC in Basutoland, (c) a stalker from Bloemfontein.

He is always keen to talk politics in the Basuto, and he has asked many questions about reading politicians.

'You must have bodyguard'

THIEVES' NOTE DISCOVERED IN WRECKED CAR

INSURANCE INSPECTOR Reuben Zunga, of Orlando East, was robbed of his car by two men when he had given a lift. When he recovered the badly damaged car on Monday, he found a warning note lying on the front seat.

The note, written in English said: "Next time when you drive around you must have a bodyguard. How much did you pay for this car?"

There was a note and address on the note. The police have taken the wrecked car to dirty paper and are investigating.

Zunga said that he was travelling from Orlando to his home in Orlando East on Friday evening.

As he entered Orlando, he was stopped by two men who asked him for a lift to the station.

Hit on neck

The men got into the back seats. After he had driven a short distance he was hit on the neck with something heavy.

He was badly dazed. And when he came round, he found himself lying on the ground. A passing motorist stopped and took him to hospital where he was treated for his injuries.

The car was found in a bush near the Baragwanath Administration.

Dead constable: two men held

TWO men were arrested in Alexandra Township last week in connection with the death of Constable Benedict Chabeli, whose body had been washed away by floods near Benoni.

The police are following up the address which was written on the note. Previously the police have been found nearby.

Photo's how the police found the car. Below: The wrecked Randfontein car in which Zunga's bodyguard was shot dead. One shot reverberated and the stones here. Lying on the driving seat was a note which warned Mr. Zunga. The police are following up the address which was written on the note that Zunga again was found nearby.

Secret sales of 'pirate' meat anger butchers

DYING CATTLE SOLD BY WHITE FARMERS

MEAT "pirates" are doing such big business in the Meadowlands area of Johannesburg that they are hitting the licensed butchers in the place where it hurts most—and that's the pocket.

Things have got so bad, with the "pirates" hawking black market meat from house to house, that the butchers have made strong protests to the authorities.

Butchers have made their own complaints into the very private trade. They find that the sellers of this underworld meat are supplied with cattle by White farmers.

Some of them buy old and dying cattle from farms on the West Rand.

The beasts are slaughtered out in the veld so that the health authorities who deal with meat markets as not permitted to control it as is the case.

Sell cheaply

The sellers move around the townships in vans and turn selling meat at prices far below those charged by licensed butchers due to the West Rand. It is actually cut where they hide delivery.

Indians and Chinese from Newclare and Sophiatown are also hawking a big meat racket.

'Raising up'

"They take African women at doing the meat by these to cause pure sort themselves allowed into the Southern Township.

"These hawkers are driving up prices and new butcher trades having to put up with the fall off in trade we find we have to destroy pounds of meat."

Rent trouble

Some established butchers are faced with difficulties in meeting their rents.

In their quest for patronage in the townships, they have noted that their rents should be reduced.

But many women who spend patronise the "pirates" say that some low-down meat are sold in low-grade meat in first grade market.

The result was that, in order to get the most on their time money, they had turned to the "pirates."

Dr. H. Rooth-Miller, Medical Officer of Health in Johannesburg, said that illegal slaughtering of cattle in Johannesburg happened from time to time but has somehow kept close watch on the meat market.

Makhethoa oa Capetown oa 1960

o khetha Cream tse holimo bakeng sa 'Mafa oa hae . . . .

Botsa Mofumahatsana Gladys Ndzela. O tie a bolelle hore li-cream tse ntle li etsoa ka Karroo. Li a loketse lebone li u neha 'mala o lesili le blakileng le se nang litlhako la lekhohlane.

Tse Peli KARROO CREAMS

tse sebelisoang Mots'eare le Bosiu

BRIDGE
COAL STOVE SPECIALISTS
JEWEL ENAMEL STOVE
CORONET ENAMEL STOVE
in Green, White, Blue.
Deposit £3.15.0 Monthly £2.6.6
133 Jeppe St., off Harrison St.

BRIDGE
COAL STOVE SPECIALISTS
GLENWOOD ENAMEL STOVE
Deposit £3.10.0 Months £2.5.0
all "DEFY" Models in Stock
123 Jeppe St., off Harrison St.

The World

Price 3d.   Midweek Edition

SOUTH AFRICA'S LEADING AFRICAN NEWSPAPER

JOHANNESBURG, WEDNESDAY, JUNE 22, 1960

TOWNSHIP RESIDENTS TO BE SCREENED

725,000 FACE PROBE

JOHANNESBURG'S 725,000 Africans are to be screened by the City Council officials before the Bantu Authorities Act is put into force in town areas.

The Department of Bantu Administration and Development has asked all Reef towns to help their survey the numbers of people who fall under the different Bantustan chiefs.

A Johannesburg City Council official told the "World" that the council would start soon on this survey.

"The names of people will probably be taken in a house-to-house campaign," he said.

"Only the names of people who consider that they fall under one of the chiefs will be taken. We do not yet know what will happen to people who have lost all their tribal contacts.

"This system has nothing to do with the council. It is a matter for the Bantu Administration Department and the various chiefs. We are merely helping in the survey," he said.

Three Johannesburg men have already been appointed as chiefs' representatives in the city. They are Mr. Hamilton Mota, for the Batlokwa; Mapedi Paulus for the Free State Smuts, and Mr. Obed Makapan for the Bakgatla.

Gang's New Look

Three youngsters and their raffeta tweed-peg-leg slacks front-page news and pictures this week. The reason? These weeks ago they were split into two battling-equipped gangs — the Black Swines and the Mic-niks. Whenever they met serious followed.

Then two dance-teachers, Mr. Dland Tshabalala and Mr. Bainey Dladla stepped in.

Now the boys have been formed into a soccer team called the Black Pirates as they are pictured above, left and right, at their first practice at a small ground near Mr. Dladla's home.

Below is Mr. Tshabalala, holding the ball and explaining the rules to some of the youngsters.

THEORY IN MURDER MYSTERY

Policeman's body hidden for a day

MURDERERS hid a body for a day, then "dumped" it away from the scene of the killing. This is the theory of the police investigating the slaying of African policeman Thomas Simelane, who was found dead in full uniform in a building on Twist Street.

Constable Simelane, who was stationed at Hospital Hill, was on his way to work when he was attacked and killed.

He did not report for duty the next morning.

On Thursday morning trace were found to early in a building under construction in Twist Street.

He was in full uniform, but his helmet, overcoat and truncheon were missing.

The police think the body is brought to the building by the men who hid it after Simelane was killed.

The dead policeman, with his left hand under his cheek, had been in the building a day.

Samson is strongest lasts longest...

it's today's best value for money

When you buy this fine Samson Denim Overall look for these features:
● BUTTON-UP CUFFS
● MADE FROM FINEST DENIM
● PLENTY OF ROOM

SAMSON

the name for greater strength

THERE'S A SAMSON FOR EVERY JOB OF WORK

Eight arrested in beerhall riot

EIGHT arrests have been made after a riot at the beerhall at Maitetane in which 700 rioting customers stoned the building, set fire to a scooter and stole a till containing £200.

More police are wanted

STAMMING, assault and pick-pocketing have become a serious affair for Payneville beerhall. During this enquiry found travelling up to recommend that the hall should close at five o'clock instead of seven.

The board is also to ask for more policemen to keep order there.

At present the area is patrolled by only one policeman, who also has to watch over a bus terminus nearby.

Miners are said to be mainly to blame for the assaults and robberies.

Latest is to beware up of a well-known resident, Mr. Biplie Kunene, and a school-boy, Both are in hospital.

The riot flared up suddenly inside the hall after a quarrel had started.

The rioters assaulted attendants and threatened the African cashier, who looted him self in a room for safety.

The riot lasted only a few minutes and stopped as suddenly as it had started.

Six claims that etc. we are found by one of the looters.

A taxi driver who tried to evacuate drove his car homewards for and the man ran away from the beerhall quick.

Advocates for PAC appeals

ADVOCATES are to be briefed to represent the accused PAC men when their appeals are heard.

It is understood that the appeals will be based on points of law which, it is claimed, were overlooked at their trials.

The date of the appeal hearings is not yet known.

They are free

SIX million Africans achieved political freedom on Monday when the West African Federation became independent.

DEAF EAR TO CRIES FOR HELP

A YOUNG Roodepoort woman calls for help shouting at a taxi stop in Dobsonville ignored by her-passers-by who were also attacked by thugs, drag-ged off into the bushes, and criminally assaulted.

This dumb was working towards the taxi stop in the evening when three men who attacked her and drag-ged her into the darkness.

Her cries, that she was raped by two of the men.

A taxi-driver who heard her screams drove his car homewards for and the man ran away from the beerhall quick.

Mr. Tihara said that trouble started when senior third policeman refused to help.

The woman panted as the policemen ran chased them through the bush.

"The twist ran through the corridor and linked with the innocent passengers," said Tihara.

Rail fight between Russians and pickpockets

MAN THROWN OUT OF MOVING TRAIN

HOODLUMS threw a young Kragersdorp man out the window of a moving train after a fight between "Russians" and pickpockets on Sunday afternoon.

The victim, John Tipani, a Witwater Station Kragersdorp resident told the "World": "I was very lucky — the train was just pulling into Windsor Mine Station when I was flung out the window.

"The train was slowing down otherwise I might have been seriously injured.

"I was knocked out of hospital and allowed to go home."

Mr. Tihara said that trouble started when senior third policemen refused to help.

The rioters panted as the policemen ran chased them through the bush.

"The twist ran through the corridor and linked with the innocent passengers," said Tihara.

Trap for robbers

A WOMAN in nurse's costume who stands in lonely places at night and captures robbers for a lift to a trap for robbers in the Reef townships.

Motorists who have stopped to give the "nurse" a lift have been attacked and robbed by men hiding nearby.

Another method

Another way the girl operates is to ask the motorist to drive her to a spot where robbers are waiting for the car to stop.

The girl is believed to use the name "Mary Moosa." She is young and attractive, and is a danger to every motorist.

VERWOERD OUT

DR. Verwoerd was discharged from Pretoria General Hospital on Saturday afternoon after an eye operation.

The operation was to replace an eye drain with plastic material.

IV

ANALYSIS AND INTERPRETATION OF THE T.A.T.

PROJECTIVE techniques for the study of personality are relatively new methods. Very few studies of their application to Africans exist and, as far as is known, the present test is the first to be constructed for the specific purpose of studying the urban African personality.

The assessment of this method is a specialized task and it will be of decidedly limited value in the hands of someone lacking a solid theoretical understanding of clinical psychology in general, and the science of personality study in particular.

While a brief interpretative outline of the analysis of this method will be presented here, the psychologist who wishes to gain competence in the use of this technique will be well advised to refer to the references given in the bibliography.

INTERPRETATIVE PROCEDURE

The main stages in the interpretative process may be tabulated as follows:

1. How does the subject define the stimulus?
2. Given his perception of the stimulus, how does he respond to it?
3. Given his definition of the stimulus and his chosen mode of response to it, what does this tell us of the subject's personality? (W. E. Henry.)

The analytical approach to arrive at the above steps is as follows:

1. The entire protocol is read for suggestive leads (mood, prevailing attitudes, unusual plots, unique verbalizations, general methods of solving problems, and the frequency of specific themes) and for the formulation of tentative interpretations and questions to be investigated further.

2. Each story is analysed for basic ideas and structural characteristics.
3. Each story is compared as a unit with the rest of the protocol in order to identify the characters, the conflicts and the relationships—to decide whether the material is wishful, autobiographical, or superficial.
4. All stories are considered as one organized, combined unit.
5. The interpretative hypotheses are integrated into a final summary evaluation of the personality.

The interpretative rules to be observed in the above analysis are as follows (from Piotrowski):

1. Proceed on the assumption that the testee identifies more with the motives expressed in the characterization than with the actual type of character introduced into the fantasy.
2. When interpreting stories, proceed on the assumption that every figure in the stories expresses some aspect of the testee's personality.
3. Take into consideration the possibility that the stories may not reflect genuine drives but superficial and stereotyped attitudes developed by the testee in order to hide his specific personality traits.
4. Proceed on the assumption that the stories frequently reflect what the subject thinks and feels about persons represented in the stories.
5. The more varied and the more incompatible the drives in a subject's stories the greater the possibility of poor personality integration, of greater tension, of fear that the unacceptable drives will undermine self-control and will prompt the subject to act contrary to his self-interests. The greater the diversity of drives, the greater the testee's indecisiveness and anxiety.
6. The chances of a particular thema being manifested in the subject's overt behaviour are positively correlated with the frequency of the thema's appearance in the protocol, with the consistency of the total record and with the emotional intensity accompanying the expression of the thema.
7. Note marked differences in the number and elaboration of ideas elicited by certain pictures as compared with those prompted by others; note bizarre notions, sudden or gradual increase or decrease of ideas; note the use of language in the stories.

The main point to remember in these tests is that the pictures presented are best seen, psychologically, as a series of social situations and interpersonal relations. To quote Bellak:

50

instead of responding to real people in real situations, the subject is responding to people in the pictures, which he imagines as certain social situations. Since he is under less constraint of conventionality of reality, his responses are more likely to depict his inner feelings. By this means we get at the contemporary patterns of his social behaviour and may be able to infer the genesis of these patterns. Interpretation is the process of finding a common denominator in the contemporary and genetic behaviour patterns of persons.

Furthermore, diagnostic statements should never be made on the basis of one story; a repetitive pattern is the best assurance that one is not dealing with an artefact but with an actual personality characteristic of the subject in question.

The following categorization of scoring categories adapted and modified from the methods of Bellak, Henry, Tomkins, Rotter and Shirley Jessor was found most useful:

1. The Main Theme: the attempt by the tester to restate the gist of the story. It is broken down into five main theme levels.

(a) The descriptive level: a plain restatement of the summarized meaning of the story.

(b) The interpretative level: assuming a psychological meaning beyond the story.

(c) The diagnostic level: transformation of the impressions into a definite statement in terms of the subject's personality.

(d) The symbolic level: interpretation according to psychoanalytic hypotheses.

(e) The elaborative level: inquiry into the subject's elaborations and free associations of specific data.

2. The Main Hero: the one who is most spoken of, whose feelings and subjective notions are most discussed and, in general, the figure with whom the narrator seems to identify himself. Consider the main hero's:

(a) Environmental stimuli—the forces in the environment affecting him.

(b) Specific stimuli—which affect him or to which he responds such as:
1. Living beings.
2. Inanimate objects.
3. Social forces, pressures and ideologies.

By virtue of the fact that the subject must structure the situation in which the hero functions, he tells us how he regards his environment. The environmental features and factors selected by the subject are usually similar to those which have importance for him or about which he is presently concerned.

3. The Main Needs of the Hero: an analysis of these needs will throw light on, and enable inferences to be made concerning the subject's needs and drives. Stein gives a good classification of these needs as follows:

(i) Activities initiated by the hero with regard to objects or situations:

(ii) Activities initiated by the hero with regard to other people.

(iii) The hero's reactions to the activities initiated by others.

4. The Conception of the Environment: usually two or three words will suffice such as succorant, hostile, friendly, dangerous, etc.

5. Apperceptive Distortion of Other Figures: as they appear in the dynamics of the hero's interpersonal relations.

6. The Manner in which the Behaviour is Expressed: we are here interested in the avenues of expression through which the hero reacts to the stimulation from the environment. These avenues of expression have been classified by Stein as follows:

(i) Fantasy—the hero does not express himself overtly but imagines, wishes or daydreams about how he would like to express himself.

(ii) Pre-motor level—the hero plans various actions but never carries them over into the 'story reality'.

(iii) Inhibited behaviour—the hero's behaviour is restrained because of fear of the consequences.

(iv) Motor level—the hero executes his plans, and his reactions to others are on an overt level. They may be in the form of:

(*a*) Gestures—'he shrugged his shoulders'.

(*b*) Active reactions—'he hit the man'.

(*c*) Passive reactions—'he did what he was told'.

(*d*) Energies directed externally—'he fought for the right to speak'.

(*e*) Energies directed internally—'he became self-critical'.

7. Significant Conflicts: we want to know not only the conflicts but the defences used against them. These may be classified as:

1. Environmental conflicts.

2. Emotional conflicts.

3. Interpersonal conflicts.

8. The Integration of the Ego: the adequacy of the hero in dealing with the problems he is confronted with in the pictures; his apperception of them indicates a great deal about his adequacy. We are interested here in:

(i) Is the subject able to tell appropriate stories?

(ii) Does he tell completely unrelated stories to the stimuli presented?

(iii) Is he preoccupied with his own problems?

(iv) Are the stories original and lucid?

(v) Are his solutions adequate?

(vi) Is there a personal involvement in the stories? ('This is what happened to *me*.')

9. Outcomes: classified as:

(i) Happy endings.

(ii) Unhappy endings.

(iii) Indefinite endings.

10. General Story Atmosphere: classified as:

(i) Calm and relaxed.

(ii) Anxious and tense.

(iii) Listless and passive.

(iv) Active and energetic.

11. Language used: the language structure gives valuable clues to the patience, intelligence, organization of thought, and decisiveness.

12. Presentation of the Summary and Final Report in terms of:

1. Motivations and Goals.
2. Outlook, Attitudes and Beliefs.
3. Frustrations, Conflicts and Fears.
4. Affects, Feelings and Emotions.
5. Insight into Self and Adjustments.
6. Personality Defences and Mechanisms.
7. Interpersonal Relations.
8. Intellectualization and Abilities.
9. Predictions and Postdictions.
10. Stress on Main Characteristics Appearing.

V

THE CARDS OF THE AFRICAN T.A.T.

AS Bellak has stated, the requirements for validity and usefulness in projective techniques can be seen as two-fold: projective methods are expected to perform as tools of both nomothetic and idiographic sciences. Originally formulated by Windelband and elaborated on by Allport, nomothetic science is concerned with the establishment of general lawfulness—as in chemistry and physics. Idiographic science, on the other hand, is concerned with understanding one particular event, for example, the results of a prolonged psychoanalysis, in which interest is centred upon the personality of one individual—the patient.

In the present context we are interested in the nomothetic implications of projective techniques, in their use in revealing general personality trends prevalent amongst urban Africans. We are primarily interested in the establishment of general personality propositions emerging as a result of our researches into urban African personality. We are attempting to isolate common factors, to determine typical patterns.

The failures and particular limitations of projective techniques as nomothetic instruments are possibly the main impetus for further research and for the increased attempts at better conceptualization. The fundamental problem is 'the difficulty of making inferences from the latent (test data) to the manifest (behavioural level)' (Bellak). In other words, in a nomothetic study of projective techniques we are mainly concerned with the correctness of our predictions made on the basis of a subject's fantasy behaviour in the test, in relation to his behaviour in reality.

The interpretation of behaviour in the translation of latent fantasy content to manifest reality behaviour is a dynamic process characterized by an interaction of four major variables: the behaviour sample selected, the psychodynamic knowledge of the interpreter, the interpreter's knowledge of the social and cultural environment of the subject, and the empathetic qualities of the interpreter. By the very nature of the variables involved, an interpretation based on such subjective functions requires statistical substantiation before the resulting assessments can be considered truly representative of overt behaviour.

The T.A.T. is the only statistically validated device in the PUTCO projective test battery, as well as the technique on which we have most data, and it will form the basis from which personality conclusions will be drawn.

> The Thematic Apperception Test is by design and administration, largely a fantasy test, not a projection test. The pictures may invoke an initial projection, but thereafter the individual develops his fantasy in a free manner . . . (Cattell).

An important aspect of the process of interpretation in this test is the understanding of the stimuli that the various pictures in the series present to the subject. The interpretation of an individual record usually proceeds picture by picture through the set. An analysis of each picture of the African T.A.T., in much the same way as Henry has analysed each card of the Morgan and Murray series, will therefore serve a dual purpose in this study:

(a) it will give interpreters specific picture-by-picture knowledge in addition to knowledge of general factors in terms of which all pictures may be described, and

(b) it will provide a basis for the formulation of modal personality trends as they appear under the stimulation of the pictures.

The categories of analysis under which each picture of the African T.A.T. will be presented are (from Henry, *The Analysis of Fantasy*):

    I. Their Description: to go with the actual photograph of the card.

    II. Manifest Stimulus Demand of the card: the manifest aspects of the card usually observed by the subjects and utilised in their stories. There are certain aspects of a card which may be taken as 'given' and other variations which may be thought to be either 'avoidance' by the subject or 'misinterpretation' and 'distortion'. Considerable caution must be used in deciding what is 'given' and hence what may be thought to be a distortion with special interpretative significance. Our concern is to so define the manifest stimulus as to enable us to develop a definition of distortions, but not to prematurely define as distorted the ordinary 'range of possible interpretations within the culture', expected in a person of adequate reality contact.

        Within this category of manifest stimulus demand, three sub-categories will be used:

    (a) Adequate Stimulus Notation—this refers to those major segments of the stimulus which reflect an adequate accounting of the card. By adequate accounting is meant the most generally

55

noted details and those out of which the usual subject builds his story.

(*b*) Other Details Often Noted—this refers to frequently observed details, other than those referred to in (*a*), that are not basic to the plot but which may be reasonably expected in normal subjects.

(*c*) Seldom Noted Details—this refers to the fact that some subjects observe details seldom seen by the majority.

III. Form Demand. Cards differ in the form pattern which they present to the subject and hence possibly reflect different degrees of task difficulty.

IV. Latent Stimulus Demand. Each stimulus presents, in addition to form and manifest content stimuli, a particular emotional issue.

V. Frequent Plots. This refers to the usual ways in which subjects integrate the preceding features and the particular stories which they tell.

VI. Significant Variations. The writer has gained the impression that some variations of response bear more close observation than others.

As the card series has been revised and altered since its original appearance, an analysis of pictures on the above lines will allow for the inclusion of cards subsequently deleted, together with the reasons for their deletion. The above approach will, furthermore, allow for judgments to be made as to the relative worth of the various cards, plus an overview of the personality areas covered by the series.

A collection of apperceptive norms, as envisaged in the above categorization, will permit comparisons of both an inter-individual nature as well as of an intra-individual type. And as Bellak has pointed out, as the 'psychodynamics of interpersonal relations revealed in the T.A.T. is much more susceptible to cultural differences than the more formal test procedures', such an accumulation of apperceptive norms will form a cultural frame of reference within which to assess the urban African. For, unless one has a series of cultural apperceptive norms, combined with a thorough knowledge of the cultural mores of the group, behaviour considered 'normal' within the particular culture, may, if judged against the standards of Western European culture, have 'pathological' significance. In urban African society this is particularly obvious when dealing with such functions as insecurity and fear, aggression, levels of inhibition, reaction to frustration and modes of verbal expression.

Apperceptive norms, especially in cultural studies, are of fundamental importance. The cultural norm, or theme, forms the basis for relative judgments and the T.A.T. is in essence a thematic device. 'Thematic tests tend to lose their very marrow if anything but the individual theme is considered' (Bellak). The true significance of urban African themes, and their subsequent assessment, must be

A.9.

B.8.

C.7.

C.7. (Revised)

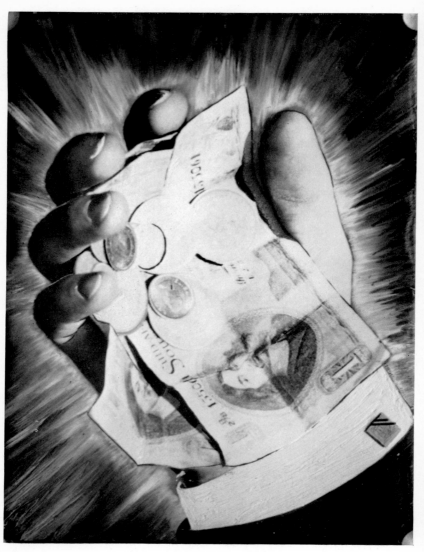

D.6.

F.4.

E.5.

G.3. (Revised)

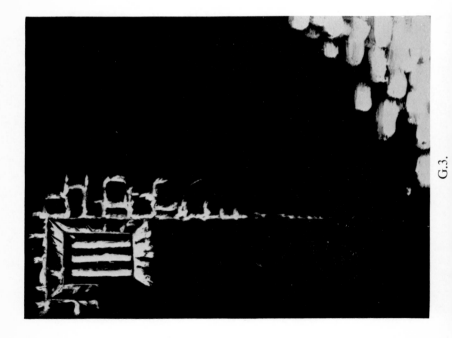

G.3.

H.2.

H.2. (Revised)

I.1.

made against a rich background of knowledge of urban African culture and a penetrating understanding of the urban African way of life.

CARD A : 9

I. *The Description:* An interpersonal relations scene with four characters—three seated in various positions in the foreground and one standing partly obscured in the background.

Their facial expressions are ambiguous. All figures are placed against a vague background depicting the indefinite outline of some sort of vehicle.

At the right-hand side of the picture an indefinite outline of a wall is indicated.

A horizontally placed picture.

II. *Manifest Stimulus Demand:*

(a) An adequate accounting of this card will involve some reference to the social situation presented. In general these figures are seen as (1) garage workers sitting down during a work break or (2) as passengers of a taxi or bus that has had a breakdown, and less frequently as (3) a robber gang discussing tactics.

(b) The social relations are very often broken into two opposing factions: the seated group and the standing man who is seen as isolated from or even spying on them.

(c) Frequently introduced are discussions on passing cars and people.

(d) In the robber theme the central seated figure and the standing figure are often seen as having masks over their faces.

(e) The background is usually seen as a bus, car, or a series of factory windows.

III. *Form Demand:* The form demand in this card calls for an integration of the figures and the background (the bus).

IV. *Latent Stimulus Demand:* Social relations problems of rivalry and ambition are very usual. It is a useful card in portraying reactions to work, to routine and to work satisfactions. This card gives a good indication of the subject's positiveness, displayed in the group's attitudes and how they are spending their leisure time.

V. *Frequent Plots:* Two main central plots are usually found:

(1) dealing with a social group of contented or fairly contented men; and

(2) dealing with an anti-social group either in terms of internal disruption or externally directed anti-social behaviour.

VI. *Significant Variations:* These are found in the extent of the co-operative or anti-social behaviour amongst the group towards others. Of interest is the response to the standing figure and his in-group or out-group status.

Anti-social behaviour resulting from unemployment gives a good indication of reactions to frustration and job insecurity.

The Cards of the African T.A.T.

I. *The Description:* A lone figure seated on a bench and leaning forward with his head in his hands and knees apart. The figure is surrounded by a completely ambiguous Dali-like surrealistic background.

On the ground in front of the character is what may be a cap, or a tin, or a box.

A vertically placed picture.

II. *Manifest Stimulus Demand:*

(a) An adequate accounting of this card involves a direct reference to the emotional reason for the figure's position.

(b) The most usual emotional reference is to the figure's despondency.

(c) The object on the floor in front of the character is usually related to his emotional state, e.g. 'a driver who has just made an accident'—it is seen as his cap; 'a man who has been drinking too much'—it is seen as a beer-mug.

(d) A rare detail is the apperception of a snake under the stool on which the character is sitting.

III. *Form Demand:* The single figure is the only basic form, although a preoccupation with minor details apperceived in the back- and fore-ground is common in emotionally involved subjects.

IV. *Latent Stimulus Demand:* This picture represents what van Lennep calls a 'being personally alone' type of situation and important attitudes toward the isolated self are aroused. As such it tends to arouse feelings of loss, inferiority, guilt, depression and anxiety. Of interest is the subject's reaction to these emotions: he may react by internally directed aggression or by externally directed aggression.

This situation highlights the subject's personal adequacy.

V. *Frequent Plots:* The central issue is usually some explanation of the reason for the man's despondency; this is usually attributed to:

(a) job insecurity,

(b) family trouble,

(c) drink.

In the drink theme, the individual is often considered to have taken to drink to overcome some emotional upheaval caused by (a) or (b) above.

VI. *Significant Variations:* The background is often apperceived as a forest and animal attacks are introduced. Blood is often introduced in the foreground.

Suicide or murder themes are sometimes introduced.

I. *The Description:* A township scene with two children in the middle of the road in the foreground. The focal point of the picture is the lone tree in the centre foreground flanked by township houses on

58

either side. The road is bordered on the one side by electric standards receding into the distance.

The whole scene is set against a wide expanse of cloudy sky. This is a horizontally placed picture.

II. *Manifest Stimulus Demand:* An adequate accounting will have to integrate the two children into the total scene, plus some explanation of what they are doing.

Other details often noted are horsemen appearing over the hill at the far right and snow on the ground.

The storm clouds are usually discussed.

III. *Form Demand:* This card lends itself to preoccupation with minor details when the story is centred on the township; if the two children are the centre of the story details in the environment tend to be overlooked.

IV. *Latest Stimulus Demand:* The situation lends itself to discussions on parental responsibility, social responsibility, civic-mindedness and criticism of squalor, an expression of personal frustration and feelings of being discriminated against. The critical faculty is given a good deal of scope in this picture.

V. *Frequent Plots:* Three types of plot occur most frequently:
   (1) The story of two lost children.
   (2) A criticism of lack of parental control.
   (3) A story (usually critical) of a township.

VI. *Significant Variations:* The treatment of the description of the township is significant, the degree and type of criticism, the feeling of being discriminated against and the race-consciousness.

The little girl on the left is sometimes introduced into the play-group.

Attention should be paid to the way in which the problem is solved: are the children found, do they die, is the township dirty or do the people move to a better area?

Revision: This card has been recently experimentally revised. The children in the foreground have been overpainted to give the story a more generalized township interest.

CARD **D : 6**

I. *The Description:* A hand holding money in silver and notes. The background is painted to direct attention on to the hand in the centre.

A horizontally placed card.

II. *Manifest Stimulus Demand:* The money is the main point in all stories.

Other details often noted and referred to are the cuff-link and white cuff. Reference is often made to van Riebeek.

III. *Form Demand:* The money and the hand are the only aspects of importance in the picture.

IV. Latent Stimulus Demand: This picture is most likely to portray attitudes toward the acquisition of wealth, to the need for security, to personal ambition, power and status. The concept of responsibility and industry is often introduced into the stories.

V. Frequent Plots: The plots tend to take three possible clues of approach:
> (*a*) That 'money is the root of all evil', followed by a discourse on money in rather abstract terms.
> (*b*) Personal gain by socially acceptable means, followed by stories of striving, hard work, education, ambition, success or failure.
> (*c*) Personal gain by anti-social means, either personally or a story about anti-social dealings involving money.

VI. Significant Variations: Included are stories about van Riebeek, historical tales, and gambling and drink fantasies. Themes on race discrimination and frustrations are of importance here.

CARD E : 5

I. The Description: An interpersonal situation, possibly a race-relations set-up. The two male figures highlighted against a black background. Their attitudes are ambiguous.
> A vertically placed picture.

II. Manifest Stimulus Demand: An adequate accounting of this picture will have reference to the interrelationship between the two figures.
> The figures are variously apperceived as in earnest conversation, aggressive conflict or an attack-retreat relationship.

III. Form Demand: The two central figures constitute the basic form demand.

IV. Latent Stimulus Demand: Attitudes towards Black-White relations appear often. Reactions to aggression and attack are often noted. The subject's relative dominance is often observable plus indications of temper and control.

V. Frequent Plots: Usually an aggressive situation is presented. The themes once again usually falling into:
> (*a*) aggression between the two members depicted,
> (*b*) aggression planned by them against others.

VI. Significant Variations: Racial co-operation for an anti-social purpose, e.g. IDB and IGB (Illicit Diamond and Gold Buying); African attacking and injuring the European; violent outbursts of racial aggression.

CARD F : 4

I. The Description: A man-woman scene. Ambiguous foreground with two trees highlighted against shadowy background.
> The man has his hand resting on the woman's shoulder. The facial expressions are ambiguous.
> A vertically placed picture.

60

The Cards of the African T.A.T.

II. Manifest Stimulus Demand: An adequate accounting of this picture will deal with the relationship between the two figures plus an explanation of the background.

Other details often noticed are the 'easy-going' attitude of the woman and the bottle in the man's pocket.

III. Form Demand: The major aspects of importance are the two figures plus their surroundings usually apperceived as a forest, with trees and bushes.

IV. Latent Stimulus Demand: This picture portrays attitudes of emotional love, sex, aggression, rape and violence. The normal phrase used in conjunction with this picture is that 'he is propositioning her in the bushes'.

The interpersonal relationships of a male-female situation are of prime importance here.

The male is seen as the dominant figure; sometimes he overcomes the woman by persuasion, sometimes by violence, sometimes he is frightened away by the police, sometimes by the woman herself.

V. Frequent Plots: Usually a seduction scene; the differences occur in what happens subsequently.

VI. Significant Variations: The man is sometimes considered to be drunk. Special attention should be paid to the way in which the interrelationship is resolved.

(REVISED VERSION) CARD G : 3

I. The Description: A dark scene, possibly an interior. Indefinite silhouettes are portrayed in the foreground, an open door is shown in the right background.

II. Manifest Stimulus Demand: An adequate accounting of this picture will require some explanation of the large upright silhouette in the foreground plus some reference to the source of light (the door) in the right background.

III. Form Demand: This picture lends itself to a preoccupation with minor details. Generally the stories deal with the upright silhouette and sometimes relate it to the horizontal silhouette.

IV. Latent Stimulus Demand: The picture usually deals with aggression/anxiety scenes. Fear motifs and attitudes of uncertainty are introduced.

V. Frequent Plots: Anti-social activities are usually the most frequent plots, robbery being the basic motif.

VI. Significant Variations: These are found in the selection of the focal point for the story, the door, the prone figure, or the upright silhouette.

(ORIGINAL VERSION) CARD G : 3

I. The Description: A very ambiguous card. In the top right-hand

61

corner is a barred window. This scene may be viewed from within or from without the building.

The background is completely black.

A vertically or horizontally placed card. Usually vertically placed.

II. *Manifest Stimulus Demand:* To the Africans this card had no form and while a number apperceived a cell-window the majority never appreciated the significance of the card, and the consequence was that, being bewildered, their fantasy was stunted. It was usually the last card attempted in the series.

III. *Form Demand:* The majority of Africans considered the card formless. Some apperceived the window.

IV. *Latent Stimulus Demand:* Usually fear- and insecurity-provoking thoughts, sometimes about cell windows, were the main theme.

V. *Frequent Plots:* Plots were usually illogical and uncertain, the fantasy stunted and disorganized. The only plot theme observable was the 'cell window theme'.

VI. *Significant Variations:* The subjects never really understood this card well enough to vary their responses with any fluency. It stunted their fantasy behaviour.

Note: Although not in the revised series, this card has been specifically mentioned because stories relating to it appear in the text.

CARD **H : 2**

I. *The Description:* A house interior scene, possibly a kitchen view looking outwards. Four characters, a boy and a man standing against a kitchen dresser and a woman holding a child seated at a table.

A window is let into the wall just above the woman's head.

Facial expressions ambiguous. The house door is partially open giving a view of the outside environment.

A horizontally placed picture.

II. *Manifest Stimulus Demand:* An adequate accounting of the home interpersonal relations is required. Stress is usually placed on the father-son relationship.

The mother is usually referred to as a submissive figure, the son is usually being scolded or being sent to the shop to buy food.

III. *Form Demand:* The picture is dominated by the four figures. The bare table is often introduced and comments are often made about the dirty floor.

IV. *Latent Stimulus Demand:* Home relationships and attitudes of parental responsibility are usually referred to. Paternal irresponsibility in not providing for the family are usually mentioned. Many stories have discourses on the causes of juvenile delinquency and social motifs.

The Cards of the African T.A.T.

V. Frequent Plots: The plots are usually of an interpersonal nature in terms of father-son relationship and their outcome. The mother is usually seen as a negative figure.

VI. Significant Variations: Some subjects have the female criticizing the male figure. Attention should be paid to the adequacy of the male figure in dealing with the circumstances. The story outcomes are important here: is the boy punished, is he reasoned with and does he respond?

Revision: This card has been recently experimentally revised. The young boy in the foreground has been overpainted, to shift the focus of attention from the father-son relationship to a more general family relationship.

CARD **I : 1**

I. The Description: A lone figure silhouetted under a street lamp; lights possibly from flats or high buildings are shown in the right background.

Facial expression ambiguous with most of the body in shadow, hands not shown.

A vertically placed picture.

II. Manifest Stimulus Demand: An adequate accounting of this card is, naturally enough, centred around the figure silhouetted under the lamp. Usually an explanation of his reasons for being there is discussed.

The flats in the background are often introduced.

III. Form Demand: The basic form in this picture is the man, the other primary details are the building lights and the street lamp.

IV. Latent Stimulus Demand: This picture is especially likely to portray fear and aggressive attitudes. The main figure is usually seen as a 'tsotsi' on the prowl. Sadism is often introduced in the attacking theme. The reaction to attack is
   (a) aggressive retaliation, or
   (b) withdrawal and evasion, or
   (c) submission and hurt.

V. Frequent Plots: Three main plot themes occur:
   (a) Anti-social motifs in which the subject associates with the character.
   (b) Anti-social motifs in which the subject dissociates and criticizes the character.
   (c) Fear motif—in which the subject is personified by the character and is deciding how to avoid danger.

VI. Significant Variations: Of special interest here is the association or dissociation with the main character as this usually indicates the direction of the fear and aggressive attitudes. Special note should be made here of violent aggression and attack, of extreme fear and insecurity and of exceptional tensions which are sometimes revealed.

VI

PERSONALITY PROTOCOL TRENDS

IN developing the methods and procedures for this investigation, the personality process was considered as being the result of the interaction between certain individual needs and demands, and certain cultural needs and demands and sanctions. Kluckhohn and Mowrer have isolated and distinguished a number of aspects or components of this process which help to clarify it, namely, the universal, the communal, the rôle, and the idiosyncratic components of personality.

These components they define as follows: The universal component consists of those attributes, behaviours and facts that are common and accepted as normal in all human beings. They spring from the commonness of certain characteristics of the physical organisms and social environments of all humans.

The communal component refers to the fact that members of any society tend to share more behavioural and personality characteristics with other members of that society than with members of other societies. These characteristics spring not only from a common cultural set of demands and trainings, but also from the commonalities of physical and biological equipment.

The rôle component refers to the distinctions that obtain between various kinds of personalities within any one society. Thus not only the personalities of the sexes, but even those of some professional groups have a certain communality that enables a person to distinguish one from the other. These rôle components of personality are some of the factors that identify various subgroups within one society.

The idiosyncratic component refers to those purely individual, unique characteristics that the individual shares with no one—those that are not determined by the training characteristic of his particular social group.

In this study interest is focused on the communal component of the personality process. To this end some 2,500 African T.A.T. protocols of urban dwellers were analysed and the communal compo-

64

nents extracted. To maintain a systematic presentation of data in the analysis of these communal components of urban African personality, it was necessary to firstly establish a workable frame of reference within which to organize and present the findings of this study.

Because of the danger, inherent in any work of this nature, of becoming too clinical, too analytically biased, and too highly abstract, the terms of reference have, as far as possible, been chosen from the more concrete, definable spheres of communal personality possibilities. The more nebulous personality functions have been purposely avoided.

Communal components will be illustrated by extracts from actual protocols.

The urban African personality will be analysed under two main headings:

1. General Protocol Trends;
2. Specific Personality Trends.

The first heading will give an overall appreciation of certain main areas of protocol presentation. It will introduce the reader to the sort of responses made by urban Africans and it will present illustrations from typical examples. The second main heading—Specific Personality Trends—will then deal with the specific communal personality trends isolated in this population. Once again this section will be illustrated with typical examples.

The main headings will be subdivided as follows:

General Protocol Trends:

    1. Level of Presentation.
    2. Emotional Involvement.
    3. Imagery and Language Trends.

Specific Personality Trends:

    1. Anxieties and Insecurities.
    2. Aggression.
    3. Motivation.
    4. Race Consciousness.
    5. Male-Female Relationships.
    6. Humour.
    7. Religious Super-Ego.
    8. General Environmental Adjustments.

GENERAL PROTOCOL TRENDS

1. Level of Presentation

The development of an intelligible story sequence requires a logical, systematic organization of ideas, an organized layout and an understandable style of presentation. This section will also serve as a general introductory review to the protocol study as such.

Africans love stories. Peggy Rutherford in her anthology of African writing, *Darkness and Light,* summed up this love and one of the main reasons for it, in the following words:

> In lands of the sun, one feels that clocks could be dispensed with, for so often the inclination is to rest when the heat of the sun has slipped into the head and fuddled the brain, and work another day. And the sun in Africa is assuredly on the side of him who sleeps. It is, therefore, with a different conception of time that one works.
>
> So it is that in this leisure of African time the habit of story-telling still survives. When the sun has gone and the fire is lit at evening, when the oxen rest, . . . tales are told; tales handed down from grandmother to grand-daughter, from father to son. On the peaceful coast of Mozambique, beyond the fringe of the village, across a valley to the hilltop kraals of Swaziland, one may hear until late into the night the sounds of laughter, of chatter, of song, of story-telling, and coming closer one may see the dark groups enclosing the fires; the children, their eyes bright with the firelight, listening to the tales of old.

Africans are great story-tellers and even the urban environment with its more synthetic pleasures has not destroyed this basically simple natural pleasure of story-telling. Their stories are usually organized and logical in time sequence, they show a definite developmental trend and maintain a thread of continuity throughout. They are intelligent, observant presentations for the most, drawing on a wealth of both urban and traditional cultural concepts. In a single protocol series it is not unusual to find a tale of urban sophistication intermixed with a story of tribal customs and magic.

Their stories make interesting reading purely from the life-interest point of view. Here is an example of the almost sparkling type of story, full of earthy wit, cynical humour and life-interest. It was written by a completely urbanized, twenty-five-year-old matriculant (the spelling and grammar are unchanged):

CARD **D : 6**

MONEY

Money is money whether honestly earned or not. A stolen florin is two shillings still. That's how I get about it. I gamble—cards, dice, chess and steal when the opportunity 'arrives'.

Take a look at the money in my hand. If I had not the brain I have I would today not be in my present position, with these crisp notes and shiny silver in the fold of my hand. Look at the shirt sleeve, the stud and the decent jacket that go with this money. Who in hell's name said

66

crooked money does not buy. I am now no more the location slut and penny-beggar that I have been for the last ten years.

I command respect and power. I can order almost anything from anybody, and it will be done for me with no questions asked. Work? Who would if fools are still being born? What I could not get with an open-hand I can now get with a rolled one and for my money's sake it's always rolled.

Maybe some day I'll go to prison for it, or some minister will pull me to church, but until then I will have to enjoy the full breath of sinful living.

Read purely as a story—quite apart from its emotional significance —it is an alive earthy tale, intelligently organized and presented. It is a real story, captivating, interesting and making enjoyable reading matter. It may well be the introduction to a Hemingway-type short-story, rather than a fantasy stimulated in the mind of an untravelled urban African by a single picture in black and white, of a hand holding money.

Without the facility of creative imagination, ingenious, original stories cannot be written. The urban Africans are an extraordinarily imaginative people. Consider the following imaginative creation, stimulated in the mind of a man living in Jabulani Township—quite an ordinary place, as far as African townships go. This illustration, chosen at random from his T.A.T., is from CARD E : 5. A card described as: 'An interpersonal situation, possibly a race-relations set-up. The two figures highlighted against a black background. Their attitudes are ambiguous.'

To this stimulus, the subject—a typical urban product, twenty-six years old, with a Standard VIII education, single, with four children —created the following story:

CARD E : 5

Tshaka's Army has been defeated by the rebellious Tsongas under Soshangane. Everywhere there was confusion. Old and young were asking each other what was going to happen to the 'Great Elephant Heaven' (Zulu) meaning Tshaka.

During that time there were two young men who were from the Cape. These two were regarded as the no goods in the country of their fore-fathers because they condemned withcraft practices.

They preached non-violence to the people. Because they were wearing the white man's clothes they were regarded with suspicion by their comrades—that they were spies, trying to overthrow the Government of Tshaka.

They were summoned to appear before the Great Elephant, Tshaka, the (Zulu) Heaven. 'Whence come ye who came and preached false Gods to my people. My Army has been defeated because you put shame on our Gods' (meaning our forefathers). Handi was the first to answer Tshaka, 'Bayete! Bayete! Zulu, I heard what you said. I preach the very God our forefathers were praying to, the God of all nations, the God that is everywhere.'

Tshaka roared like a lion 'Please take them away for the Spirits are angry. And do not kill them but banish them to live in the forest where their God stayeth, for they might be right.' Handi and Bandi were banished to the forests of Zululand. And there they prayed many moons and when the white man occupied Natal they were allowed to return. They had grown beards and it became a tradition, that today all the Zion Ministers have nursed their beards, it was because of Handi and Bandi, the first Africans to come into contact with Christianity.

Their story presentations illustrate the three cultural influences to which the urban African is exposed. The ideas which they present are sometimes tribal in influence:

CARD **A** : **9**

We are sitting at a place called (the) 'Kgotla' where matters and cases (of the tribe) are discussed and settled. Here we also remember our forefathers by offering them a slaughtered kid to appease them. We also ask them to send us rain. Without rain we cannot live because the fields provide us with food . . .

Sometimes urban in influence:

CARD **A** : **9**

. . . One day these men came together and discussed the position of the township, the township they were staying at was becoming corrupt and bad. Gentlemen, said Piet, do you see that our township is becoming dangerous, at night you can't walk about as you like, during the day you can't walk about as you like, because of these two gangs of tsotsis. Now what can we do to get rid of them . . . let us call the residents of the township and suggest to them that we must form our own protection (society) namely the 'Civic guards' and if they accept our proposal then we can form the body.

And sometimes European in influence:

CARD **G** : **3**

. . . Gas is a very thin element which no human eye can see—but very dangerous. It kills without warning of any kind.

Regardless of their motivating influences the presentations of urban Africans are characterized by a certain spontaneity and 'aliveness'. Drab, uninteresting fantasy presentations, although they certaily do occur, are not typical. The headings which subjects often give to their stories are indicative of their sense of drama. An example of the headings appearing in a single protocol series highlights this:

CARD	F : 4	DARLING TAKE MY SOUL
CARD	H : 2	PILFERING
CARD	E : 5	I'LL OPPOSE YOU
CARD	I : 1	EVENING
CARD	B : 8	HEAVY FEELING
CARD	D : 6	MONEY
CARD	C : 7	THE BABY-SITTER
CARD	A : 9	SUN BATHING
CARD	G : 3	MODERN ART

or from another series:

CARD	B : 8	GO TO PUTCO
CARD	D : 6	THE RAT
CARD	F : 4	TENDER LOVE
CARD	I : 1	CHILD PRODIGY
CARD	C : 7	THE PROFESSOR
CARD	H : 2	THE LITTLE TOUGH
CARD	E : 5	GOOD MANNERS
CARD	A : 9	AT PUTCO
CARD	G : 3	(No heading)

The vivid world of urban townships, a kaleidoscope of birth, life and death, of cultural classes, of tribal customs and of European influences; a multitude of often conflicting ways of life, a conglomeration of primitive ideals and sophisticated ideas—all these find outlet in the fantasy world of the urban African, and are reflected in the presentation of his responses to the T.A.T. Cultural contradictions in such society are numerous; take the example of religion as an instance. One man speaks of how:

CARD **A : 9**

. . . We also remember our forefathers by offering them a slaughtered kid to appease them. We also ask them to send us rain . . .

while another says:

CARD **B : 8**

. . . when you are worried and miserable as if all your relatives are dead do not despair God is there. I see that this man is praying that God should help him. It is how it should be.

Story presentations show considerable variation in the type of introduction or opening line used. Although the story-book theme of 'Once upon a time there was . . . .' is possibly the most popular introductory phrase, considerable originality is nevertheless evidenced. This is illustrated by the following series of examples, taken at random, from the opening lines of ten subjects all responding to CARD G : 3:

1. Once upon a time I was alone at home.

2. The most thieves today likes to go about with torches in the night.
3. The room was dark and gloomy, the door was half open, a woman lay in bed, her husband was standing beside her, bidding her goodbye.
4. Long ago my father used to live in the wood deep in the Bushveld.
5. In the Drakensberg there is a big rock.
6. There was a man who belongs to the Jewish tribe. He was a king. This man was called Nicodemus.
7. There once lived a family of two on the outskirts of town.
8. The man in this picture reminds me of the first day I entered in the mine.
9. One day I was going to hunt bucks when I was in a big forest, I saw a big round hut there.
10. In the old days when they caught anyone for a crime the law would punish a man in such a way that he never try to come back again.

A noticeable tendency observed in a great many story presentations is the 'story with a moral' type of ending. For example, such endings as: So look before you leap; A friend in need is a friend indeed; Never take no for an answer; and A stitch in time saves nine.

Nor is it unusual to have the story addressed to the reader in the form of a letter, ending with a formal, 'Yours faithfully'. Take the following example:

CARD C : 7

Dear Sir,
It will be a good thing to provide the people living in this shanty town with better accommodation . . .

or

CARD E : 5

Dear Sir,
In this picture I can see that there are two men . . .

A common protocol trend is found in stories dealing with particular current happenings. This is not unusual since a great many urban Africans read newspapers and listen to the radio.

Increasing education and closer contact with Whites has brought mass media to the African. The African press has grown rapidly in the past decade. Where there was only a handful of weeklies, there are now, in addition, three mass-circulation magazines, a Sunday tabloid, and a number of small circulation magazines . . . Radio has become part of the lives of Africans. Around 11 per cent of urban Africans now have their own radios and there are others, like domestic servants, who have the opportunity of listening in at the places where they work (N. Mekele —'The African as a Buyer' in *The Southern Africa Financial Mail*, Vol. II, No. 2, 1960).

'Current news' is often related in T.A.T. protocols. During the 'Bride of the Year Competition', run by *The Golden City Post*—an African newspaper—stories like the following appeared:

CARD **F** : 4

BRIDE OF THE YEAR

The picture on F : 4 reminds me of the best wedding I've ever seen. At the Orlando Stadium recently, Miss Mirian and John Esquire were the happiest couple. The wedding was on a Saturday . . .

While a mining disaster at a South African coal-mine, which received world-wide publicity, resulted in stories like the following:

CARD **A** : 9

These four sad men are the rescuers at the Clydesdale mine in Coalbrook where over *400* men are entombed.
    Wives and relatives of the entombed men we understand asked the Minister of Mines Senator De Klerk to send the drilling machines again . . .
    The poor whites and my own people stood in open veld throughout the night watching and weeping as they heard the noise created by the big drilling machines. Mr. Kleinhans, a 'seer', claimed that there are some who he says are still alive, surely how on earth can a human being be without water and food from 21 Jan. 1960 and be alive now?

The level of story presentation is a function of the literacy standard, which in turn is closely associated with the educational level of the population. All the protocol examples given come from literate people with educations ranging from Standard IV to Matriculation —a population representative of the educated African populations of the Witwatersrand urban complex.

2. Emotional Involvement

While any apperception theoretically implies an emotional involvement, we are here interested in the general level of involvement, its type and degree.
    A good story-teller must 'live' his stories, he must use his imagination and really 'give of himself'. Africans are good story-tellers. They really immerse themselves in their stories. One can sense the emotional pathos in the following fantasy:

CARD **B** : 8

Why! Why did I have to do it? What urged me on and on to do this foolish thing? . . . What caused me to kill a man only to get twopence in his pockets?

or in the following:

Dejected with hunger and listless with hopelessness Paul threw his weary body on a dilapidated couch, legs astride, head bowed, and face covered with both his hands. He was crying—crying like a child.

The use of the first person in stories is most common. Take the following example:

One day I was walking along Kerk Street. That day I lost a five pound note. It was not my money. I was sent to the bank by my master when I was working. And that made me very unhappy. I was very sad. I kept asking myself what shall I do? Who will help me? What shall I say to my master at the firm . . .

It also occurs that the reader is sometimes invited to accompany the writer in his fantasy:

Let me take you to Somfene Village. When you get into this settlement you will notice its muddy avenues during the rainy seasons, the dilapidated mud-houses that are built near the streets. Mongrel dogs are everywhere, fowls, pigs and other livestock mix freely with human beings. But among such surroundings you can see well-to-do houses like Mr. Ndlovu's on Gula Avenue.

or as in the following opening lines:

This is big trouble I am going to tell you about, it is not exactly trouble if you are a man with good brains.

The African definitely becomes emotionally involved in his stories, in a direct, outspoken fashion. He fantasizes, but he lives his fantasy, he is directly associated with it, he makes very few attempts to divorce or dissociate himself from it, and he expresses his emotional involvement in it with verve and feeling.

Consider the following story for example, written by a thirty-year-old man, with a Standard VII education:

It was a surprise for John when he received a letter from Maggie saying she does not love him any longer. She did not point out any reason for saying so. John became worried and did not know what to do. He was so much in love with Maggie. For the first time he went to work earlier than before. He boarded the train and never wanted to speak to anybody. He chose a seat right in the corner where he would be alone. The train pulled off. Still he was thinking of Maggie. He just wondered what could have happened in the world that she should turn against him without any reason after they had been so happy together. He looked round and round at the passengers. He found that no one was looking at him. He thought to himself that there is nothing more he could do. He got off at the next station where he always gets off when he goes to work. He worked the whole day in a sad mood and in the evening tried to sleep but kept awake all night. The next day it was worse. He never went to work. He reported sick and remained in bed for 3 hours after sunrise. To his surprise when he woke up after having a bad dream he put on his gown and went out and when he opened the door there she was standing right in the middle of the room. Maggie! he said. There was no waste of time. She was in his arms. Oh, darling forgive me it was my fault for writing that letter. I was mad because my friend Jane told me she was getting married to you. I did not see it was a lie. John said forget it darling, you know you are mine and will always be.

As is to be expected, criticism of prevailing social conditions often finds outlet in subjects' fantasy involvements—criticism which shows a thorough grasp of the causes of many urban social problems. On the question of juvenile delinquency, for example, a thirty-year-old had this to say:

CARD **I** : **1**

Many times in the dark streets of Alexandra Township you will see young tsotsis sitting at dark corners of streets, especially on weekends . . . in the township as you know it is dark, there are no lights, people get off the bus, and just as the bus drives off these thugs attack and rob them of their watches, money, clothing, etc. These thugs are very very strong men, who could go to town and look for work, but because Alexandra Township is outside the urban areas, some of these tsotsis are discharged and told to go and look for a job in Alexandra Township . . . so they sit and sit, until all their money is worn out . . . then they think of mischief and go to bioscopes and see American pictures of hold ups and robbery . . . then they wait for fathers as they come home from work with their pay . . .

It is not surprising that such stories form so large a part of many subjects' fantasies. When one's fear of attack by tsotsis is so real one tends naturally to apperceive along such lines. Similarly one finds feelings of being discriminated against, being openly voiced by frustrated urban dwellers—feelings which are expressed by the subjects with conviction and directness. Feelings such as the following expressed by a forty-year-old man with a Standard IV education:

CARD **C** : **7**

South Africa is a very nice country to live in, but now-a-days it is not of the best, because of the new Nationalist Government. Our own Black-race for every day when the sun rises, we get very hard laws that makes or leads the black race to slavery, in so much that a man thinks, if there can be War in this country might things work better afterwards.

73

Political emotional involvement is often voiced, sometimes in a gentle evasive fashion, sometimes with bluntness and directness, as in the above example.

Africans are a naturally expressive people. The urban dweller has not yet fully adopted the sophisticated veneer of inhibitions characteristic of European society. In his T.A.T. stories he speaks with a naïve directness, he associates story elements in a direct fashion, and he expresses his fantasies with an emotional involvement born of a personality that is not hampered by the inhibiting restrictions of European tradition.

3. *Imagery and Language Trends*

The means of expression, the idiom used, the mode of description and the phraseology in which the urban African presents his fantasy world, are important factors when studying general protocol trends prevalent amongst these people.

This population, it must be remembered, is relatively educated and English was the medium of education used. But the fact that they have been taught in English does not preclude them from thinking and feeling and describing as Africans. Indeed, a study of the language used in their protocols not only indicates the African's vivid appreciation and expression of imagery, but it also indicates the elasticity of the English tongue. As Can Themba, an African journalist, has put it: '. . . Africans are creating out of English a language of their own: a language that thinks in actions, using words that dart back and forth on quick-moving feet, virile, earthy, garrulous.' The English used is consequently not Oxford English, it may more correctly be referred to as Township English.

A translation of Shakespearean thoughts into Township English thoughts can be seen from the following extract:

CARD **D : 9**

When one is alone with one's thoughts life assumes the character of a mystery. The World is a stage and we are the actors. Some of us have leading rôles and others are ordinary members of the cast. We re-act in varying degrees to given circumstances.

To the African, English is the language of the superior status group, and he delights wherever possible in using 'superior sounding' English words and phrases, even to the extent of being completely irrelevant and not a little illogical in his presentation.

Classic examples of this love of high-sounding words and phrases are the following letters reproduced without modification or alteration. Written by a twenty-six-year-old man, with a Standard VII education, the first letter is a request for employment; the second, by the same individual, is a complaint to the Management on the general inefficiency of the company, after he had been rejected for employment, on personality grounds, by the Aptitude Test Centre.

The Request for Employment

> . . . , ... Avenue,
> Alexandra Township,
> Johannesburg.
> . . . May 1955.

Director,
P.U.T. Corporation Limited,
Wynberg,
JOHANNESBURG.

Dear Sir,

Timely considerations and momentary decisions have entrusted me with the wonderful gift you bestowed to our human kind of race, so that my humble heart was obliged to reveal and express my gratitude towards your unquestionable and unapproachable responsibility. Hence these inevitable compliments.

Having in mind such significant factors and being touched by such honourable meritorious achievements, I have decided to do everything in my power to join and spread this civilization which you are expanding amongst the non-European society, and which is a debt to mankind by the Welfare Department. I am sociable, long tempered, and well educated as well as hard working. If only you could give me a chance, I shall convince you of my ability and aptitude. In regard to a position I would like to be either in the Welfare Department or to be an Inspector of Buses.

An interview with my lord will confirm my fluctuating thoughts.

> I remain,
> Your humble servant,
> . . . .

Letter of Complaint (after he had been rejected)

> . . . , ... Avenue,
> Alexandra Township,
> Johannesburg.
> . . . August, 1955.

Divisional Superintendent,
P.U.T.C. Ltd.,
Wynberg Division,
P.O. Bramley,
JOHANNESBURG.

Dear Sir,

Unmindful of the fact that you are ignorant of the system prevailing in your buses along the routes, you look contented of things, but I deem to let you know and unveil the sardonical and prejudicial drama undertaken by your employee's characters of spotless reputation, and men of responsibility and authorities of recognized social and welfare missions, namely the event that befell me on Monday, . . . , August, 1955, which was not only barbarous but also points out your failure to eschew that and thus revealing your incongruous incapability and inaptitude in your responsible task.

I paused alone for the last bus from Germiston to Alexandra at Edenvale Hospital bus stop, and the Driver drove right through, and never stopped, even when I blew a whistle. Do not forget that I occupy a responsible position in a big Association and all the Association's money and records were with me. Because that was the last bus, I commenced my journey on foot, looping my eyes and fighting my path amongst the hungry eyes of the Tsotsi Gangs that shoved me up the road like a sweeping hurricane and had to suffer all the tremour-causing elements, the Author of which is your Bus Service, Sir, I pause to hear your views, and demand nothing but your direct redress of your Bus-system.

> Remaining,
> Yours greatly perturbed,
> . . . .

Fowler's Pocket Oxford Dictionary is not the urban African's sole authority on the English language. The influences of American films, yellow-back novels and comics are also apparent. Take the following story, written by a twenty-nine-year-old man, with a Standard VII education, as an example:

CARD **F : 4**

The evening breeze blew from the southern part of the station, the pine trees were sighing in their usual manner. Henry took advantage of the inspiring surroundings. Immediately in front of him was a sight to improve any sane man's vision tremendously. When I say sight, I truly mean that.

Here was an explosive package of African beauty swinging some part of the anatomy called hips, her mannequin type of gait spoke a language of its own, her shapely legs with the stocking seams in the right places was just about enough to send some sort of sensation up Henry's spine.

One more pace and another yet another and our friend Henry was almost abrest with this little bit of T.N.T. Luck is luck in any language and Henry had a bit more, 'cause this sweet piece of this and that is nobody else than his old schoolmate Kiddie.

Did I tell you that Henry is not bad at all. 'Oh! Sorry.' Here was a manly physique that would make any right thinking lady look twice in case the first impression was wrong.

Kiddie beamed: Boy! it was as though the sun on second thought decided to rise again. Henry swung Kiddie round so that her broad back was against the fence and he was looking directly into that young and clear yellowish brown complexioned face unspoiled by Western cosmetics. Her lips parted once more and our hero went soft around the knees, as a set of pearl-like teeth were displayed. In that split second all the poets flashed into his mind, J. Keats, Byron, Shakespeare, etc. Which one was he to recite to this dream on legs?

The language used in this story is English, the idiom is American, the author is African, but the type of apperception is universal.

Americanisms abound in the stories and a great many statements are highly original and many unintentionally humorous:

CARD **H : 2**

. . . these children are so lazy that they hardly can pass water in the w.c. . . .

CARD **E : 5**

When Richard arrived in Johannesburg he could not tell which person was a crook and which was a lawyer . . .

or the following original simile:

CARD **B : 8**

. . . and the man was crying like a train when it nears the station.

or in romantic mood:

CARD **F : 4**

. . . he kissed her as if he was given an ultimatum to quit the country . . .

In stories with dialogue, 'tsotsi' slang is often spoken by the various characters introduced. As one subject expressed it:

CARD **E : 5**

There is a place in the city where the boys have what they call a paradise . . . they call themselves with peculiar names and speak adulterated Afrikaans, which is mixed with English, Zulu and Sesotho . . . when the band stops you will see a young man with scars going to the band-leader with his hands in his pockets and say 'speel' meaning play . . .

Strange contradictions often occur when modern 'tsotsi' slang becomes mixed with traditional African custom. The following story is a good example of what occurs. Here we see the traditional custom of 'lobola' (a payment by the man's family to the family of the woman for her hand in marriage) expressed in 'tsotsi' slang:

CARD **F : 4**

Dick had an appointment with his beautiful girl friend Ivy in the woods. 'I have got good news for you Ivy.' 'What gives Dicky?' the girl asked. Continuing Dick: 'My uncle has agreed to pay the £100 lobola, the

77

military overcoat for your father, the travelling rug for your mother, and a tin full of snuff for your granny.'

'So you mean we're getting coupled-up Dick?' the girl asked.

'Sure darling, me and you are going to be one thing in life from now on, provided I give a third of what I earn every week to you,' Dick said. And the girl agreed. She also told Dick she would never go to Rock 'n Roll shows without him.

The majority of the urban Africans speak an English liberally flavoured with American slang and enriched by a conglomeration of Afrikaans, Zulu and Sesotho words and phrases. Township English is a colourful, highly expressive slang, used with complete grammatical abandon, in an atmosphere of devil-may-care originality.

One speaks for the most as one thinks. And when one's ideas are presented in aspects of four languages—the resulting thoughts are voiced in the verbal potpourri which is the basis of township slang and the 'tsotsi' language.

These language developments are highly dynamic entities, especially amongst the 'tsotsi'. Words and phrases are being added almost daily. The dominant base language is also constantly changing, the present mode being an Afrikaans base, with English, Zulu and Sesotho 'frills'.

This 'tsotsi' slang, or 'Wittisha', mirrors the 'tsotsi' way of life— a way of life in which id-directed motives predominate. It is a life of gang warfare, of robbery, assault and rape, of uninhibited cruelty and sadism, a life with no social conscience and few moral standards.

Examples from the 'Wittisha' of the four main township gangs (1959–60), The Vultures, The Black-Hawks, The Spoirings, and The Tomahawks, will serve to illustrate the use of the Afrikaans base, plus the original language innovations which have evolved to make this slang the colourful, highly expressive, secret means of 'tsotsi' communication that it is.

The 'tsotsi' is constantly in trouble with the police—or more correctly stated, the police are a constant source of annoyance to the 'tsotsi', rather than a real danger to him. For unlike other members of opposing 'tsotsi' gangs, the police simply arrest one, they do not kill. Their opinion of the function of the police expressed in 'tsotsi' 'Wittisha' is that: 'Die gatas neining jou net' (The police just arrest one). And unlike other 'tsotsi' gang members who 'Will jou hinti maak' (Want to kill you), 'Die gatas is sweet' (The police are safe, as far as that is concerned). The main danger to life lies in meeting members of other gangs: 'Want die motlanas sal jou chumerchu' (Because these gang members will kill you with a sharpened wire).

If we analyse certain of the above 'Wittisha' statements, we will

78

notice the Afrikaans base plus the use of English and Bantu languages. Take the last statement for example:

> 'Want die motlanas sal jou chumerchu' (Because these (other) gang members will kill you with a sharpened wire).

Want	Afrikaans for 'because'
die	Afrikaans for 'the' or 'these'
motlanas	Tswana for 'young boy'. 'Wittisha' interpretation of the young boys who make up the 'tsotsi' gangs.
sal	Afrikaans for 'will'
jou	Afrikaans for 'you'
chumerchu	A Baca corruption, meaning a sharpened object. 'Wittisha' for needle-sharp tempered wire used by the 'tsotsi'.

In this one short sentence we see the predominating Afrikaans base, the use of Tswana with a 'Wittisha' interpretation, and a Baca corruption with a special 'Wittisha' meaning.

To analyse one further example, consider the following short sentence used above:

> 'Die gatas is sweet' (The police are safe)

Die	Afrikaans for 'The'
gatas	Sesotho for 'to step'. 'Wittisha' for the police who are always stepping after or following the 'tsotsis'.
is	Afrikaans for 'is' or 'are'
sweet	English word 'sweet'. 'Wittisha' interpretation, 'all right' or 'safe'.

A sentence with a combination of Afrikaans and English with a 'Wittisha' innovation.

Certain 'Wittisha' words and phrases have filtered into the everyday township slang of the law-abiding individuals—a slang which is often used in their T.A.T. stories. The money in CARD D : 6, for example, is sometimes referred to as 'ching' and 'squal' ('Wittisha' for money), the woman in CARD F : 4 is sometimes spoken of as a 'cherie' ('Wittisha' for girl), and the scene in CARD G : 3 is sometimes described as being in 'Number 4' ('Wittisha' for the Johannesburg Gaol).

The township African, in addition to his usual knowledge of two or three Bantu languages, English and Afrikaans, usually speaks the township 'Wittisha' slang—a slang which finds outlet in his T.A.T. fantasy presentations.

Entirely new words have also evolved—words whose etymological history it is impossible to trace. European words, taken completely out of context, have been combined into outwardly meaningless, yet symbolically significant phrases, phrases like the 'tsotsi' reply to a greeting, 'Corvette under corset'. In 'Wittisha' this means 'Everything is fine'. Its symbolical derivation is, however, both interesting and revealing of the 'tsotsi' way of life. 'Corvette' refers to the trade name of a most satisfying brand of fish-paste sandwich-spread sold on the South African market: 'under corset' refers to the female's sex organs under her corset. The hidden implication of the greeting is thus: I'm sexually satisfied, therefore everything is fine with me.

VII

SPECIFIC PERSONALITY TRENDS

1. Anxieties and Insecurities

TOWNSHIP living is dangerous living, living for the most in rather drab, dirty surroundings. The reaction of urban inhabitants is well expressed in the following story:

CARD A : 9

Once I travel by bus between Johannesburg and Alexandra Township I always feel happy and enjoy my journey. I see Public Utility buses going to different destinations. Most of them going to Johannesburg and Sophiatown and others to Rosebank and Germiston. I usually see people crossing the street while the robot shows red. Native women crossing in the middle of the street with big bundles of washing on their heads. Other people cross the street with their eyes looking to the direction they come from. Cars and cyclists to the direction of Pretoria travel at high speed. I admire European school-boys ranging from the age of five to seven years when they play in the school premises teasing each other in joy. My joy ends as soon as I reach Alexandra Township.

Or in this brief story introduction:

CARD C : 7

This is Moroka Township where it is not safe to send a boy to the shop at night . . .

Why is this so? For the answer we turn to this story extract:

CARD F : 4

Hooligans, more especially in the locations have become a menace.
   They are dangerous to the public and it is not safe to send a girl to the shop in the evening. These hooligans think of nothing else except robbing people of their money and outraging girls. They anxiously wait for sunset in order to do their dirty job properly. What they start with is to drink kaffir beer and smoke dagga. From there everyone they meet is their victim. When they meet a girl they give one of their comrades an opportunity to propose love to that poor soul . . . if the girl shouts for help she is stabbed without any hesitation . . .

P.U.A.—G   81

It is small wonder that law-abiding citizens live in fear of these 'tsotsis'. Their assaults have become daily occurrences:

CARD E : 5

It is one of the usual scenes in the townships to see young boys and even grown ups brandishing knives in the street in an attempt to stab either rival gangs or even those suspected of having money.

This fear of assault and attack is a constant anxiety facing the urban dweller. It has become part of his life. It is the most constantly recurring apperceptive distortion found in the T.A.T. series. Attack with robbery is standard practice in the urban township and, as such, the fear of attack and its resulting anxieties have become ingrained aspects of the urban dweller's personality.

This fear is not alleviated by the presence of police protection, for the township dwellers know that the African police who patrol the townships are ill equipped with their sticks and handcuffs, to protect law-abiding citizens from 'tsotsis' armed with razor-sharp knives, revolvers and rifles. Furthermore, the police, as such, constitute an additional source of personal anxiety to the urban African; because they have the unenviable duty of checking the numerous documents which the law requires the urban African to carry, they have come to be accepted by the township dweller as an additional social hazard. Urban Africans are arrested in their tens of thousands each year for technical contraventions of the Pass Laws. Such arrests are often described in their stories:

CARD A : 9

. . . I was once arrested for not having a pass with me. In fact I had forgotten it at home. It was too late for tears. I was handcuffed to a certain person who was also arrested . . .

We came to the charge-office and the police unlocked the handcuffs. I was fined (two-pounds) £2 for not being in a position to produce a pass . . .

. . . the bus came but it was too full. Jacob had no time to waste and decided to walk to Sophiatown. He was stopped by the Police who asked for his pass and unfortunately he had forgotten it at home and he was arrested and taken to Auckland Park Police Station. The following morning he was taken to Court and was sentenced to 5 days or 10 shillings fine. As he did not have the 10 shillings he was sent to the Fort . . .

Both the fear of attack and the fear of imprisonment are constantly with these people. The following story of a subject's reaction, when faced with both of these fears, describes the situation excellently:

82

Specific Personality Trends

The evening lights of a white suburb are reflected on this man . . .

The poor fellow has been overworked, exploited and underpaid. He fears going to the buses or the taxis, lest he be reluctantly compelled to expose his earnings to some unreliable eyes. It won't be long anyway walking home in the safety of these lights and quiet atmosphere. But the poor fellow fears even his shadow when he comes to think that at the end of this suburb will be the beginning of the stench, noise and unsafety of his township—lurking with darkness and unseen shadows. But providence saves him when a policeman flashes a torch upon his face and demands his pass. He tells a lie that he has none so that he can spent the night in a cell . . .

Gang warfare Chicago style further adds to the distress of law-abiding Africans. The following T.A.T. story written at the height of the gang-warfare period reveals the fears and anxieties of such people:

The people of this place lived in fear because their lives were in danger. The cause of this was that there were two groups of dangerous gangsters, one group wanted to be superior to the other. They were forced to settle this by blood. As a result a warfare was started. Every week people were killed, robbed, assaulted. Even women and medium sized girls were raped by these gangsters. People had to stay home in order to spare their lives by not going to work. These gangsters were cruel and dangerous day and night. They themselves killed each other merely for superiority . . .

The above story is the fantasy production of a resident of Alexandra Township. A 'fantasy production' which was reported by the *Rand Daily Mail* (16 February 1960) in the following words:

. . . Alexandra was the home of the rivalling Msomi and Spoiler gangs . . . who were responsible for as many as 93 deaths in 10 months.

In such an atmosphere of attack, robbery and the fear of imprisonment, it is small wonder that law-abiding urban Africans develop an anxious, insecure outlook. It is small wonder that a twenty-seven-year-old man remarked in a story about farm life:

. . . In the farms we live well without any fear of tsotsis or police . . .

This constant fear of attack has tended to warp the perception of the urban African, so that even innocent people come to be viewed with suspicion and distrust. As one subject put it:

One day I saw a man standing in a dark corner. This man was waiting for the people who were from work with their pay packets. This man stood there for a long time. No one passed near him. At the end it was discovered that he was only waiting for his wife who had gone to town in the afternoon.

It is therefore of no avail to keep on watching everybody with fear . . .

Ignorance of the law is no excuse, but in African society this ignorance is very often one of the fundamental bases of the fears and anxieties of the urban dweller. Individuals are sometimes imprisoned through sheer ignorance, especially newcomers to the urban areas. Such occurrences are by no means rare. A subject describes such a happening in the following extract:

CARD E : 5

So when Joe's parents died, Joe had to come to the city to work, he felt like a fish whose pond has suddenly run dry.

He had just got off the bus in the township when a shabbily-dressed individual approached him and roughly demanded to see his pass. Joe had never heard of a pass. So promptly the shabbily-dressed individual produced and snapped some handcuffs on to Joe's wrists. The shabbily-dressed man was a member of the 'ghost-squad', and this incident led to Joe's long ordeal in the labour gangs.

The constant strain of the bewildering and attacking environment in which they live has developed in the urban African deep-seated feelings of anxiety and insecurity. They fear their own people and they fear the law. This undercurrent of anxiety and insecurity is the most widespread and general factor characteristic of the urban African personality.

2. Aggression

The township African lives in a most aggressive social environment. A survey of protocols revealed a high trend of aggressive responses and reactions by these people. The Africans as a group appear to be an aggressive people. Witness of assault and robbery is almost a daily occurrence and is reflected in stories such as this one:

CARD B : 8

The story I'm about to relate happened a few weeks ago in the city of Alexandra Township . . .

One day I decided to pay a visit to one of my old school mates who stays in Alexandra. As I was coming along Seventh Ave. having two more streets to cross I saw a gang of about twelve people. Few yards from them was a couple strolling in the opposite direction. They were neatly dressed. All of a sudden these gangsters jumped on them and assaulted them severely. The two people were undressed and left naked. After some seconds after the gangsters had left, one of them came back

84

fearing that the assaulted people, if they regain their consciousness, he would be recognised among those gangsters. He stabbed them with a big jungle knife until they died.

Familiarity with assault and attack, coupled with a certain lack of emotional control or moderation, quickly develops in the urban African the violent emotions of primitive aggression. This aggression is obvious in his fantasies:

CARD **E : 5**

. . . Bob tried by all means to explain to him that he was making a nusense of himself in front of people, but Jim drew out a knife and tried to stab his friend.

. . . Bob took a lash and lashed him until he threw that knife away and ran fast towards home. The next day Jim went straight to Bob and thanked him very much for proving to be a good friend . . .

CARD **A : 9**

. . . They caught him from behind, telling him that you do not want to hear when we tell you do not ride the buses. They then cut his ear off altogether . . .

CARD **E : 5**

. . . the one man asked the other man to move away if he is not look-ing for trouble. The other man started to put his hands in his pockets and promised to kill the man.

The man did not waste time, he lifted his stick and knocked him down on the head . . .

CARD **I : 1**

. . . He told me that he hired a taxi from Johannesburg to Orlando Township. On the way to Orlando the taxi driver stopped his taxi. The taxi driver demanded the whole money that his passenger possessed, threatening to leave his passenger at the lonely spot. The passenger preferred to be left there than to surrender his money. In a struggle that took place the taxi driver stabbed his passenger several times. The man told me that he was saved by a car that appeared making the taxi driver leave him and drive off.

CARD **F : 4**

. . . this man was very angry for his wife, the wife seems to be frightened. In the end the man lashed her . . .

CARD **D : 6**

. . . As Mr. Brown tried to retreat into the house, Jose jumped at him with a knife in his hand. He stabbed twice with such speed that Mr. Brown could not defend himself. He just went down like a block of wood and lay sprawled on the floor. Meanwhile Jose ran into the night . . .

. . . Before he could shout for help they started hacking him to death . . .

These examples of savage violence are very often found in the T.A.T. protocols of urban Africans. Such violent aggression and such sudden uncontrolled surges of fury are very common story themes.

Aggression in the African flares up with frightening suddenness, annoyance ignites into violence with alarming speed, and emotions change from relative calm to crazy killing in a flash of anger. While African stories are characterized by a considerable amount of aggression, the interesting fact is not so much the undercurrent of aggression displayed, but the extraordinary speed with which the personality changes from relative aggression to the uncontrolled violence of an almost completely id-dominated being.

It is interesting to note that Laubscher, writing in 1937, when referring to a tendency he noticed in the Cape Bantu for fighting in play to develop into fighting in earnest, arrived at very similar conclusions. He says:

> I come to the conclusion that once an emotional impulse is aroused and the stimulus continues to be present, the native just drifts along with the impulse and exercises little if any inhibitory power . . Resultingly, the intellectual mechanisms of foresight, judgment and self-control are readily submerged by the instinctive impulse.

This uninhibited aggression, this id-domination of the African personality, has been also noted by Shelly and Watson who, in their discussion on murders committed by Nyasaland Africans, mention that:

> Temporary insanity in the form of sudden and violent rages is well-recognised by the natives . . . The killer will assault his victim with great ferocity, attacking him with a spear, axe, or some other implement, until the body of his supposed enemy is horribly mutilated. Immediately after committing such a crime, the murderer appears to be so greatly relieved that he neglects to take any precautions to cover up his guilt . . . A little later, as the sense of relief passes, he 'returns to earth', and ideas of safety or of covering up his guilt occur to him . . .

3. Motivation

Ambition in terms of social advance and an increase in personal status and wealth are constantly recurring themes. The urban African considers that the most socially acceptable means towards achieving this end, is education. Education is seen as the answer to problems of status, recognition and wealth. Education is considered as an essential prerequisite to success. The urban African both admires and desires education, and educated men have considerable status in his society.

It is the supreme desire of the vast majority of urban parents to give their children the opportunity of an education. Success themes are usually associated in their stories with educational achievement. Educational achievement and personal success are considered as almost synonymous by the urban African. Those sentiments are well expressed in the following story extract:

CARD **A** : **9**

For seven years my father had been a spanner-boy at Risdon Motors . . . I used to tell my teacher of how my father was working hard and how he usually came late at home . . .

So every day I kept on thinking about my education until I could not go further for my old-man could not afford to support the family . . . Then I decided to leave school and help my old-man by working . . . You can see how heavy it is for us Africans to look for a job while you are still interested in schooling . . . its through lack of education that we Africans have got to work so hard . . . Education pays more than anything else.

In urban African society, while education definitely gives an individual increased status, and the aspect of social service by education, in terms of school teaching, medicine, social work, etc., is a further motivating influence to become educated, the main advantage of education is seen by the majority of urban Africans as purely economic in nature. Educational achievement is considered by them as synonymous with success, and success spells more money.

CARD **D** : **6**

. . . with enough money one can always lead a good life. One can also be able to maintain the family well and support his children.

One can also educate his children so that they meet the future being prepared for good well-paying jobs. The children who are from good families and have good qualifications are always prosperous in their lives . . .

Or in the words of a young man from Moroka:

CARD **D** : **6**

. . . Today we live in the age of money. That is why we go to school in order to acquire a higher education in order to get higher wages . . .

While a matriculated man expresses the association between money and education as follows:

CARD **D : 6**

Education plays the most important part in the life of a modern man. Educated men earn money and are proud of their titles.

This is the hand of a wealthy man who earns money easily. He is showing his friends who left him at school and started to work with little Education . . . He realises that Education is powerful.

The Greek concept of education as knowledge for the betterment of the 'persona' has virtually no place in urban African thinking. As one subject expressed it:

CARD **D : 6**

I am convinced that money is one of the ingredients of life itself— by this I mean that to lead a sound and steady kind of life, you must command a good amount of *money* . . .

Not only is money directly associated with happiness:

CARD **H : 2**

. . . The house itself is a typical Moroka house, which of course suggests that these people are quite decent, but owing to the conditions under which they live, you immediately arrive at the idea that they are not quite happy. The appearance of a house, what it holds, and the general outlook of its occupants, can readily reveal a good number of facts. The fact is that the mother and baby are not properly dressed or clothed. It would appear that the poor child is not quite content, probably due to hunger as the father does not earn quite enough . . . the baby in arms is in a bad state of health, and as such the father is about to send the young man somewhere for some financial help . . .

but the urban dweller also fully realizes that the money problem is at the bottom of many other social evils:

CARD **A : 9**

Bad homes that lack parental control results in the upbringing of tsotsis.

Poor parents are both forced to go out working to feed and clothe the children . . . the children wander up and down the streets, not attending school. On every corner, in dark lanes you'll find these tsotsis waiting their prey . . .

Education is a socially acceptable means of achieving the urban African's ambition of financial success; there are, however, other less desirable ways: The following story by a Dube Township inhabitant gives an alternative avenue to success:

CARD **D : 6**

Always dapper and with an unmistakably natty tie is the only way in which one can describe James Ndaba. Yet still one may add that he was even as proud as a peacock. He had no straight—what you call decent—employment yet he so loved to jingle money in his pocket or sometimes in his open hand that even in his sitting room hung a picture of his hand filled with money. His friends called him Natty Natty, because he always looked smartest. But the dicks who had all his criminal records had a name for him: they called him 'The Rat'. They believed he was a rat of a man because he flourished on what some people earned by the sweat of their brows.

The increase in the cost-of-living has naturally reinforced this desire for money and gambling has become a favourite means of obtaining it:

CARD **D : 6**

Long ago when money was too scarce in the country people had to work on the farms for 6 months and their wages being five shillings and to them it was too much. On the other hand food was not so costly as today. People used to buy a bag of mealie-meal for just only half-crown and meat too was plenty for they had cows to slaughter. They did not worry about clothing for they used skins of dead animals . . . The people of nowadays . . . all they do is to steal money from poor hardworking people. This one gets money from a different angle. All that he has to do is to gamble day and night either in playing cards or throwing dice.

Although the above statement of working six months for a payment of five shillings is undoubtedly an exaggeration of the increase in living standards, the story nevertheless indicates the money need and a means of satisfying it. Other less respectable money-making schemes are:

CARD **A : 9**

Shebeen-Queens spread out day after day . . . dagga was also one of the best business rackets ever run. Brothels too . . . outside the house when passing along the street you always find a group of five or eight people waiting for their turns . . .

The fundamental motivation of the urban African is to have more money, to acquire wealth. Education is seen as the most socially acceptable means of achieving this ambition, as far as respectable people are concerned. Others with less social conscience brew beer, gamble, attack and rob, organize dagga smoking-dens and run brothels.

While the fundamental ambition of the urban African is to acquire wealth, the means to this end tends to vary according to personal predisposition and upbringing. Money has come to be regarded by him as the panacea for all social and personal ills;

CARD **D : 6**

. . . In life as it affects almost everything money is the Key to Life. Anything today means money . . . Our very lives today are worthless without money. God! money means all . . .

Driven by this money ambition the urban dweller moves from job to job:

CARD **D : 6**

When I started my first job after leaving school I received a wage of £1.10.0 a week, and thought it far too little to cope up with my demands. Then I started drifting from one job to the other and I still thought the money was little, in spite of the fact that I now earned £5. a week compared to £1.10.0. Then I got a job with a musical company that paid me £10. a week. I nearly hit the ceiling at the offer given me. I immediately abandoned my £5. a week job and thought that, that was for the birds . . .

Money, and more money, is the driving force in this occupational drifting. It is not at all uncommon to find individuals who have had between five to eight different jobs within a period of three years.

The quest for more money has become almost an obsession with urban Africans; increased financial status is their primary ambition in life, greater wealth their constant ideal, the acquisition of money their basic motivation.

Summing up the situation in the words of one subject:

CARD **D : 6**

In days of yore money was never known. As the Whites came over from over the seas they taught us that their 'cow' was money. So they pleaded with us to exchange our stock through silver and brass coins. If you have money nowadays you have everything. In the cities everything is money. Food, wood and what not, is money. To live a decent life you must have some coins in your pockets.

This money obsession, however, has tended to have assumed the status of almost an end in itself. As one subject put it:

CARD **D : 6**

You will remember this: God made man, man made money, money made man rich . . .

The motivation is money, but the desire is purely self-gain. Philanthropic ideas, community development schemes or social betterment programmes have no part in these money fantasies. The stories are characterized by individual selfishness and personal greed, rather than by personal generosity and a broader social conscience.

Wealth is desired for one's personal well-being, or for that of one's immediate family. Personal gain themes completely dominate the fantasies in the money sphere. To use one's money on social projects for the betterment of the rest of society is a foreign concept.

The urban African is extremely money conscious—a consciousness, however, which is characterized by greed fantasies and selfish desires. He wants money but his fantasy desires are completely personally biased.

4. Race Consciousness

Urban Africans living as they do in such close contact with European society tend naturally to develop certain ideas and attitudes about the question of race.

The most obvious trend observed in the T.A.T. stories is a feeling of being discriminated against by the European group. As one subject put it, when referring to the character standing under the streetlamp in CARD I : 1: 'Poor fellow he has been overworked, exploited and underpaid' . . . a statement which typifies the feelings of the urban African responses in this sphere.

While personality differences cut across all other influences, the usual trend in matters of race and colour is: the better the education of the individual, the more liable he is to feelings of being discriminated against.

A thirty-four-year-old man with a Primary Teacher's Certificate expressed this feeling of being discriminated against in the following story. It features a discussion between a Bus Boycott leader and an Anglican priest who is trying to persuade the leader to stop the boycott. The boycott leader replies:

CARD E : 5

. . . At once Mr. Nkomo felt very angry and told the Priest the following: 'If only you had the African interests at heart you would not have said all this. An African is underpaid, has no wealth of his own in the land of his birth; no house of his own, and each time the White-man delights in robbing him of his birthright; he lives on wages below the breadline. As a result disease and poverty are rife. Why don't you stop your own white-skinned brothers from all these evils? Surely you could put some sense into them. This Boycott is one of the only ways of showing you white people how we feel about all this rubbish of robbing the under-privileged. You are only encouraging your own brother whitemen to continue sucking the last pint of blood left in the Native', concluded the big Nkomo.

Criticism of prevailing conditions and events is voiced, sometimes openly and bluntly, as in the above example, and sometimes in a more subtle, veiled form, as in the following cynical commentaries.

The first is on the Sharpville riots, the second on the Sophiatown removal scheme.

CARD **I : 1**

What happened at Sharpville, was it war or not?

The Police had guns, Saracens and sten-guns. I understand the Police were shooting.

What did the poor Africans do? I hope they were doing the same with their knop-kieries.

How many bullets does a knop-kierie load?

CARD **C : 7**

In the year nineteen hundred and fiftyfour, it was passed in the Parliament that our township Sophiatown must go because it was a black spot on the white spot.

We at first thought it was just a topic to keep them busy, as we thought they had nothing to speak about that day. To our surprise it was also passed in the Senate that it should be.

Later, we were issued with notices that a place called Meadowlands was built for us in the south western areas of Johannesburg.

We decided not to move for we loved our place of birth. We were moved by law from our beloved homes to our new homes.

We had it very hard at our new homes for we used to get lost and you would find yourself in a wrong house, for the houses look alike there.

Our beloved home Sophiatown exists no more now, with only a few houses there.

Instead of many homes crowding on the same place, you see heaps of ground and ashes, old cars and tins, bewildered dogs and cats, street lights and big fruit trees. Those are the only things that can prove to you that this place was once a home of many people.

Dissatisfaction with the social set-up of the urban areas is expressed in different ways. Some prefer the boycott methods, others choose a return to the tribal way of life:

CARD **C : 7**

Once upon a time there was a chief who bought land, and took his people away from the control of the whiteman, to go and build a beautiful land . . . It was a pleasure and relief to see the nice open land in which they had to rule themselves, under their mighty Chief . . .

Yet others feel an appeal to world opinion is the best method:

CARD **E : 5**

These two men were discussing about their journey to overseas where they want to meet Britain's Prime Minister about their living in South Africa. They are not satisfied of (the) new Government in South Africa. They hope to fly tomorrow morning at Jan Smuts airport.

92

While others simply blame the government of the country:

CARD **C : 7**

. . . the South African Nationalist Government is planting or creating conflicts amongst whites and blacks, for you find in *Native Townships* robberies, murders, and all kinds of crimes; more crimes are happening on weekends in the Townships, because of hard to get work because of the pass-laws and no pleasure resorts or accommodation for native people. . . .

Such outspoken critical responses do not, however, explain the crux of the race problem. The main criticism of the social set-up is made in stories dealing with the urban Africans' low wages. The feeling of racial discrimination tends to be centred on the financial implications of the industrial colour-bar.

Urban Africans, as a group, are extremely money conscious, and as has been pointed out in the section on 'Motivation'—their basic motivation is reducible to the acquisition of money. The industrial colour-bar thwarts this ambition, and consequently tends to become the main bone of racial contention for the majority of urban dwellers.

When one path to the accomplishment of a strong need is blocked, the personality seeks out substitutes or other approaches to the fulfilment of its desires. If sufficient money cannot be earned legally, illegal methods are often resorted to, as evidenced by the tremendously high incidence of illicit liquor brewing in the urban areas and the deep resentment of the township inhabitants at police beer raids. Beer brewing is the most popular home-industry organized to supplement the 'honestly earned' but usually inadequate wages of the urban dwellers.

The crux of black-white antagonism in the urban areas is centred on the restrictions placed by the Europeans in the paths of the urban Africans who, in their constant quest for satisfaction in their desire for more money, become frustrated, annoyed and antagonistic towards the Europeans as a group.

This desire for more money is by no means the sole motivating force moving urban Africans; it is, however, the need which was found to be most stressed and most widely spread amongst this population. So much so, that urban Africans, when discussing race discrimination in their stories, are almost stereotypical in their use of such phrases as:

CARD **I : 1**

. . . he has been overworked, exploited and underpaid . . .

and

. . . he lives below the breadline . . .

Black-white race consciousness in urban society spells money consciousness. And while individual experiences in the race sphere certainly influence the African, the money problem is the root problem.

Apart from race consciousness in the sphere of African-European contacts, the urban African is also very conscious of inter-tribal differences and of his own cultural heritage. Western standards are undoubtedly urban African ideals, but such people are still very conscious of their tribal ties and proud of their tribal past.

Tribal traditions and customs are often incorporated in the story presentations or urbanized subjects. Here is a typical example taken from a story written by a thirty-five-year-old who has lived all his life in the urban areas:

. . . we Swazis we are not allowed to stay or play with girls thats our tribal law.

When you are still under age you look after goats and sheep . . . Until such time your parents would like you to get married to somebody's daughter, they will arrange everything for you and they will tell you where you must go and propose a girl friend . . .

Tribal tradition and custom die hard, even in a strongly urbanized society. The urban African is proud of his tribal name and affiliations —however distant they may be, and in the overwhelming majority of cases such associations are by no means distant.

Story presentations dealing with tribal customs and mores are often found. And while the Pass Regulations require a tribal designation, and the Governmental policy of ethnic grouping has stressed the requirement of a tribal association, urban Africans are still nevertheless genuinely tribally biased. They speak of their black group collectively as Africans or Bantu, but they associate individual members tribally. For example, on CARD C : 7 a twenty-seven-year-old urban subject wrote:

These children in this picture, they are Xosas . . . we find this nation in the Colony . . . (i.e. Cape Colony);

or in the words of another subject:

On the picture we see a gentleman standing with a lady. The name of the gentleman is Mr. Duma, he is a typical Zulu in nationality.

While a young man from Orlando Township expressed this feeling of tribal difference as follows:

Specific Personality Trends

The people are running to the scene where the British Prime Minister is said to be.
There were Zulus, Sothos, Xosas, and Coloureds who came to see him.

The concept of Africanism is used politically and finds impetus in the 'unity is strength' type of argument, but tribal affiliation is still the fundamental individual association amongst the vast majority of urban Africans. Detribalization in the urban areas is exemplified rather by the neglect and disuse of many traditional tribal folkways than by an absolute rejection of tribal customs and affiliation and a complete acceptance of the mores of European society. The completely tribally emancipated African is a psychological rarity.

The urban African personality has evolved not through the europeanization of the township dweller but through the breakdown of a number of his tribal concepts and the integration of urbanized values (sometimes European) into the 'left-overs' of his tribal past.

The resulting dilemmas of such cultural changes have been expressed by a 30-year-old African stores clerk as follows:

'We African races have many customs, and these customs to some of us are the things of the past, but with some of us they still continue . . . These customs have with them behaviour. If you are a child you are told of things not to do and things you can do . . . The first is that you are not supposed to eat what an elderly person eats, you are told not to be among the old people when they discuss their affairs . . . If an old person talks to you, you must kneel down, let him or her talk and finish then you can answer. If there is a party of some sort a goat is slaughtered and the children are given the insides of the goat and not the meat, and before they can eat those insides they must fight for them with little sticks, and the winner takes them for himself and if he pleases he will give the children some of it to eat. Now as I said to some of the children these customs and behaviour are things of the past, they don't do them. If an old man gave you a piece of meat you would be so glad and you would take it with both hands, if he gives you bread or tomatoes or anything at all you would take it with both hands. This custom is now out of date, we eat with our parents at the same time, eat the food they eat, be among them when they discuss and even take what they give you with *one* hand no matter what. (The emphasis is the subject's.)

African myths, customs and tribal beliefs are oft-used themes. Here is a beautiful example of African mythology related by a thirty-four-year-old urban man. Related possibly in the same words that the story was told to him by his father, and as he has subsequently relayed it to his own children. His name is Walter Mazibuko, and the story he tells is a myth on the origins of his tribe—the Mazibuko:

CARD C : 7

Once upon a time, it was at night, a noise of bellowing and of lowing of cattle was heard in the cattle kraal. Among this herd of cattle there was one with black and white colours. It was given the name of 'Gwag-was-Gwilike'. The whole herd forced their way out of the kraal led by the black and white one. And all the people at that village awoke and followed that cow. Let me explain that such an incident was an omen of war—that village was to be attacked at the dead of night. The black and white cow was like a 'Sangoma', that is a witch-doctor. Let me say this war or battle was declared by the King of the Zulus to invade this little village. Some of the warriors fought hard at this, the battle of 'Kwasosbangane'. In the end the black and white cow chased the enemy away. This battle lasted for a very long time. The houses were deserted. Kraals were empty, it was a mournful spectacle. The cow led the people. It went as far as the Tugela and never even stopped on the way to eat until they were safe. They started to build houses and kraals. When they arrived at that place they had already multiplied for it took three years to get there. Most of the children grew on the way and others were also born on the way. When they had finished to build, they then waited.

The owner of this mysterious cow was Hlathi. They then changed their name and called themselves the Mazibukos because when they arrived at the Tugela, the river was flooded and they could not cross for six months. The cow would wade through the river and come back. In so doing it was testing the strength of the river. When the river was no longer over-flowing they crossed it. The cow now started to bellow for one full hour and they praised it. This cow never calved, it was barren. From that day these people adopted the name Mazibuko.

The tribal name Mazibuko, the plural of 'isibuko', means the number of crossings of the river, as was made by the cow in the story.

The urban African, while he has European ideals, has maintained much of his tribal cultural heritage; he is very conscious of his tribal affiliations and proud of his tribe and its traditions. Race conscious-ness in African-to-African relations becomes tribal consciousness. A consciousness which even in the urban areas has tended to maintain much of its insular, isolationistic attitudes:

CARD F : 4

... my mother told me I could not marry that man because she hated the Xhosas ...

Race consciousness amongst urban Africans follows two lines: race consciousness in the black-white sphere, characterized by feel-ings of discrimination, and motivated by a frustrated money drive (a universal phenomenon in the black-white sphere): and race con-sciousness in the black-black sphere, characterized by feelings of tribal difference and motivated by traditional isolationistic attitudes (a widely spread phenomenon). The former phenomenon is increasing in strength with time, the latter is decreasing in strength with urbanization, but it is, nevertheless, still very strong.

5. *Male-Female Relationship*

In the atmosphere of general moral laxity prevailing in the urban areas, the male-female relationship is characterized by an almost animal-like primitivism:

CARD **F : 4**

. . . It was the beginning of the year when a decent and respectable girl came to the township to further her education. When Phillip saw her, he was fascinated by her charms. He tried all he could to see her but she always turned him down because of his behaviour. On one occasion she was on her way from school, when Phillip approached and accosted her. Threatening her, he said 'Do you know that I'm the boss around here?' 'What do you mean?' she said. 'How long did you think you could evade me?' he asked. Before she could answer, he slapped her across the face and she fell to the ground.

The typical boy-meets-girl theme is characterized by the following story:

CARD **F : 4**

. . . As men and women danced I scrutinised the best of them all— a lady. At a far distance I saw a lady with all curves. I mean she had all the necessary things to be married for.

Hey! I say! I called the lady outside and by St. Pete the lady was mine. She gave me a real smile that no women ever gave me. I crept to the ground to give her a bear's hug. Did we romance. O! man, that was a night for me.

The fantasy is frankly sexual, the approach is uninhibited, the ego controls weak. It is a story which typifies the male-female relationship of the urban areas. It is a relationship which is very, very often characterized by aggression and violence:

CARD **F : 4**

Doris and Ben were a happy and ambitious couple with the hope that one day they would team up and build a home of their own. This was one of the reasons why you would find them together all the time.

Doris unfortunately became unfaithful to Ben and she found herself another partner. It was during that time that Ben noticed radical changes in Doris' behaviour. One night he as usual paid her a visit. When he entered the gate he met Doris obviously going out for an appointment.

He explained to her that he had come to pay her a visit. To his surprise she became restive and insisted on going out alone. Ben infuriated by this type of behaviour decided to mete out a severe beating to Doris. It was the end of a happy association.

Specific Personality Trends

The urban African male's approach to the male-female relationship is frank, direct and aggressive.

CARD F : 4

This man is proposing love to this woman, she is resisting hard . . .

CARD F : 4

Well, well, Sarah was a fine dame. I say so because she was a beauty. You know something, you could never get tired of looking at her. You don't feel hungry when you are with such a thing like Sarah. She had them curves and good legs. Man! her eyes would send you to bed before your actual time.

CARD F : 4

In the darkness of Alexandra, the black township where people live in fear of their lives is Zorro. He is trying to persuade this poor girl to fall in love with him. She was sent to the shop to go and buy some meali-meal and Zorro just felt like stopping her to make love to her. Zorro promised to kill her if she doesn't love him.

The girl went home late in the evening crying because Zorro had held and slapped her.

The girl's parents said 'Tomorrow we shall take you to your aunt at Sharpville Township because Zorro will take you away if you stay here.'

CARD F : 4

This girl who had no happiness, was seeking for love, but could not find it until she met up with a guy called Masters. A guy who was a masterpiece in his profession of making love . . .

CARD F : 4

Once upon a time I lived in Orlando Location and I fell in love with a lady but before I could marry her we were sort of street lovers.

One day she came to me in the Shebeen house where I was drinking. We went outside the house and stood there for a long time kissing until it was nearly morning. We then went to the place where I hired a room still holding hands and that happened for a long time . . .

In a society where might is to a very great extent right, and the law of the jungle a very real law, the id emerges as the dominant personality force—especially in the sex sphere:

CARD F : 4

We see Tom and Mary right inside the bush where they are just alone. Tom saw Mary passing towards the shop. She was sent by her mother to go and buy sugar and bread from the shop. When Tom saw her he called and forced her to accompany him to the bush. Mary tried to refuse but all was in vain as Tom showed her a knife to convince her. They are now alone in the bush.

98

Specific Personality Trends

The urban African's approach to sex is uninhibited and unembarrassed. Sex is an animal drive to be satisfied in almost an animal fashion. It is in this sphere that the id domination of the urban personality is most obvious. Sex is very often coupled with violence and aggression and no attempt is made to hide the individual's motives; if he is not satisfied he uses brute force. The tribal mores governing courting behaviour and sex practices have been dropped by the younger generation and an increase in illegitimacy and unhappiness is the result. As a man from Sophiatown puts it:

CARD **F : 4**

HOW ILLEGITIMACY STARTS IN TOWNS

It happened that a certain high school girl who was staying next door to us got attracted to a married man due to the fact that he was always in American clothes, neatly dressed and she always got money from him to buy clothes and everything. She thought that that was the man of her life, not knowing that the man was married and had six children. The man used to take her out to the movies and to all sorts of places, so that on some nights she used not to come back home. Time went on and she got pregnant. Anyway she did not mind thinking that was the time for marriage. But the reverse was the case because she found afterwards that the man was married, and that he had run away from her for good. Now who is the father of the child? This picture reminds me of that young school girl being embraced by that man.

One practice which has been largely retained, however, is the payment of 'lobola'—it has an economic basis and is in conformity with the urban dweller's tremendous money drive:

CARD **F : 4**

Lobola is common among Africans. You can go all over South Africa and in the African territories and you will still find lobola. All that counts is money when you first propose.

While the urban African has adopted many European modes of behaviour, European chivalry has not been one of his cultural acquisitions. The male-female relationship in the urban areas is characterized by aggression, brute force and sadism. It functions on the id-directed internal logic of: 'I want, therefore I take.'

A study of the ego functions in relation to the drive helps to indicate the possibility of the impulses breaking through. In sexuality, as in aggression, the ego controls of the urban African personality are very liable to break through.

While the latent sexuality in their fantasies is clinically interesting, the striking factor is the violence, aggression and complete lack of control of the almost id-dominated personality, with which it is usually associated.

99

6. *Humour*

The urban African laughs easily and with uninhibited hilarity. And while the preceding sections have dealt with the more serious aspects of his personality makeup, one must not lose sight of the fact that the urban African spends a great deal of his social life laughing at jokes and telling them.

What kind of humour does he appreciate most? What type of humour is most prevalent in urban African society? We will attempt to answer these questions in this section.

When dealing with urban African humour one must distinguish clearly between true humour as such and the cruder sense of the comic.

An excellent definition of true humour has been given by the novelist Meredith, who considers it to be the ability to laugh at the things one loves (including oneself), and still love them. As Allport has stated, 'the real humorist perceives behind some solemn event, himself for instance, the contrast between pretension and performance. That which he values becomes, for the time being, vain show.' True humour, Allport considers, seems to have a development entirely parallel to that of insight. He feels that personal insight—or self-objectification as he calls it, which is the ability to perceive one's personal incongruities and absurdities, in settings where their own pretensions are disclosed—is fundamental to the possession of true humour.

The sense of the comic, on the other hand, is far less subtle than true humour. The comic consists of absurdities of the custard-pie-throwing variety. It is described as 'slap-stick' humour. It is usually laughter provoked by the degradation of some individual, or by the sly and abrupt release of some emotional suppression.

Landis and Ross, discussing this difference, came to the conclusion that true humour requires a high level of intelligence, while the less sophisticated prefer comic episodes derived from their own repressions, usually expressed in terms of 'dirty jokes' and risqué stories.

The urban African appreciates the comic, and his laughter is almost wholly derived from comic situations. True humour, as described above, is seldom if ever found; for, in personalities struggling for recognition, acceptance, and status in a Western European society, the ability to perceive personal incongruities, in settings where their pretensions are disclosed, tends to be almost completely inhibited.

The test situation in the present study is hardly conducive to producing comic responses from what is normally a very fun-loving people. Yet even in a test situation the urban African's sense of the comic is by no means completely stifled; it does break through every now and then.

M- 03414

Sophisticated humour, true humour, containing insight and self-objectification, is rare. One of the few exceptions, which borders on true humour, is the following example of an urban African's ability to laugh at African suspicion and gullibility:

CARD E : 5

Hi! Jack why you look worried? Indeed I am worried. I am not feeling at all well. True as God my kidney troubles me a lot. I have tried most of the tablets but they all seem to be doing me no good. So much so, that I have thought of consulting a doctor, perhaps a doctor will help me.

Ah! no Jack, if you go to a doctor he will not help you but he will give you an injection and that injection will just overpower the disease and not cure it. If I take you to a certain well known witchdoctor he will give you some Bantu treatment. Honestly, I tell you Jack he will give you two bottles and I am sure you will be cured within six months. Doctors, yah! are O.K. when treating other things but not kidneys, because when somebody is seriously ill in one kidney the doctor will simply operate and try to take out the whole organ and replace it with a sheep's kidney.

Ah! yah! it is so. No I will take your advice my friend, I shall come with you.

Another example, in a sophisticated vein, is contained in the following story extract:

CARD F : 4

Lovemaking is one of the oldest arts in creation. The only creatures who had an advantage were those that were taken by Noah in the Ark. The Bible has it that they were selected in pairs and this eliminated competition.

An attempted pun by an urban African results in the following comic situation between master and servant:

CARD E : 5

'Well I am going out now Jim to play golf with the other bosses. The madam will be coming just now, she is working at the Post Office. But before she comes, see that you have an egg fried for her, a nice cup of coffee and please make us a cake for three o'clock tea-time. Do you understand?'

'Where, under what sir?' asked the boy.

'I mean do you hear what I am saying?'

'Oh! yes' replies the boy.

'What did you think I am saying?' asked the boss.

'Well boss I thought you said can I stand under, and that is why I am replying by asking under where.'

Humorous episodes related at the expense of another person occupy a great deal of the urban African jokers' time. Episodes such as the following:

101

CARD **B** : **8**

Here is Mack, now this man is a funny man, because on Friday or at the end of the month after getting his pay he goes to the Beerhall; after a few drinks he says no this beer is no good I will now go to the Shebeen and buy myself a nip of cane spirit, when he gets to the Shebeen he calls for a nip of cane spirit and drinks it out and then he calls for a second nip, and then people gather around him praising him for his generosity and wealth as he buys more drinks until his money runs out; when the time comes for the people of the house to go to bed they order everybody to leave and they go through this man's pockets and then throw him out. He does not know where he is, he slept in the snake house and the snakes were surprised to see an uninvited guest.

Comic involvements like the following, showing the influence of the European music-hall variety act, are also not uncommon:

CARD **I** : **1**

. . . When I came home my wife asked me where I got the red eye, I said to her 'Never mind my red eye, you should see how the other guy looks.'

CARD **B** : **8**

This man is in a bad condition, he is Elvis Presley. One day he was travelling with his two little boys in a train to Mexico, suddenly the guard of the train warned him to tell his boys to behave as they were making a noise in the train, and they were looking for trouble.

The man stood and answered the guard: 'Trouble, you don't know what trouble is, my wife has just born twins, my father was knocked down by a car yesterday, the other boy has just chewed up our train tickets and I've just discovered that we are in the wrong train—so what do you know about trouble.'

The guard was annoyed to hear such words, he immediately informed the police who locked Presley up in a cell as trains in America have got cells and Magistrates inside.

Presley was charged with High Treason and he was sentenced to make records. That is why we hear Elvis Presley records at every corner.

While blatantly exhibitionistic comic fantasies, such as the following extract, form a large part of the repertoire of the African comic:

CARD **F** : **4**

Gee whiz, there comes a strange beautiful figure in town. What a doll, wonder who's the guy for her. Anyway I might be the first one to see her. 'The early bird catches the fly.' What a joke??! No attention!!! Am I as ugly as all that?! Oh, she thinks she's her majesty. Anyway Grapes are sour. I better go for Shebeen dames who care not what kind of a guy I am.

Urban African humour, as can be seen from the examples given, has been greatly influenced by the European sense of the comic. European jokes of the comic variety are very popular in the urban townships, where they are altered slightly to give them local colour. African periodicals contain many European cartoons, sometimes in their original English, and sometimes with Zulu or Sotho captions. A feature of practically all present-day African tabloids is the joke section, in which European wit is presented, either in English, or translated into a Bantu language.

With their relative lack of inhibitions and their love of comic-humour, urban Africans appreciate jokes most when they are told with the aid of exaggerated gestures, facial expressions and voice changes. The appreciation exists not only in the telling of a joke but also in the accompanying actions.

Urban African humour finds its greatest outlet in the farcical comic story, usually European in origin, related with considerable gesticulation and action.

7. *Religious Super-Ego*

The acceptance of Christian belief by the African of necessity implies the rejection of many established tribal customs. Religious pressure is undoubtedly one of the most highly organized 'urbanizing' forces which the tribal newcomer to the townships has to contend with in his adjustments to the new environment. The churches of the urban areas are far more numerous and active than the missions of the rural areas.

This pressure is both externally applied by missions and churches directly seeking converts to their faiths, and internally motivated by the personality need of the urban African to find something stable to cling to in the culturally bewildering urban context about him.

His T.A.T. stories portray his bewilderment. They range from tales of traditional tribal ancestor worship, like the following:

CARD **A : 9**

. . . we also remember our forefathers by offering them a slaughtered kid to appease them. We also ask them to send us rain . . .

CARD **B : 8**

. . . this man is asking his ancestors for help . . .

to more Christian concepts like:

CARD **B : 8**

. . . when you are worried and miserable as if all your relatives are dead do not dispair God is there.

. . . they believed in their ancestors, and sacrificed to them at mountains. Those people will be forgiven by God, because they never knew, but we who know and do not want to understand will be blamed . . .

to fantasies like the following one, showing the contradiction in Christianity, which is for ever in the urban African's mind:

In the suburbs of a certain city, in a shanty township, lived a native that earned his living by making drawings and selling them to people for small takings.

Some of his drawings were indeed very beautiful and had some meaning in them, as a result people would go to his shack for selection.

When one day a minister of religion came to his shack to find out if there could be anything that would interest him, he thought he must also have religious drawings for religious people.

His first religious drawing was that of Jesus Christ and because he painted him black the police arrested him and he was deported to his original district.

Such bewilderment and contradiction have tended to foster the growth of African religious sects. A private communication with the Bantu Affairs Department—who have recently (1959) undertaken a survey into African religions—reveals that there are 81 recognized religions and 2,254 non-recognized religions, the vast majority being in the urban areas. Government recognition, established by the Native Churches Commission of 1925, is necessary before a church can be granted a site in one of the urban townships, before its ministers can be issued with railway concessions or can be registered as marriage officers, and before the church can obtain sacramental wine.

This separatist tendency, with its African cultural colouring, is not particular to the Johannesburg urban areas only. Kuper, Watts and Davies in their study of the racial ecology of Durban, published in 1958, found that:

> The major differences in the Christian population are in the strength of minor sects among the African. Almost half of the African population—44·67 per cent—belongs to minor sects. Many of these combine Christian observance with elements of African belief and ritual.

African religious practices are deeply ingrained aspects of traditional tribal culture. They are closely bound up with ancestor worship, and with special offerings to appease the spirits of the tribal forefathers. They include witchcraft aspects—practices which still prevail in the townships. Indeed, witchcraft is regarded as a very respectable profession amongst many urban dwellers and many stories are written about it. As one subject wrote:

CARD **B : 8**

. . . I was educated as a witchdoctor. To be a witchdoctor is nice. Our Superintendent witchdoctor sent me to Stoffberg to go and cure a man whose leg was broken and I helped that man . . .

The power of the witchdoctor is still considerable, even in the urban areas. A man living in Jabavu Township told the following story:

CARD **I : 1**

The Public Health Department inspector was travelling through our location to see what we have done. He found a flowering tree in my garden and ask me why do I plant that kind of tree because that kind of tree is harmful to children. I was taken to the police station. Later I went to the witchdoctor, the witchdoctor told me that he will come and kill the Public Health inspector with his drugs.

While a Mofolo Township inhabitant wrote the following:

CARD **H : 2**

This is a small house in Mofolo where Butelezi stays. Butelezi is a witchdoctor. He always tries to help people when they are sick.

In the personality trends evidenced in urban African populations at the present stage of their development, the influence of witchcraft is still a powerful determining factor. References to African magic appear in many stories.

The majority of the non-recognized sects which abound in the Johannesburg urban areas are a weird mixture of Christian faith and African custom. With their colourful individually decorated regalia, their use of tom-toms and their circumbulatory rituals about a sacred tree or stone, plus their establishment of prophets (usually the origin-ators of the various sects), these religions are attempts to compromise between Christianity and tribal beliefs, attempts to find an answer to the many religious bewilderments which exist in the urban areas. Most 'ministers' take regular Sunday collections, plus payments for extras like 'baptisms' and 'consecrations' and 'blessings' of various personal objects.

It is not possible to differentiate clearly between professing and nominal African Christians as individuals. It is possible, however, to form certain trend assumptions on the basis of available evidence.

An analysis of the fantasy productions of urban Africans as a group has revealed:
1. the existence of a definite religious bewilderment;
2. the presence of strong tribal influences and biases amongst these people; and

105

3. the existence of a strong belief in witchcraft and the power
of magic.

These personality trends, coupled with the great number and tremendous growth of African non-recognized churches amongst the
urban population—2,254 in January 1960—tend to indicate that
Christian conversions amongst the urban Africans have been more
successful numerically than spiritually.

Translated into psychoanalytic terminology, the religious super-
ego of the urban African is still very strongly tribally conditioned—
a fact which is supported by Bascom and Herskovits, who write:

> Despite the intensity of Christian missionary effort and the thousand
> years of Moslem proselytizing which have marked the history of various
> parts of Africa, African religions continue to manifest vitality every-
> where. This is to be seen in the worship of African deities, the homage
> to the ancestors, and the recourse to divination, magic, and other
> rituals. A growing number of Africans, to be sure, have been taught to
> regard the religion of their forefathers as superstition and to reject
> other beliefs and customs as outmoded. But there is no evidence which
> supports the assumption that so often underlies thinking about Africa's
> future, that African culture, whether in its religious or other aspects,
> will shortly and inevitably disappear.

8. General Environmental Adjustments

In the urban areas the African is exposed to many influences, some
good, some bad, some traditional and familiar, some foreign and
strange. To all these the urban Africans must adjust, but, like all
humans, some of them do and some of them do not. And these
adjustments and maladjustments are reflected in their T.A.T. stories.

Here is a story reflecting the trials of urban adjustment, written
by a twenty-six-year-old man:

CARD C : 7

I was born in Oudshoorn and I never realised what location life was
like, until we migrated to Johannesburg in 1943. Since that time I have
always stayed in one Location and that was Alexandra. In its hay-day, I
thought the place was a human jungle. The place was really fast and
rough, only to find the situation the same in other locations which I
visited at a later stage. I never saw so many nations put together as in
Alexandra, you see where I come from you only find Xhosas and
Coloureds. Well I gradually adapted myself to the means and ways these
people were living . . .

Since then I met a lot of ups and downs and so did Alexandra. Here
we are now, its 1960 and we have lights all over the place, and Bars
where you can always quench your thirst. We have a Stadium etc. etc.
Even the crime rate has subsided through the improvement Alexandra

has achieved. A location is really a hep place. There's never a dull moment unless when the police have cornered our blood streams—that is the 'Shebeens'.

A typical urban adjustment, he has the 'cops and robbers' outlook, the American slang and the 'shebeen' complex.

Criminal techniques also become adjusted in the urban areas. Here is a typical American gangster adjustment—note the language used. The story is set in the Mooiplaas Location, west of Pretoria:

CARD **F** : **4**

One day last December I was walking down a lane in Mooiplaas where murder is rife. The men and women will assault you without any provocation. You'll be assaulted, carried away and dumped somewhere after taking all your personal belongings. As I say that any day in Mooiplaas a gang of youths and their molls will be seen in every lane, waiting on law abiding people to be slaughtered like cattle. These molls will first approch their victim, and she will suggest where they can go and have a nice time. She will take you to the appointed place where these gangsters are waiting on you. They will first accuse you of molesting their sister (their moll) then assault you and leave you where you are. This picture might be of a taxi driver or a bus driver who was assaulted and robbed of his takings by these youths and their molls.

Urban adjustment for the African requires amongst other things the fundamental qualities of patience and compliance.

Patience with the overworked housing authorities:

CARD **H** : **2**

Blessed are those who live luxuriously, for I say this because I once lived in what you would call a slum area. It happened during the shortage of houses and we had to wait indefinitely for houses on a new sight promised us by the authorities. Well, if I recall now it took nearly two years before we could pull into our new house.

. . . Through perseverence and hope we eventually survived.

Compliance with the intricacies of European law which they don't fully understand:

CARD **B** : **8**

. . . we were made to understand from our father that our uncle was to be deported to his home town that is out of the Union. He has been in the Union since he was six years old and was now in his early fiftys. The evictment came to him as a shock . . . If it was money trouble, my father could have tried to lend a hand, but in this case it was the hand of the law of the country governing us, and against that there is nothing we could have done.

Patience with the authorities who are doing their best to curb the steady incidence of crime in the townships:

CARD **C : 7**

There is a place which is called a Native Location in the north of Johannesburg which is Alexandra. There live many people of different races. Some of them work in Johannesburg, and some in other towns. . . . every weekend they get their wages and go to their homes. Along the way homeward there comes the little boys called tsotsis.

These boys are no good because they kill the poor people and take their money and their passes. And every weekend people are worried about these tsotsis.

And the police are all trying to stop these boys from doing so, but these boys are also wise. It seems to me these boys called tsotsis are also improving in their actions. The police are also improving to stop these boys. After a few years if the police can improve their job these boys will end their actions.

And patience with the slow progress of wage increases compared with the rise in the cost of living:

CARD **D : 6**

I have in my hand the value of my labour output for the week. It amounts to two pound notes, seven-shillings, and two-pennies and after having calculated my expenses and credits for the very same week I am left with a defecit of eighteen shillings and a tickey. What with schools reopening and a further burden of income and poll taxes; and this and that. What shall I do? . . . but I shall not give up hope 'Where there is a will, there is a way.' How true the saying is. It is years old— my father once said so. Strangely enough, the money I have in my hand, part of my labour which I have sold, vanishes into hundreds of channels over the week end . . . I do not drink, but the cry for an increase in money is more. What shall I do; perhaps the coming week will be more fruitful.

The American influence is extremely strong in the urban areas— story themes and the use of language indicates this. Consider the following piece of typical Afro-American writing, note the language used; it is English written in 'Chicago style' by an African living in Jabulani Township:

CARD **A : 9**

Luckdip was a small township for a hoodlum like Twinny. Twinny lived with his Pa and Ma, down in the country at a place called 'Kurulen' (which means a 'place of peace'). Twinny hitched-hiked to Luckdip. It took him three and a half days. On entering the township he met Buta, a reputed Tsotsi in the township. Twinny arranged for an appointment, Twinny was a born gangster. City-life was what Twinny envied, I would say he loved city life, Buta was the Gang leader. And they called themselves the 'Swindlers'. Why? because they hi-jacked people every now and then. One would find them hanging around the street corners, some playing cards, some playing dice.

Twinny was promoted, next to the boss Buta. There at the corner called The Corner of Billy's as they called it, they did their planning on how they could dodge the Cops. Yet Twinny because he was ambitious pointed out to Buta, that, running away from the Cops, wouldn't pay them, so they all agreed that they could swindle the Cops by blackmailing.

One Friday morning after they had counted their loot which was amounting to £800 Buta decided that they shouldn't share the loot and the rest of the boys got sore about Buta. They thought, Buta was trying to be a wise guy, so they drew their big daggers, and Buta when he saw what was coming to him, drew his 32 pistol. He got the first two who were near to him, then Twinny. And as you all know the pistol ran out of bullets and Pete who was the youngest of the gang got Buta in the chest, and thus ended one of the most feared gangsters. Pete collected the loot and fled to Lourenco Marques, where the Cops got him after nine years, thus ended the life of the 'Swindlers', the creators of Billy's Corner.

The urban Africans are continually exposed to the influence of American comics, novels, advertisement themes and films. Their stories abound with Americanisms such as: 'life here is really hep'; 'the guys and their molls'; 'the cops'; 'that was for the birds'; 'one of the boys'; 'the dicks caught up with him'; 'the chief of the underworld'; 'Daddy watta we gonna eat?'; 'this girl here double-crossed the gangster'; 'he is going to shoot her down'; 'Hiya baby!'; 'What gives?'; 'So she gives him the eye'. Living in this pseudo-American gangster atmosphere, the urban African's sense of values has tended to become rather id-biased:

CARD **D : 6**

One day my brother said to me, it is better to be a criminal than to work for a white man who always give you a certain amount of money a week or monthly .

To have been imprisoned carries no shame:

(Original) CARD **G : 3**

I was in a cell at the Fort . . . So it happened one day we were transferred to Boksburg . . . When we reach Boksburg, I was shocked by seeing cells with unclosed small windows and three iron bars . . . I found my cell was very wet even the blankets too, were very wet and as a prisoner I was forced to sleep with those wet blankets, that is why I am not well.

This is admittedly a fantasy and may or may not be true, but the interesting aspect is the naïve criticism of prison treatment, rather than any indications of shame or injustice at being imprisoned. He is not defending the fact that he was imprisoned, he feels no need to do so; what he is criticizing is the fact that it affected his health.

Specific Personality Trends

Immature exhibitionism is another factor constantly emerging. The urban African loves to show off, to attract attention. He usually drives not a car but a 'super American Buick Special'. If he is wealthy (in fantasy) he lives, not in a well-built house, but in a 'piece of edifice built by the hands of a skilled builder'. If he considers himself educated and intelligent, he will blatantly indicate this presumed superiority. Statements such as 'I command respect and power' are by no means uncommon. Exaggeration for effect is very often found in their stories. Delusions of intellectual grandeur are favourite exhibitionistic fantasy themes. Here is a typical example written by a twenty-five-year-old man from Western Native Township:

CARD A : 9

. . . Charlie is a tuberculotic, Jimmy a drug-addict (the smoke in the picture); Willie never had anything, inclusive of brains and a pass. Well, me I have everything—the brains! That's my team.

The urban African is a character of extremes. He is not inhibited in the expression of his feelings by the cautioning influence of moderation. His fantasy productions are remarkably blatant, and his exhibitionism naïve and unsophisticated. This aspect of personality immaturity, this outspoken personal selling, this blatant exhibitionism, is typical of the urban African personality.

If he decides that the best way to obtain work is to curry favour, he will proceed to 'butter-up' his potential employer in his T.A.T. stories, without any semblance of tact, delicacy or finesse. For example, a story written by a PUTCO applicant from Dube Township:

CARD A : 9

Asked how he felt about his employment, one of the men sitting outside the PUTCO canteen said 'What? We are at home here, no bother, nothing. As long as we do our work properly, PUTCO is always interested not only in our labour, but in our welfare as well.'
. . . They spoke of the free medical check-up they received, the provident fund, and a thousand and one facilities.
. . . Ask anybody and you will be told that both her patrons and servants are a contented lot. Nothing is left to chance at PUTCO. You find everybody—from bus inspectors to the canteen worker exhuding friendliness. Why? You may ask yourself. Well the reasons have already been given. They are a contented labour force.

To use an Americanism, even in Plato's utopia 'they never had it so good'.

African urban adjustment allows the id impulses considerable leeway. This freedom is obvious in their fantasy themes. They are outspoken, sometimes amazingly so:

110

Specific Personality Trends

A school girl on the way from school to home saw a man coming along and she looked at this man, she saw that the man was very angry and his eyes were red. When the girl was not even three feet far from the man, the hooligan said, 'Here you girl, where are you from, lie down just where you are and take your clothes off. I want to specialise on you.' The poor girl cried but the hooligan did not fear her crying until the girl seeing nobody to rescue her, she started pulling her things off and lied down. Then the stupid hooligan got on top of her and done his duty until he was satisfied. The poor girl went to report the hooligan and the hooligan was arrested. But the hooligan was not found guilty because of how he spoke himself innocent. He told the Court that he proposed the girl, and the girl didn't want to agree with him. Well then he requested her to sleep and fortunately the girl didn't refuse, she took off her clothes and lied down, 'Then I done what I needed on her,' he said. Now the magistrate found that he was right, because he didn't take out her clothes, the girl made herself naked.

Not only is the above story most uninhibited and outspoken, but it indicates the peculiar concepts present in the mind of many an urban African regarding the workings of European law.

In his fantasy, as in his life, the African laughs loud and long when he is happy, and weeps bitter tears when he is sad. There are no half-measures when it comes to his fantasy life, and there are few half-measures in his reality.

The African has adjusted to urban requirements, but his adjustments, while fairly adequate, tend to be immature; his personal revelations, while naïve, tend to be exhibitionistic; and his trains of thought tend to be based on stereotypical bias rather than on individual reasoning. He is easily led, he is easily influenced, he is very amenable to mass reactions and he tends to function a great deal on group influences, rather than on personal assessment and conviction.

VIII

CASE ILLUSTRATION

IN his T.A.T. responses the urban African is not only indicating his own personality predispositions, he is also recording a series of observations on the life about him. His views on his world are both revealing and interesting. They are observations made on prevailing urban conditions, on its joys and sorrows, on its social problems, on racial problems, on urban crime, on sex life; a vivid, colourful range of verbal portraits from the pens of philosophical, humorous, bitter or contented men. Some are pure fantasy, some reality, but all are indicative of urban African attitudes, thoughts and ideals.

In this section we will consider an urban T.A.T. *in toto*. A T.A.T. which has been chosen from the 2,500 available cases.

A completely typical case-study, representative within itself of all the communal personality components isolated and discussed in the foregoing sections, just does not occur. Such a personality would be a textbook figment rather than a living reality—a statistical hypothesis rather than a human being.

We have, therefore, in our choice selected an essentially human being—a man of Dube Township. We shall approach his T.A.T. not as an individual record to be idiosyncratically interpreted and analysed, but we shall consider what he says from the broader social aspect—as an observer of urban African life, rather than as a single case-study of a specific personality.

With this approach in view, we have selected a man who is a 'social philosopher' by disposition, and, when he wrote these stories, a job-seeker by necessity.

Our choice is a keen observer of social conditions—the primary reason for his selection. Consider the following informative views on juvenile delinquency in the urban townships:

CARD **F** : 4

Johannesburg is surrounded by African townships. These townships are teeming full of juvenile delinquents. But ruling and setting a bad

112

example to these juveniles are the older and hardened criminals. These gangsters hang around corners in these townships. These corners are of strategic importance to them because they are always at places frequented by passers by. These passers by vary between schoolchildren and the honest working class.

These criminals operate on a systematic and well planned programme. During the night they rob and molest honest people. During the day they forcibly make love to the schoolgoing teenagers. The innocent teenagers will fall for these flashy-clothed won't workers.

Starting in the street corners this love drifts to the backyards behind the trees. In a few months the girl is expecting a baby—an illegitimate baby. The hooligan that sired the baby will not maintain it. Naturally, as you may see, the days when the hooligan of a father professed the most exclusive love he had for the innocent, ignorant girl, ends when she expects a baby. It is then that she will realise how foolish she was. But too late.

Yet in another corner, in another backyard a similar malady is beginning. The end will be just as bad, or even worse. Because it may result in a concealed birth, or an abortion.

The result will be the evergrowing immorality amongst African teenagers in the townships.

Yet it all started at a street corner!

A well-written observation, an introduction to African criminology, a simple factual statement on one aspect of township life. There are other aspects; there is the economic aspect of township living, for example:

CARD C : 7

To the west of Johannesburg is situated a township—Sophiatown, the streets of this township are barely lit at night. The streets are very dusty. The houses look shabby and derelict but they are full of life within. Most of the people living in these townships have to work in order to earn a living. Those that don't resort to illegal means.

During the day the mother and the father will be at work. The mother is also forced to work as soon as baby is not suckling in order to supplement hubby's meagre salary. The elderst child is left in charge of the younger ones.

A very down-to-earth statement on basic economics. Yet even economics has its human sidelights—it affects lives, it touches emotions, emotions known to many an urban dweller, emotions like the following:

CARD H : 2

Old man Mabaso stayed with his family at Orlando Shelters. Pain and grief struck him one day when he was assaulted by thugs on his way home from work. He was so severely beaten-up that he had to stay in hospital for two months. During those two months, the wife had to fend for the two kids and herself as Mabaso was the sole breadwinner for the family.

When Mabaso returned to his employers he was told he had since been replaced as he had been away too long.

Now Mabaso was on the streets. Each day Mabaso would leave his home in the early morning without even a cup of tea He would roam the streets, stop at each factory gate. The reply would always be 'No Vacancies'. He would know he cannot go home for lunch. There was none. A friend might help with a sixpence. He'd have whatever he could for a sixpence, take a little rest and carry on looking for work. The day would end with no success. He'd have to go back home.

That was the most tortuous part of the day. His son would be gaping at him for something nice he's brought from town. The mother would stare at his empty hands and bow her head as if praying. From the look on his face she'd know there was no luck. The fire would not burn, nor would the pot be set on the stove.

It was another day of hunger.

A pathetic tale. Yet at times even the most gloomy philosopher can smile—even if his humour is a little bitter. Consider the following rather cynical observation on the pass laws:

CARD E : 5

Many men work in the city. They will always work as long as the employers are satisfied with them and can keep them. They shall always work as long as their documents are in order. If their documents are not in order they shall be arrested and sent to goal. Dahwa did not know about this. He was fresh from the country. He was honestly coming to work in the city. Early in the morning he left his cousin's place to look for work in the city. There were many others. To Dahwa they looked mad. They were rushing in all directions. Not one seemed to care for the other except for a casual 'Excuse me' as they accidentally bumped onto the other. He realised that he would be silly if he enquired anything from any of these people. He decided to mind his business. He still thought everybody was minding his or their business when a policeman confronted him and asked with a jerk 'Pass!' With a frown of confusion he answered saying he did not know what the man was talking about. Within seconds he was bundled into a van and off it started.

With a sorrowful grin he mumbled 'So I was wrong. They mind other people's business too.'

Still, pass laws or no pass laws, life must go on. And while pass problems become a part of the urban dweller's life, what really counts is money. Even if it means working for it.

CARD D : 6

It is every Monday that begins like the normal working week. Oh! what a lousy day it is to everybody. The weekend's over with all its gayness and enjoyments, you feel lazy. You even think of how to dodge work. You are nursing and toying with this idea when a slight, lingering idea touches your mind. I may loose my job or even the confidence of my employer. If not, then, on pay day, surely your pay won't be full and you don't like that. On the spur of the moment you are up and preparing for work. The day tolls on into the next. Oh! you're working the week through and enjoying it so immensely that each day you come to work bright and full of energy and enthusiasm for work. Comes payday and you are one of the millions of hardworking citizens with money in their pockets. You will proudly hold your money in your hand and say: 'I have honestly worked and earned this money. I shall not go hungry. What a pleasure it is to earn money honestly and not by foul means at the expense of others.'

A very human story on the urban dweller's basic motivating force —money. However, in the urban townships where the money drive is universal, there are innumerable 'shebeens', run by women who also want money:

CARD **B : 8**

It was payday—Friday. John left the premises where he was employed. He proceeded at a brisk pace towards the bus stop. He was in the queue when Jack came up to him and patted him on the shoulder. 'Aren't you going to visit Sis Katie for a drink?' he asked. 'No, I'm not' John answered curtly. 'But why not, or have you forgotten it's payday today?' 'Yes, I know' John answered. 'That is the reason why I'm not going. I owe her but I have to take my kid to the doctor tomorrow. If I pay Sis Katie I shall not be able to afford it,' he explained. 'Okay John I'll stand you a drink at Sis Joyce's, come along,' proffered Jack. John agreed and they went to Sis Joyce's place.

The first two drinks led to two more. In fact it was just the beginning of a drinking spree. John found himself buying drinks; though he had inwardly vowed not to. To make matters worse, there were women at this shebeen. The very presence of the weaker sex made John very free with money and drinks. He had to show that he was not just John but a working John and therefore he was Big John. He did not know when and how he had left Sis Joyce's. The next time his mind cleared he was sleeping on a bench in somebody's backyard. He sat up, searched his pockets. They were empty. Their emptiness made his heart throb. His child would not be able to see the doctor. His wife and other children would have nothing to eat. What a very bad thing drinking was, he cupped his head in his hands.

Not only the 'shebeen' queens like Sis Katie and Sis Joyce mentioned above want money. There are others; others who supply nothing in exchange for the money they take. The urban dweller has to constantly be on his guard against this element. However, township conditions, especially at night, make this a very difficult task:

Case Illustration

It was after 6 p.m. one Friday. Dahwa Ngcobo alighted from a bus and proceeded, whistling a gay tune, along Gerty Street, Sophiatown. That is where his shack was situated. He was whistling because, there in that shack, his wife Mandlovu was fondling their four-month-old baby boy. Their other two kids—a boy and a girl—would be sitting near their mother. The one would be pulling his shirt and the other shouting at the top of her voice. Or sitting 'round the fire as it was cold.

With hands in his pockets Dahwa was happy. He could feel his pay envelope, and the crumpling sound of the crisp notes in it. But the streets of Sophiatown are ill lit and hordes of gangsters terrorise them.

He was about to turn into the little stoep that led to the back of the house where his shack was, when something hard struck him from behind. He fell forward, tried to get up; but another blow sent him crumpling to the ground, and into a world of darkness.

When he came to he was only clad in undies, all his clothes and money for the upbringing of his kids were gone.

'But why do they not light the streets of Sophiatown after dark,' he mumbled: his head throbbed and he fell back.

Such happenings are daily occurrences in the townships. The social set-up is such that it tends to breed criminals. Consider the following causal factors which combine to develop the urban African criminal:

John was born of a respectable, God fearing family. As a boy he went to church and attended Sunday School. He was a bright scholar and was very much loved by his teachers. Even John's parents were proud of him. His father hoped that one day his son would be a doctor or a lawyer. Little did he realise that his hopes were to be dashed to the ground.

At Standard Seven John made friends with a boy who later induced him to leave school and run away from home with the promise of getting a job in town and earning tons of money.

Things never turned out bright as expected by John. He landed in prison for a pass offence. He came out and he was back again for theft. He could not find employment, however honest he tried to be. He eventually gave up.

Today he is a pickpocket, a bag-snatcher, a thief. He would do anything to get money so as to eat and dress like others.

Lurking in dark corners for anybody's purse to prey on he knew deep within himself that this was not what his father was grooming him up to be. Nor was this what he imagined he was going to be when he reached this age.

A bad friend, he knew, was his downfall.

A sort of Township Rake's Progress, told in a matter-of-fact manner, as if by one who has witnessed this degeneration many times; a story told in a philosophical vein, based on keen social observation.

116

Case Illustration

An observing mind which can find something of interest in most aspects of life, even in the routine of daily work:

CARD **A : 9**

John woke up always early in the morning to queue up for the bus to transport him to work. It was the dreary intercourse of daily life. The bus would drawl slowly to the town. From there he would walk it to his place of employment.

At 6.45 a.m. work would begin. And with John it was really work. Loading and offloading bags of sugar for transit. This would go on until 9.30 when he and the others get their teatime break, what a relief it becomes. Ten minutes later they are at it hammer and tongs, singing and chanting.

On and on the process will go until 12.30 when the lunch hour break comes. Some will come out jumping and rush to the beer hall for a quick one. The others will go and have a meal at a nearby eating house.

But the others who, like John, bring their own lunch prepared by their dearest ones will sit anywhere possible and enjoy it with intermittent jokes between mouthfuls of 'mealiepap' and meat. Cold though it may be, they'll enjoy it. If there is a park nearby they'll sit there, on a bench, or even enjoy it on a pavement in front of their premises. They will finish their meal and sit and talk happily until the siren summons them back to work and the day is making its end. It will be home again to their dearest ones.

A story from the mind of an educated African—the type of mind for which the present social system will have to find a satisfactory occupational outlet, if it is not to be turned by frustration to bitterness, antagonism and disillusionment.

We have obtained in this presentation a glimpse of the urban African world. The responses to the nine cards of the T.A.T. series have given us an informative overview of the main aspects of urban living—its money drive, its crime and social evils, its 'shebeens' and juvenile sex delinquency, its illegitimacy, its economic stress, its fears and anxieties of unemployment, of attack and police arrest, its unwholesome environment, of its cruelties and its kindnesses, some of its frustrations and some of its simple joys.

It is as near a typical picture as one could hope for—a survey of urban conditions contained in one protocol series. Much is admittedly missing, but much has also been explained and discussed.

It is the type of presentation that one has come to expect of the better-educated urban African, a literary presentation full of interest, information, emotion and vivacity.

117

IX

THE AFRICAN NATIONALIST

IN the last section we presented and discussed the protocol trends revealed in a 'typical' T.A.T. series. No attempt at a personality assessment and interpretation was made, primarily because in this study we are interested basically in communal trends and not in idiosyncratic personality characteristics.

Recent developments in Africa, however, have focused attention upon a particular type of individual, an individual usually referred to by the Europeans in Africa as an agitator or an African nationalist. The nationalist, whether one likes him or not, is definitely a key-man in Africa. In this chapter we will study in detail the personality of one such individual and we will formulate certain hypotheses on the 'African nationalist personality' as it has revealed itself in the T.A.T. protocols of a series of individuals known to be 'actively political'.

One of the most recent, most comprehensive and best-informed statements on the African nationalist was made, in December 1958, by Sir Andrew Cohen, sometime head of the Africa Division of the Colonial Office, ex-Governor of Uganda and a present member of the British delegation to the United Nations. He described the African nationalist in the following words:

> Some people see a nationalist as either a hero or a dangerous fanatic. He may of course be either, as anyone else may. But this is not the correct image . . . (the nationalist) has to bridge the gulf between his home, often in the village, and the university he attended. He has to work with people who are often uneducated and know nothing of the outside world; with his education and knowledge, he is thereby subjected to great temptation, because many of those he talks to will have no standard by which to judge much of what he tells them. He nearly always carries a slight, or a fancied slight, by Europeans in Africa, Europe, or indeed North America. But in spite of this he is usually friendly to individual Europeans, and is almost always deeply attached to the ultimate goals of the West. He is distressed by the great gap between the existing state of affairs in his country, with all its physical

118

and human limitations on rapid advance, and his own ideal for it as he would like to see it, with self-government, a respected culture, and a modern economic apparatus . . .

This statement was made more specifically within an East, Central and West African frame of reference. Let us consider how it agrees with our findings in the Union of South Africa. We will consider first the personality make-up of an active African nationalist, a member of the Pan-Africanist Congress—a breakaway extremist group of the African National Congress of South Africa. The Pan-Africanists were the group who organized the 'anti-pass' campaign at the Sharpeville and Langa Locations in March 1960—a campaign which resulted in disastrous rioting and the death of 67 Africans.

The following protocol was written and analysed six months before the 1960 riots. Each T.A.T. story will be presented on the right of the page, the relevant assessment comments being recorded on the left-hand side.

STORY **H : 2**

An opening paragraph reflecting anxiety, insecurity and tension.

In the bare stricken home of a family of four. The boy in the absence of the mother puts up a strong case against his hunger. He

An appeal to authority to alter the situation.

pleads with the father that some change in the situation must come for them to have food. He has just returned from playing and feels dry for something to go down his throat.

The description of an unsatisfied need, and an indication of the personal frustration resulting from inadequate environmental compensation, in an unsatisfactory, frustrating, apathetic social set-up.

The father as usual is listening attentively to the story of his brood and gives from his face, all promise of making good for the hunger not only of the boy but that also of the sister who is sitting quietly and expectantly for the results of this meeting between the father and the brother. She is also very hungry but she chose a different form of protest. A protest of sitting down privately and in this position, to invoke the sympathy of her parents.

Personal insecurity, anxiety and fear. An attitude of uncertainty expressed in an inconclusive ending.

From the look of things, it does seem there is some hope of getting anything to eat. The cupboard is packed with clean plates and cups; the table has just been cleaned. Woe poverty.

119

A slow, emotional build-up, an attitude of expectancy, a prelude to tension.

A criticism of township conditions, a disgruntled, actively outspoken criticism. Hostility to the social set-up and the unhelpful, unsatisfying environment is expressed.

Uncertainty of the future, with a stress on personal self-sacrifice to alleviate suffering and to gain satisfaction. An indication of financial frustrations and the satisfaction of money.

Personal anxiety about the future, frustrated ambitions, unsatisfied needs, thwarted desires, combine to increase the uncertainty of the future.

Despondency caused by frustrated ambitions and hopes.

A regression, a need for guidance in a confusing, unhelpful environment.

STORY C : 7

One summer morning with dew or shall I say rain having settled heavily on the ground. The sky is overcast, there might be another shower. The air is quiet scarcely a twig moves. This strange quiet is usually a lull before the storm.

The ground is of black loam, the kind that becomes very fertile if mixed with sandy soil. On the road it can mean hell for a driver. The houses are of mud with old iron as roofing. They present a dilapidated look not fit for habitation. One wonders if the shade of this tree has ever been enjoyed, no scenic beauty here.

There are these two children in the foreground; where are they going to? One perhaps could safely deduce that they are sent for sugar to the nearest shop for the thirst for tea will always press the poor mother to spare that last sixpence in order that her young brood may enjoy a morning sip.

STORY B : 8

Life has come down heavily on this man. One sees life's ceiling weighing heavily on the shoulders of this lad. 'Oh! man I'm gone', he seems to say. He has just been sentenced to a long term of imprisonment. His future is dark, he cries for himself, for those of his family he has been a breadwinner for. He imagines the waste of time entailed. He definitely had plans—and good ones for that matter—for the future, all this has now been dashed.

He remembers his humble beginning, he prays the prayers his parents taught him then. He remembers the advice he received so often in his home, at school, at

The African Nationalist

A feeling of loneliness, of isolation from one's group, of bewilderment and disillusionment.

A yearning for success, for acceptance, for status.

An indication of determination to continue.

A philosophical vein, with indications of personal worry and insecurity, and despondency, in an unhelpful anxiety-provoking environment. A personal money need expressed, the frustration of unfulfilled ambitions being indicated.

An uncertainty, and a personal despondency is shown. A certain hopelessness at the existing conditions is given.

An inconclusive ending, indicating an expression of frustration.

An energetic, active approach, extroverted, hopeful and determined. A happiness at anticipated success.

Sunday school and from those dear friends of his family. His mind is in a mess. He craves for the comfort of all those he loved. The fact that they are not there breaks his heart. What concerns humanity is not that he has got into trouble, but whether or not he will retrace his steps to rejoin society as a good man. Too late for tears.

STORY A : 9

These men are having a breather from a spell of hard work. Teatime, lunch or just resting. All are in some meditation, is it about the pay packet, the family up-keep, or the son has got into some trouble of an armed robbery. One thing certain is that nothing of joy beams from these faces. Their way of dress decides, their category as a working class of poorest pay. But what are they holding? Is it their lunch that they are busy with? In the circumstances one safely must conclude that these people are having lunch.

Trying to imagine what type of work they are doing, the background of this picture can help in solving this question. There is the faint view of a heavy duty vehicle. The vehicle gives the impression that it deals with coal. The conclusion can therefore safely be that these men belong to a coalyard firm and carry bags of coal, therefore their dull look of the face.

STORY F : 4

This young man has a chance of his life time. He has always looked for this opportunity, a moment when they could be together with a dame of his love. The bright sun-lit day, the trees with their cool shades and their foliage, the corn

A self-confident directness of approach, with a personal determination to succeed.

Egoistical and vain with an air of superiority, of confidence and of domination.

Personal domination leads to success.

fields all harmonise in beautiful background for the romance of these two children of nature.

He begins his story by telling her how fortunate he is to have been provided with such an opportunity by the goddess of love. He woos her with sweet words, telling her how beautiful she is and how they are both made for each other. He promises her heaven and earth if she only says yes to his pleadings. The fellow wears a confident face, he is determined to win her for himself. He has given that bewitching pat on the shoulder. His eyes have hypnotised the poor girl. From her way of standing she has no alternative but to say I belong to you.

A build-up to tension with interpersonal antagonism between superior and subordinate figures. An active criticism of social conditions, a trace of cynicism and distrust of management.

STORY E : 5

There is some trouble in the firm, the workers have gone on strike. The leader is talking to the boss. The master is showing his point to the leader. He argues that their approach to the situation has been wrong, that the workers had not given the management time to consider their complaints and that in fact their coming out on strike has been a breach of faith in that certain stipulations in the last agreement have not been respected by the workers. The strike is therefore illegal he contends. He urges that the workers do one thing—go back to work and that the dispute goes to a board of arbitration.

Suspicion and distrust of authority figures.

The leader of the workers wears a serious look, so that perhaps he may safeguard himself against any tendency to compromise on the issue involved. He is adamant that the management had ignored the demands of the workers, that the workers had time and again

An attitude of determination reinforced by continual frustrations.

122

Uncompromising determination, and an unyielding attitude with an air of defiance, of challenge.

brought their case to the management and had been deliberately ignored and cold-shouldered. That it was not possible for the workers to call off the strike without certain guarantees. There is the likelihood of an impasse being reached.

STORY **D : 6**

A spontaneous beginning, active and alive.

An appreciation of the power of money.

The financial strength of the European and the need for it by the African is expressed here.

This is the story of money. The song goes 'Money is the root of evil'. I hope it is just for the singing of it.

Here is money in hand, no! money in a right hand. This hand is of an immaculately dressed man; under the hand a bulb of electric light is placed to give the wonderful glow of white race. This money is money in a social function held by the Master of Ceremonies as people give freely on this occasion. It is an occasion to say farewell to someone leaving for further studies. It is common on such occasions that we say farewell to a person by making a little collection that we can call provision.

An expression of national pride, an association with the African group.

An acceptance of the power of money.

This is always a sign amongst Africans of good neighbourliness. The Blacks are very liberal with gifts. They always want to show outwardly what their hearts reveal. The person also that is given this present accepts this with great gratitude. It reveals also an inherent sense of man in money as a purchasing power.

Whatever one can do with money, there is always this intriguing question, what is money and why has it been adopted internationally as a means of exchange? To a student of mercantile Law and commerce this question may be easy to answer, but to a layman it is as elusive as the Scarlet Pimpernel of fame.

The adoption of a superior, teaching approach to conclude with. Egoistical in attitude.

An attacking anxiety provoking hostile environment.

It is in the night, the old man is walking home from work. He is an engine driver with the railways. He is passing a street lamp. It is not too safe these days so one has to be on a look-out for tsotsis.

A need for support in a desire to satisfy personal longings, desires and ambitions, personal needs and wishes and hopes.

He reassures his mind on the power of the Almighty to enable him to reach his destination. His mind goes also into the ever-present problem of a responsible man and that is the family upkeep. He plods his way thinking deeply on the schooling careers of his sons and daughters; he wonders if he could make up the necessary fees that are needed yearly. He becomes annoyed at the rising cost of living. 'What can I do in the circumstance,' he asks himself time and again.

An expression of bewilderment and frustration at his personal insecurity and uncertainty.

A direct comparison between African and European opportunities, causing personal frustration resulting in an aggressive outburst against European domination. A desire to be free of the frustrations and restrictions of the present social set-up, ending in a deep-seated resentment and hostility to the present circumstances.

He compares his efforts to those of a man who has been able to build this magnificent Flat to his right. He asks why he has not been able to build this kind of building himself. He curses himself for having been unable to make headway. Above it all he curses the conditions that have not been able to provide him with any opportunity to develop.

An indication of personal insecurity, yet with a desire to achieve his goal even in the frustrating circumstances of an unhelpful environment.

This is a puzzle picture to me. I am lost to know just what is taking place here. One thing certain is this that a man in a dark room is looking earnestly for something which he badly wants to regain. It does also seem that this poor fellow has no light save that which comes through this window.

A determination to achieve success, a drive to overcome adversity and to succeed.

The light that comes through the window is very bright but because it is not direct, it cannot help him much. He nevertheless comforts

A personal determination to succeed in his ambition, to satisfy his needs regardless of the environmental restrictions imposed on him.

An intense personal determination to succeed in his activity.

himself with the hope that as he looks carefully through he will finally find what he is looking for.

From what I can judge of his posture and concentration, this man is determined that he will finally retrieve what he has lost, never mind how small it may be in relation to light in the room.

He says to himself, 'Where there's a will there's a way.'

It is obvious that because of the subjectivity inherent in the interpretative process, T.A.T. reports can very easily deteriorate into a series of empty phrases and erroneous inferences. Possibly the greatest inherent danger in projective testing is, however, the tendency of the uncertain analyst to assume an 'interpretative fence-sitting' position —a technique whereby phrases are used like a double-edged sword, giving the analyst protection either way. In a blind analysis this temptation must be constantly guarded against. It is essential therefore that one maintains and strictly adheres to a definite, organized system of approach. The following report will, consequently, be presented on the lines already laid down in the chapter on 'Analysis and Interpretation':

ANALYSIS

Main Themes: In eight of the nine stories we find the hero or heroes in conflict with the environment. Insecurity themes predominate.

Main Hero: (a) Frustration by the environment shown.

(b) Deep personal insecurity and anxiety expressed.

(c) Feelings of personal bewilderment shown.

(d) Hostile reactions to his environment evidenced.

(e) Personal conviction and determination to overcome the environmental pressures are indicated.

(f) An attitude of personal superiority is expressed, he is egoistically inclined.

(g) A deep suspicion and distrust of authority are shown.

(h) A deep feeling of being discriminated against is indicated.

(i) A resentment of the European is expressed.

Hero's Needs: A strong security need, coupled with a desire for recognition and status. A yearning for acceptance, for guidance and help, and for a definite change in the social conditions of the frustrating environment. A determination to overcome environmental obstacles and a well defined money need are present.

125

Conception of the Environment: An environment which is seen as unyielding, at times hostile, at times restricting and inhibiting—an irksome, frustrating environment, restricting by its poverty, by its laws, by its hostility, by apathy and by race discrimination.

Apperceptive Distortions: The subject shows a preoccupation with a criticism of the present social conditions; people are seen as 'poverty stricken', houses as 'dilapidated and not fit for habitation', facial expressions as 'dull' and as indicating 'nothing of joy'. The African who 'curses the conditions that have not been able to provide him with the opportunity to develop' is seen as a 'responsible man'. Europeans are envied as possessing 'the wonderful glow of white race'—money and opportunity.

Behavioural Expression: The expression of behaviour is outspoken and direct, even aggressive. The energies tend generally to be directed against the frustrating environment with determination and drive: 'He says to himself: "Where there's a will there's a way" '; 'This man is determined that he will finally retrieve what he has lost'; 'He reassures his mind on the power of the Almighty to enable him to reach his destination'; 'the leader of the workers is adamant'.

Significant Conflicts: (*a*) A constant conflict with a frustrating environment.

(*b*) An internal conflict in terms of personal uncertainty, anxiety, insecurity, and the need for support on the one hand, and feelings of superiority, determination and personal conviction on the other.

(*c*) Interpersonal conflicts are shown between superior and subordinate figures and between African and European.

Integration of the Ego: The subject tends to be preoccupied with his own problems yet uncertain of their ultimate solution. He is bewildered by the environment, yet convinced that it must be changed. He is too personally involved at present with sorting out his own problems to bother about their eventual outcome—he is preoccupied with himself rather than with the story outcomes. He is definitely not adjusted to his environment.

Story Outcomes: These fluctuate from anxious, apathetic, defeatist, bewildered endings, to determined, aggressive, egoistical attitudes. Social outcomes are either indefinite or unhappy, the sex theme contains the only truly satisfied and successful conclusion.

General Story Atmosphere: The atmosphere is characterized by anxiety, tension, bewilderment, and embitterment, coloured by such statements as 'Woe poverty', 'this strange quiet is usually a lull before the storm', 'His future is dark', 'his mind is in a mess', 'Too late for tears', 'He becomes annoyed at the rising cost of living' and 'He curses himself for having been unable to make headway'.

Language: The language is lucid and fluent, it is direct and outspokenly presented and tends to become clipped when the subject is concentrating: 'Trying to imagine what type of work they are doing', 'He definitely had plans—' and 'I am lost to know what is taking place'.

Interpretation: The subject is definitely not adjusted to the prevailing social conditions. He shows very strong insecurity and anxiety feelings and is frustrated in the satisfaction of his needs, desires and ambitions. His resulting embitterment and his feelings of being discriminated against find outlet in criticism of the prevailing social set-up in general and of Europeans in particular. He wants recognition, status, acceptance and wealth, yet he fluctuates between bewildered anxiety and the need for support, and an aggressive determination and firm conviction to achieve what he considers his rights.

Egoistically inclined and personally involved, with feelings of superiority, he is outspoken and direct in his criticism, and is suspicious of and aggressively inclined toward authority figures.

A personality that is very preoccupied with what he considers are social injustices, he writes in a systematic, fluent, literate style.

An African of above average intelligence.

Such is the personality of an agitator, of an African nationalist, of a member of the extremist Pan-Africanist movement in South Africa. It is interesting, in this context, to note the results of extreme anxiety and tension, the effects of a frustrated money drive, and the influence of restrictive measures, upon an egoistically inclined, intelligent and ambitious personality.

African nationalists are, on the whole, intelligent men—men with ambition, egoistical men. They are outspoken in their criticisms and are all extremely discrimination-conscious. They are not all anti-European, nor are they all Communistic in their viewpoints. They are, for the most, essentially African—conscious of their traditions, rather ashamed of their tribal affiliations and of their 'inferior' racial status in the world, suspicious of European motives and very aware of the prevailing African social and industrial conditions in the urban areas. Extremist views are the rule, moderate tendencies are the exception. Like his fellow Africans, the African nationalist seldom does things in halves, he tends to love with all his heart or hate with all his soul.

If there is any single function which distinguishes the African nationalist from the African rank and file, it is his extreme feeling of being discriminated against. While others may feel it, with him it becomes an all-consuming obsession. The African nationalist personality is a personality in which discrimination-consciousness predominates.

127

The African Nationalist

This discrimination-conscious obsession is characteristic of the majority of African nationalists seeking independence. It is not surprising therefore that nearly 'all the petitions received by the Trusteeship Council of the United Nations have to do with racial discrimination' (Cranston: *Human Rights Today*). Such petitions, the majority of which are forwarded by African and Asian nationalists, are as much a reflection of their own personality needs as they are of actual social conditions in their particular countries. As in a T.A.T. response, so in real life: one's perception of a social situation is coloured by one's underlying personality formations. Possibly due to this function, there is a tendency in Africa today for quite innocent, well-meaning European motives or actions to be misconstrued by the African nationalist as being discriminatory in nature.

In his T.A.T. responses the 'political' individual levels most of his criticisms at the Government or at some legislative body:

CARD E : 5

. . . (These two men) . . . they are not satisfied of (the) new Government in South Africa . . .

CARD C : 7

South Africa is a very nice country to live in, but now-a-days it is not of the best because of the new Nationalist Government . . .

CARD C : 7

. . . the South African Nationalist Government is planting or creating conflicts amongst whites and blacks . . .

Antagonism or aggression is seldom voiced against individual Europeans as such. The police, however, as the upholders of 'Government law', come in for considerable criticism and hostility. In the T.A.T.s of such politically-minded individuals, boycott movements and labour strikes are oft-voiced themes, aggression and rioting being associated with police beer raids rather than with any show of political strength. Realizing the economic power of African labour as a political weapon, strikes and boycotts have become militant concepts to the African nationalist: the boycott being especially favoured, as strikes involve legal entanglements, whereas boycotts at present do not.

X

THEME ILLUSTRATIONS

A FUNDAMENTAL step in T.A.T. assessments is the classification and interpretation of the theme content running through the various stories which comprise an individual's test response. The more strongly evident a particular theme is in fantasy, the greater is the likelihood of its being displayed by the individual in reality.

In this section we will present a series of complete T.A.T. responses, chosen to illustrate the clarity with which this continuity of theme is found in the story series of the urban Africans. We will illustrate the manner in which a specific emotion so often tends to predominate throughout an individual's stories.

Take the following example of an anxious, insecure personality, an inadequate personality with ineffectual adjustments. Note the constant reference in this protocol to the need for help from outside, observe the continuity of this theme and its constant repetition throughout the stories. Here is the complete T.A.T. series:

CARD H : 2

These two people and a child were living in difficulties. They were very poor and were trying their best to make a living, but the man did not get enough to support his family. The money he got was too little to cover his expenses.

The family tried to get their friends to lend them a few pennies, but they never got any help from anybody. They had no money to buy clothes, no money for food.

They are just like me and my family, we have been the same for many years. We got help from nobody. The money I get is just enough to buy food and coal and clothes for the babies.

CARD A : 9

John, Samuel and Simon are thinking of going somewhere to loan some money to buy food for their families. These three men they are penniless. They have got no shoes and no clothes to put on. They have got children and wives to look after. They are really worried. They do not know who can help them. They are resting on the pavement, they are really hungry and thirsty. They are thinking about going and borrowing some money from friends. They are not quite sure that they will get help from anybody.

CARD E : 5

These two friends meet each other unexpectedly. The one is poor, he has been looking for a job for nearly four years. Most fortunately he meets his best friend. He tells his friend of his trouble and how he has walked all over looking for help from anybody who can afford to give some help. So he told his friend 'Man I got no money to buy food for my family and for the last two days I never go home. If you have got some money, please just lend me some and I will pay you back as soon as I get a job.'

CARD G : 3

This man has got no money to buy clothes and hardly money for food. He has got a big family. This poor man he was in bed for about two years. He is in the street, he really does not know where to go and what to give his family. He is really in trouble and needs some help from his friends. He does not know where to go to borrow some money.

This picture it is me. I want to go upstairs and take the test for a license. I am really worried about it.

CARD F : 4

This man is me, my wife is asking me if I met my boss and told him of the difficulty we have. Did I discuss with my boss that I need some help? If my boss will just help me I will be really pleased. Did I ask my boss if I can go and take a license? Then I can be a driver.

But there is only one that I am worried about, it is the licence. I cannot sleep at night, I am really worried about it.

CARD C : 7

This building here in this picture is where I am going to get my licence. In the licence department there are many people waiting to get licences. I am also waiting to get a licence. I just pray that I must go through with my test. If I can get the licence I will be very pleased. A licence is the most important thing, especially for an African. Because some of them have got no education. That's why once you have got a licence you know very well that you can get a better job and money.

CARD I : 1

This man is from the licence department. He is a happy man at last. He was worried for many years about the licence. He used to wish God will help him to get a licence.

Once you need a thing you really need it with your whole heart. It is not to say that you need it for just pleasure. No. I really deny this.

You want something because you know very well that this will help you when you are in trouble tomorrow.

The same with me. I want a licence with my whole heart. I know that it will help me tomorrow.

CARD **D : 6**

This is the hand of Mr. Strauss. He has got the results. He tells us how we have done our best in the test we have taken. He tells us that we can go to the driving school and to work hard there.

To get a licence is a very hard thing. It is not to say that you can do as you like just because you have got a licence.

A licence is the most important thing for African people especially.

CARD **B : 8**

This is me. I can really cry for a licence. I am worried about it. I think that to have a licence is a really good thing.

Really this man in the picture when I saw him I just think of myself. This poor man is worried to have a licence. I am also worried about the licence. If I can get the licence I will be really happy indeed.

Compare the above stories of self-involvement with the following mature statement by an individual adjusted to his environment and interested in its problems. Note the air of moderation in which these stories are related, note their almost philosophical vein, and above all note the theme of mature perception and reasoning which runs through all the stories:

CARD **D : 6**

MONEY

Time and again we have heard, 'money is the root of all evil'. There are many points for and against this saying. Here are a few points in favour of the saying.

Firstly, it is true that if there was no money we would not be talking of 'the crime wave' that appears in newspapers daily. Those who have no money and must have it usually resort to foul means of getting it. Sometimes a good and honest person turns a criminal because of lack of money.

Secondly, if there were no such thing as money people would be less greedy. Self-preservation is a natural law and no one ever wants to be poorer than the next person. Because money buys so many things— and if you have it—so many luxurious things, people usually envy those who have it. Now envy is against the laws of God.

Now for the points against the saying 'money is the root of all evil'. Certainly many people in modern times would refute this so-called fact.

Money is very convenient when business transactions must be made. The old method of bartering is out-of-date and would serve the modern world no good. In order to buy the bare necessities of life—food, clothing, etc., money must be used.

Secondly, money is an incentive to hard work. The man who is not prepared to work must do without it—lose the benefit of good food and clothing—or get it by foul means and, of course, get to gaol.

Thirdly, without money, no industries would develop. Mines and their subsidiary industries would just not be there if there was no money.

The respected person, industrialist or business concern can only get repute through acquiring money in an honest way.

CARD **F** : **4**

LOVE

Love is the most wonderful gift of God to man. Love is not only found in human beings but is also found among all creatures made by God. As St. Paul puts it 'Without love I am nothing.'

With human beings, love first begins at home where father, mother and children show love towards one another. This love goes on—unless other circumstances arise—till death. In animals it is less so.

In this picture we see where real love begins. The young man Jack and his girl-friend Jill will stand at street corners when they cannot be seen by their elders and make love. This goes on until the pair feel they should let their parents know about it and it usually ends up in marriage.

In order that the young couple may get married the young man must go out to work for money for lobola. No girl—at least a decent one—would waste her love on a good-for-nothing fellow who is a won't-work.

If parents encouraged their sons and daughters to make love at home and not at street corners there would be fewer illegitimate children brought to this world. If children (of love-making age) made love at home and their parents each contributed in teaching them about sex, love would and should be what it really was meant to be.

How happier would Jack and Jill have been if they were sitting in Jill's home with Jill's parents' consent rather than them standing in the street corner when they look so ardently in love.

CARD **H** : **2**

HOME SWEET HOME

How happy and contented this family looks! They may be poor as they apparently are but they are content with whatever they have.

The head of the family has provided a home for his family. That is of great importance. No family can be stable without a suitable home.

When a suitable home has been found, the head of the family must buy the necessities of a house—a table with chairs (perhaps benches), plates, cups, etc. They will be her pride.

But in order that these may be obtained, the father must go out to work in order to earn money. Sometimes, especially during these difficult times, the mother too must go out to work.

With a stable home, children are usually brought up in an upright manner. The children realize how hard their parents work for them and they in turn help in the small odd jobs that have to be performed at home like washing dishes, scrubbing floors, etc.

Theme Illustrations

A home is the pride of everyone, especially a newly married couple. Above all, when a home is blessed with children, so much more can we say 'home sweet home'.

WORRY

Worry is one of the worst things that at one time or another a person suffers from. There are many causes of worry, some of which are the following.

The man in this story is definitely worried, and could be worried by lack of employment as he appears. Very likely he has a family to look after but fails to do so because of lack of employment.

Worry may also be caused by illness in the family. Once a man has one of his loved ones ill, he cannot do his work efficiently.

Worry may also be caused by loneliness. Sometimes because of misfortune one feels so lonely that the story picture may reflect one's feelings. One may be lonely because of frustration caused by the loss of a wife, a child, property, etc.

The man in the picture is deeply in thought and is definitely worried, perhaps, because he is not at peace with his conscience. He might have been responsible for the death of some innocent person and the law has not yet caught up with him. His worry is the dreadful deed he made. He cannot rest until someone knows about it and he can be brought to book. But he also fears the consequences and does not know whether to give himself up to the police or keep his secret which definitely worries him.

There *is* a way by which one can avoid being too worried. That is for one to try at all times to lead an upright life. Perhaps another way of avoiding worry is to stop being selfish and envious of other peoples' belongings and achievements. Nevertheless one cannot altogether avoid worry but it should always be reduced to the barest minimum by engaging oneself in games, entertainment and occupation.

NIGHT PROWLERS

Nowadays with the ever-increasing amount of gangsterism, people dare not leave their doors open at night in fear of being attacked and robbed of their belongings.

Some time ago, when no such thing as crime was known people lived peacefully and in the evenings would keep all doors wide open for fresh air which is so necessary for health. People even slept with windows open. But today the story is different.

The story picture shows a typical night prowler who will take the earliest moment to get into a house whose door is open and either murder the inhabitants or terrorize them into giving him money and other belongings. It is clear that he feels and perhaps knows that he is not being watched and will take the owners of the house by surprise.

133

Theme Illustrations

The hazards of life in the crowded townships make people to be uneasy even when an innocent stranger knocks at their houses. When night falls all doors are locked and bolted and whoever knocks is asked who he is, what he wants at the time of night and many other such questions. Unless the person who knocks at the door can identify himself the owners of the house will not let him in.

LIFE IN THE TOWNSHIP

Life in the township is so different from life on the farm that when one who lives on the farm gets to a township he gets bewildered at the buildings, street lights, cars and so many other things. The one from the township wonders at the easy-going life on the farm—the quietness, the peace and behaviour of the people.

Townships had to be there because of the discovery of gold and diamonds. As men migrated to towns which sprang up as a result, their families had to follow them and the men who lived in compounds had to be settled in townships with their families.

Life in the townships has its good points as well as bad ones. Here are a few bad points about townships.

In the early days of the discovery of gold and diamonds the diggers were mainly concerned with getting the minerals and did not worry much about proper housing. Even today there are still places called slums which are a result of the discovery of minerals.

In slum areas there is a lot of disease and crime. When people live close to each other disease is bound to crop up and people die in many numbers. Crime also lifts up its head when people are crowded. Some of the worst crime areas in Johannesburg are places like Alexandra, Sophiatown and the Orlando 'Shanty town' (which, fortunately, has just been cleared by the City Council).

Gradually the authorities have realized the squalor of these slum areas and modern, well-planned housing schemes are being carried out.

In the modern townships more and more amenities are provided for the inhabitants. The houses are well built, beautifully tarred roads have been made and these are electrically lit. Beautiful schools have been built and a drastic change has taken place as far as illiteracy is concerned.

The people in the townships are more or less satisfied with conditions in the townships as water is laid out, there is proper sanitation and the health services are excellent. The people here are getting more enlightened and are grasping the western civilisation.

TRANSPORT

Long ago transport facilities were very inadequate and as a result industry was slow. In order that our industries can be pushed up we need plentiful and efficient transport.

People live far away from their places of work, knock off late and start early. The modern electric train is fast and many people can be transported to and from their places of employment. Because of their efficiency, people do not have to wait long for trains or que long for tickets.

But railways alone are not sufficient to transport people to and from work. Motor cars and cycles are also extensively used for transportation services. Those people who cannot afford motor cars have buses at their disposal.

As the picture story shows, these men are from work and are waiting to be transported home. The bus services are numerous and efficient. Where trains cannot reach, they do the work. Fares are reduced to a minimum as these are government-subsidized.

With industries spreading farther and farther afield of big cities, the motor transport plays a very important role in the transportation of people from place to place. The people leave their homes in good time to get to work and get home in good time before it is too dark when the bad element takes hold of the places and people can be attacked and even murdered.

CARD E : 5

QUARRELS

The two men in the story picture appear to be in a fighting mood. It is quite common today to come across people quarrelling. Quarrels are caused by a number of things.

People will quarrel over money as it is sometimes termed the root of all evil. When one person borrow another's money and the terms of the contract are not fulfilled by one of the parties, a quarrel usually ensues. Often blood is shed and sometimes lives are lost.

Sometimes people quarrel over money, not because there was borrowing, but because the one who does not have it must rob the one who has it. It is very common that people have been robbed of their pay when coming from work especially if it is at night. This happens because there is an ever-increasing number of people who have made up their minds that they won't work but shall live by the sweat of other people.

At other times we find people who are naturally quarrelsome. Wherever they go they must fight somebody or another. They just love to bully and terrorize other human beings. When the tempers of two people rise there is bound to be one who will be hurt and sometimes blood is shed.

The root of being quarrelsome is being inconsiderate to others. If only people could know that everybody has feelings, how wonderful would this world be!. If only people knew that it takes two to make a quarrel and that if the two sat down to settle the quarrel the world would be so much happier. Using force on another human being is not only brutal but beastly.

CARD I : 1

ELECTRICITY

Electricity is one of the best discoveries that the science has made. Today electricity can be put to numerous uses. It is used to heating as well as cooling.

But the best use for electricity is the generating of light. As the picture story depicts, the man is going to or coming back from work. Not that he would not do either without the electric light, but that it is so much safer for anybody to walk about at night when there is light.

In our cities and townships today streets are lit and this is a boon for the inhabitants. We have read time and again of the brutal murder and slaughter of human beings in our unlit streets.

Not only is electricity useful in the lighting of our streets but it is also being used in the lighting of our homes. Where a thief or murderer would have thought there were no people in a house, he would fear if he saw the illuminating light of electricity.

What is really good with electricity is that it is so much cheaper than other means of getting light. With proper care and understanding electricity is quite safe to use. But with no understanding of electricity it can be fatal to our lives.

Recently electricity is used for moving our electric trains which take people to and from work. Journeys which took a number of hours have been shortened by the use of electricity which today is fast expanding into country places for convenience and speed.

Electrical appliances in the home make work which was formerly done by hand so much easier and quicker.

Contrast the above T.A.T. with the aggressive and violent theme running through the following series. These eight stories of violence and fear contain no less than six aggressive attacks, four deaths and two cases of black magic and superstition. In all the fantasies the environment is depicted by the subject as threatening, unhelpful and aggressive:

CARD **C : 7**

Once upon a time when Moses was driving his taxi along a dusty road carrying passengers, he observed two children walking along the road. He saw those children did not take much care about the traffic on the road. They played and walked in the centre of the road. When Moses approached them they did not even care to look back when he hooted at them.

When Moses applied the brakes and swerved his car near the children they became so frightened that one of them fell down. The driver got out of his car and chased after the children. He caught them both and thrashed them with a lash.

CARD **A : 9**

One evening at a bus rank there were four men, three sitting down, one standing. They looked for work since daybreak but they could not find any. They had many things in their minds. They looked very hungry and you could see in their faces that they were up to mischief. They sat and planned how they would rob some people of their money. They would follow someone from the city and prey upon him in some dark corner.

Theme Illustrations

That evening Frank was from the race-course and had won over fifty pounds. They heard in the conversation of two racegoers about the fortune Frank had just collected. Fortunately one of these four men knew Frank very well. They waylaid him in a dark corner. Frank came walking happily along but to his surprise somebody got hold of him from behind with both hands. He was struck on the head and fell down. The crooks searched his pockets and got away with the fifty pounds.

They ran towards a café at the bus terminus and bought themselves food. In the meantime Frank recovered. When he discovered that his money was gone he became mad. He ran about the streets shouting and luckily he met three policemen on duty. He told them what had happened. The police went for a bus that was just loading and started searching all the passengers. They eventually found forty-eight pounds in one of the crooks' sock. He was arrested. He pointed out his other friends and they were pulled out of the bus. They were each sentenced to six years imprisonment.

During their spell in jail the crooks made many attempts to escape, one day, of course, they succeeded by opening a small hole in the wall. They went out one by one. They attacked the warder and took his pistol. They left him unconscious. In the morning the police went after them. They found the men in a bush. They exchanged shots with the police. At that time a bus was just passing and they attempted to stop it by standing in front of it. The bus was too close and could not stop at once. It killed three of them and the other one was taken by the police.

CARD **D : 6**

Tom had a grocery shop in Orlando Township. He employed a certain young boy to work in the shop. His name was Solomon.

Tom taught Solomon how to handle the business so that when he, Tom, was absent Solomon could take care of his shop.

They worked together for quite a long time until Tom trusted Solomon so much that time and again he remained at home while Solomon managed the shop.

Solomon was a young man who was still full of youth. He made love to many girls. He would use the shop takings as much as he liked. He gave some of the money to his girlfriends. Really he did not see that he was letting the shop down, but when Tom realized that his profits were less he suspected Solomon. So he trapped him when one day when he rushed into the shop to find Solomon giving away six pounds to one of his girlfriends. He took it out of the till. Tom asked him what he was doing. Solomon said 'I am running the show, don't you worry.' Tom became very angry and asked him 'Why do you give my money away like this?' Solomon said 'I only just gave her six pounds.' Tom swore at him and chased him out of the shop. Solomon became very angry. Tom tried to snatch the money from the girl and he succeeded. The girl went out crying bitterly. Solomon became very furious when he saw Tom manhandling his girlfriend. Tom came out with a fiver and threw it in front of Solomon and told him that he would hit him if he did not take it and go. Solomon did not want to pick it up. Tom lifted up his hand and cracked Solomon's angry face. Solomon put his hand in his pocket and drew out a very big knife. He tried in vain to stab Tom. When they were still fighting the girl came with a big stone and knocked Tom on the head. He fell down and they ran away.

CARD **B : 8**

Accidents today are very common. Bus 118 left Alexandra with sixty-seven passengers. It was roaring along Louis Botha Avenue. The driver had one thing in mind, to deliver his load in town on time. At the corner of Louis Botha and Harrow Road the robot stopped him. All of a sudden a coal lorry smashed the rear mudguard of Bus 118.

The impact was so terrible that the passengers sitting on the rear seats were injured. Some had broken legs, blood streamed everywhere. People were screaming in the bus looking for help. Some were jumping through the windows. Many fell hard on the pavement increasing the number of casualties.

The truck driver was called to make a statement to the police. He said, 'I did not sleep well last night because I quarrelled with my parents. I became very angry and wanted to leave home and go somewhere else. I was still thinking and planning when I found myself almost killed.' The police locked him up.

The truck driver was allowed a bail of fifteen pounds. He was superstitious and immediately went to the witchdoctor to ask for his fortune and to get some medicines that will initiate his discharge. The witchdoctor told him that he had been bewitched by the woman next door, because he had refused to give her some milk. She wanted him to be killed by the truck he was driving. The witchdoctor gave him some ointment to smear on the steering wheel and on his face. He also gave him some roots to chew when he went to court so that he will be discharged. He did what he was told and he was discharged. He really thought it was the medicines that initiated his discharge. But the truck owner paid a lot of money to the busowner.

CARD **F : 4**

Once upon a time a man called Ben had a quarrel with his wife.

Ben wanted to marry another woman, but Lilly refuse because she was legally married and told Ben not to make the attempt. But Ben insisted on marrying another woman. This was how the quarrel started. Ben did not listen to Lilly in spite of all the bonds of legal marriage. He went and proposed to a young girl.

Ben did not come home as usual. He came only after two weeks. This made Lilly cross and she decided to part from her husband on legal grounds. She reported the matter to the Native Commissioner. Ben was already preparing for a big feast in the meanwhile to celebrate his second marriage. He had paid twenty head of cattle and fifteen sheep for his new wife. He slaughtered two oxen.

Two weeks after the feast Ben received a summons from the Commissioner. The case between Ben and his wife went on for many days. Ben sold many oxen and paid a lawyer to defend him. The case ended in Lillys favour however. Lilly was given all the lands, the cattle and the sheep owned by her husband. Ben lost everything. When the new wife saw that she could not enjoy the riches that Ben had before, she deserted him and ran away with another man to a far-off country.

That same night Ben hanged himself. He was buried the following day.

CARD **G : 3**

One time not many years ago a certain woman was living alone in a house in Randfontein. Her husband had died two years back. She did not have sons, but two daughters. She liked to go to bioscopes in the evening and come back home very late in the night. She always found her children fast asleep.

Their house had six windows, and one of these windows became the most dreaded window of the house. For in this window the haunting ghost came through into the house. This was the ghost of her husband. He usually came when the children were alone. The ghost would ask the children where their mother was. It would kiss their hands and wished them a good night. Then it would disappear through the window.

One day the children told their mother that their father comes to them when she is not there during the night. She would not believe their story and said they spoke nonsense and that if he ever come to them again he is just a ghost. The children became frightened. The mother told them to put the light on when she is not there because ghosts are afraid of light. Despite the light the ghost came to visit the children when she was not there. When she came back that night she saw that the light was on and asked the children what happened. They told her that it was there again. She then decided not to come home late.

The children told their mother that the ghost of their father had said that if she neglected them again he would take them with him. She then cooked better food for the children and washed their dirty clothes and the children were happy.

One night when they were having their supper they heard sounds on that window. The mother saw a figure like that of her husband standing near the window. Then it moved slowly towards where they were sitting. They were all quite, waiting to see what would happen.

The ghost called the woman by name and told her not to leave the children alone at night and that she must take care of them. Then it left through that window.

She took a horse-shoe and nailed it on the troublesome window. The ghost never came to visit them again.

CARD **E : 5**

Once a man becomes a driver he should take care of all things around him. Careless driving does not do any good.

Theme Illustrations

I remember one day how a driver knocked a cyclist down at a robot. The motorist was going against the light.

A certain lady who was there when it happened had taken the number of the car. She was also nearly run over by a double-decker bus.

The motorist who ran away was found by the police and charged. In the mean time the cyclist died in the hospital.

CARD I : 1

Jane was a very lazy girl. She did not hear her parents' advices. She could not even cook porridge. She always said, 'I will do everything when I am big.' Jane loved jiving more than anything in the world. When she wakes up in the morning she could not even prepare her bed. Her mother did everything for her. She would wash herself nicely and smear herself with all the assorted creams and go to jiving. It was in one of these entertainments that she fell in love with a certain boy called 'Wise Guy'. This boy loved Jane very much because she was very beautiful.

Jane refused many proposals from rich people and thought that 'Wise Guy' was the only heaven to her. She did not want to go to school also. But 'Wise Guy' was a criminal. She did not know. Even if she knew she did not care. 'Wise Guy' was hers.

One day he told her that she should come and stay with him in the house that he had hired. Jane agreed. She left her home without a farewell. She went and lived with 'Wise Guy'.

It was hardly two months they were staying together that 'Wise Guy' was arrested for murder. 'Wise Guy' ran away from jail one evening. He came home with a stolen car and told Jane that they had to leave for his home in Pietersburg. She packed quickly and they left. They were travelling at a high speed of about 90 m.p.h. He dropped Jane at his home and went back to town to abandon the car. He came back by bus in the morning.

They stayed for three months but 'Wise Guy' was rearrested again. Jane had a baby boy when 'Wise Guy' left her. She did not have enough money to live on. She did not have enough clothes for the child and herself. She was only left with the hope that 'Wise Guy's' parents would help her. But they were primitive people who still enjoyed in wearing skins. She was not used to the primitive way of living. But what could she do. There was no tea, bread, rice or any food. Her husband-to-be was sentenced to death. She wanted to come back but she did not have a penny. She then decided to walk from Pietersburg to Johannesburg.

She left early one morning and did not even bid farewell to her supposed-to-be-in-laws.

On the way she became so hungry that she looked for some houses where she could ask for some food. But there was no sign of a house nearby. She was tired and the child began to cry. It was already dark and she wondered where she would sleep. She saw a bush about four yards from the road. She went there to try and sleep. But the child was

140

crying and she could not sleep. Jackals were also howling nearby. She was trembling with fear. She started very early the next morning. Very luckily, at about 10 o'clock she met a certain man who was going her way. He felt pity on her and gave some food to both of them. The sun was very hot. She could smell the dirt from her skin-clad body. She walked for five weeks in her long journey, asking for food from passersby and from some houses along the road. When she reached Pretoria on the first day of the sixth week her feet were swollen and the child was in a state of collapse. She found relatives and were given some money to come back to Johannesburg.

Her mother cried bitterly when she saw Jane clad in goats skin with a baby at her back.

She bought her some clothes and she became a good-looking woman again. She will never forget all her troubles in the future.

We have illustrated the clarity with which the continuity of theme is so often found in urban African T.A.T.s by presenting three complete, individual test responses. This in no way implies that all test responses maintain only one theme throughout all stories. A great many story series contain more than one main theme. What we have attempted to illustrate is the clarity with which a theme emerges— a clarity which is so frequently found in urban African T.A.T. responses as to be almost characteristic of them.

It is possibly this clarity of the theme, or themes, running through their stories, coupled with the urban African's spontaneous, relatively uninhibited, direct type of style, that makes the African Thematic Apperception Test such a rewarding device for the assessment of urban African personality.

XI

INTER-CITY COMPARISON

THIS study has dealt almost exclusively with assessments of the urban African population living in and around the Johannesburg areas. The question now arises: How do the communal personality components of Africans living in an urban area distant from the Reef urban complex, compare with those of the Johannesburg urban dwellers—assessed on the same test?

The urban area selected to make the comparison was Durban. The sample was composed of men of the same age range as the Johannesburg sample, and satisfying the same educational minimum. It was a sample made up from men who had applied for jobs at the Durban Division of Public Utility Transport Corporation.

As a group, however, they differed from the Johannesburg sample in the extent and degree of their 'intensive' urbanization, and also in their tribal homogeneity—most were Zulu speaking, and in closer proximity to their traditional tribal homes in Zululand.

No attempt will be made, here, to go into detail about the Durban urban African social conditions. The reader is referred instead to the excellent survey undertaken by Kuper, Watts and Davies: *Durban— A Study in Racial Ecology*.

We will confine ourselves merely to an overall comparison between the Johannesburg and Durban type of response.

Once again one finds the same spontaneity, vivacity and sparkle that one has come to associate with the stories of the Africans of the Johannesburg area. Take the following example, written by a twenty-six-year-old man living at Kwa Mashu Township:

CARD F : 4

'Paul, I am expecting a baby' Maud cried in Paul's arms. Something in her voice, something, he could not say what it was, made Paul push her vigorously away from him. He looked deep into her eyes—as if looking at her for the first time. 'Yes, its true, Paul, I know how much it will hurt you—your reputation in the village will be ruined! But I couldn't keep it from you any longer.' Maud was now sure of herself, all the shame gone from her face. She stood there now with all the dignity and self-assurance making a bid for her future with Paul not to go to the drain which she had feared so dreadfully. 'Maud.' 'Yes, Paul?' 'Are you sure of what you are talking about?' Paul relaxed his grip on her shoulder. He looked all around them. For a moment he thought he heard something moving behind him—for the first time in his life he felt frightened. Yet there was no reason for him to be afraid. Maud searched his eyes. She could detect nothing. She thought maybe it's the surrounding atmosphere which was gradually becoming tense that was worrying him. Behind him, there were tall pine trees, and a little bush immediately behind the pines, stretching towards a dense forest beyond. Maud drew closer to him now. She wanted to explain but no words came.

'Who is responsible for this Maud? You know quite well that I have been away from home for the past six months. Now how could I have . . . ?'

'You are not responsible Paul,' Maud cut his words. 'But how I wish you were! Only God knows how much.' Maud finished her last word on Paul's shoulder, with both her arms around his neck as if she would never let him go.

'So, Maud, you are in love with another man?' he talked to himself rather than asked Maud.

'No, Paul. I am not in love with another man.'

'But how can you account for the baby?' begging her instead of scolding.

'You see, Paul, I thought you didn't love me, and fell for a man who had just come to our village. We got engaged. It was so fast. I couldn't think. I was so lonely Paul without you—I fell. James, then, who was supposed to marry me died a week after the engagement party. Later I realized I was two months pregnant.—Oh! Paul, will you hit me, punish me, do anything hard, but please forgive me Paul, my darling!'

In that moment Paul found his lips against hers—and they remained entangled in each others arms for a long, long time.

Like the Johannesburg stories, the Durban responses often mention, and discuss, the close relationship between township conditions and juvenile crime. Here is an example by an inhabitant of Cato Manor:

CARD C : 7

Simon Dube lives in Cato Manor where some of the shacks have been destroyed. Cato Manor is named after the first Station Commander who was Mr. Cato. Before there were few shacks and now there are thousands which were built after the clash between the Indians and the Natives. This place is so dirty that even a pig sty at some places is better. Death occurs almost daily in this place because some of the people who live there have nothing to eat and some come from outside the town and so they are not allowed to stay in town without a permission from the Court where they come from.

Inter-City Comparison

In this place the transport is run by the Indians and a few by Corporation. The government together with Corporation have decided to build better houses somewhere at a place called Kwa Mashu and at Umlazi Mission but the people who stay at that place still do not want to go to Kwa Mashu because they have a good chance of brewing Shimeyana and another sort of a thing called Izingodo and out of it they get nice and drunk. This place where Simon lives is full of flies and when its raining you do not get a chance of walking because of the mud. Some of these shacks are leaking and some of them have no windows. The parents of the children who stay there are not able to send their children to schools and the children start their way of living by making groups in the streets and at night they start pickpocketing everyone they come across and they spend most of their lives in jail.

Like the Johannesburg stories, items of topical interest or stories relating to 'local news' are not uncommon. For example:

CARD **B : 8**

Thoho! This afternoon I want you to buy me a *Star* (Johannesburg newspaper) . . . on the first page they are talking about the Queen. Good luck she got a baby boy and her sister is engaged to Mr. Armstrong Jones.

CARD **E : 5**

This picture reminds me of Elias Msomi who was killing other people but at last they got hold of him and he was sentenced to death.

The character in question, Elphas Msomi, was a notorious killer who was active in the Natal area for months before he was eventually captured, brought to trial and hanged.

Tribalism, as one would expect from a population with an even shorter and less intensive background of urbanization than the Johannesburg sample, is a very prevalent factor, often mentioned in their stories. Stories such as:

CARD **F : 4**

The letter was written by a boy to his girl friend. The boy mentioned the day and the time of his arrival and asked his girl friend to meet him at the station. When the girl received this letter, she became very happy to know that her boy friend will be coming home, since he has been away for two years.

She started preparing for the journey to the station. She went to the station, when she came to the station she waited. In about an hour's time the train pulled in. She looked carefully and saw her boy friend looking through the window of the compartment. She was so glad. As soon as the man got off, they flung into each other's arms, they even forgot that the tribal law of the Bantu is not to kiss each other in public. They remembered that after they had deeply kissed each other . . .

144

Inter-City Comparison

On this picture I see a hand full of bank notes. When I see this hand I remember the day when I received my first pay after leaving school, when I was employed as a Doctors interpreter. I, immediately after receiving my salary, went to the post office to post part of my money home to my parents so that they could buy cattles for me. This applies to all natives, when they get their first pay they always post the money to their parents so that when they want to get married they will have a number of cattle bought for them by their parents.

'Lobola' payments in the rural areas are made in accordance with tradition—mainly in cattle. Africans either send the money to their parents every month, who then purchase the cattle, or, if they are far away, the African saves it and brings a lump sum home for immediate purchase. Amongst the younger men the main impetus to work is to earn money to pay 'lobola' for a wife:

One day I shall go home and marry the girl I love, a man whispered one day to his friend in one of the hostels in Johannesburg. The young man worked hard for three years saving for the only woman he loved . . .

This stress on tribalism is naturally enough coupled with a preoccupation with black magic. Take the following examples expressing the power of magic:

Dick, a mine worker, worked in Johannesburg gold mines for fifteen years, and when he came back after that time he had a new coat called 'Jazz Conch' and a big trousers with a wide bottom called 'bula umngeni'. After these years he brought all his money to his father who told him to get married because he was old and had no wife. One day when Dick was hunting early in the morning he saw Fumane and started talking about love but Fumane refused saying that Dick was very old and Fumane was a school child. On another day Dick woke up in the morning and waited for Fumane where Fumane used to fetch the water. Fumane went again to fetch the water and again Dick started talking with Fumane about love but she said there is no love.

On the third day Dick told his father who gave him a small bottle containing the fat of animals and said you must hide in the bush and smear your face with the fat but before you do that I will give you a bottle of water mixed with some roots of trees. When you wake up at one o'clock you must shake the bottle, put some of this mixture in your mouth, spit it out and call her name three times. So Dick did what his father told him and early in the morning he went again to where Fumane used to fetch water. He hid himself in the bush when Fumane came past and he jumped out of the bush and said 'Here am I'. Fumane got such a shock that she stood still and Dick put his hand on her shoulder saying: I love you. After that Fumane said: I love you. And all was over. After a few months lobola was paid and they got married.

CARD **F** : 4

There was a man called Barnabas. This man was living near the Umfolozi River with his wife but they had no children.

One day this man called his wife and told her that after a long time together they still had no children. He asked his wife what they should do about it and she replied that she knew quite well that he must go and see the doctor who would give him the medicine because he was very sick.

The man said he was not sick at all and that maybe there was something wrong with the wife, so after that they both went to the doctor who said they were both sick and if they wanted help they were to bring two cattle which would be the equivalent of two children. The man said he wanted twelve children and said to his wife that if she is old enough he will take on another wife and marry her so the wife agreed as she did not want a lot of children. They then returned for the twelve cattle which they brought back to the doctor and he gave them medicine. After a while they had two children, but he married another woman who had ten children, so in the end he got his twelve children and they stayed there very happy until they died.

While most stories dealing with magic are related within the context of African culture, at times the belief in the power of the supernatural is put to rather specifically civilized pursuits—as the following example shows:

CARD **G** : 3

We Zulus believe also in dreams; if the dream is related to horses, then we go for betting and we sometimes come right.

Even with all this emphasis on tribalism, civilization is slowly encroaching on tribal tradition, the influence of money and of urban living is slowly causing the youth to forget their traditional obligations to their parents:

CARD **I** : 1

On this picture I see an old man sitting outside the house. When I see him, I remember the old man I saw last year in Zululand, sitting near the house thinking about the only son he had who went to work and as he got work he forgot all about his parents.

This old man has nowhere to go and no one to support him.

A pathetic story of cultural clash, where the protection and respect for the aged, so characteristic of traditional society, has been broken. The perplexities of civilized advance, however, present some unconsciously humorous observations. Take the following example:

Inter-City Comparison

This is the home of civilized people. Though civilized, this was a very poor family for they only had one chair for the mother to sit on, the husband had to stand. So one could agree with me in saying that these people are civilized for if it were not so the man would have been sitting, and let the wife stand, as our native custom is vice versa to that of the Europeans . . .

Such are the trials of civilized advance, where small aspects of European culture which, while they remain almost unnoticed by Europeans, are readily perceived by peoples with different customs and patterns of social living—a perception which, as the African comes to accept more of European culture, becomes more of a habit and less of a deviation.

Amongst the less-sophisticated Africans of Durban, of whom there are a considerably greater number than in the Johannesburg area, the material aspects of civilization are especially prized:

Here in South Africa civilization is growing beat by beat. The picture in H.2 shows how smart it is to be civilized. Africans usually buy stoves, cups, pots and kitchen equipment . . .

A naïve conception of civilized progress admittedly, but nevertheless a desire for the material culture of the white man, this last story is typical of the less-urbanized African's ideas of civilized advance— the acquisition of European material culture. Such people have a 'fine feathers make fine birds' complex, they tend to associate only the observable elements of Western culture with civilized advance—a shallow conception of civilization but nevertheless with such people a very real identification. The material culture of another society is always more obvious than its vague, unseen, traditional, legal and religious institutions. The acquisition of material cultural items is a first step to cultural change.

Such material acquisitions are naturally enough still prized and desired by the Johannesburg urban Africans, and while many of the latter have what we have called a 'brief-case complex'—that is, a rationalization that a brief-case gives intellectual stature and status to its owner—the general appreciation of civilized advance has, with them, progressed to a desire for the more subtle aspects of civilized progress, such as education and knowledge. Just as the desire for pots and pans, in Durban, marks the first stage of cultural change, so possibly, the 'brief-case complex' in Johannesburg marks the beginning of the second and more important stage—the desire for the white man's knowledge.

The less-sophisticated attitudes of the Durban sample are observable in a number of different spheres. Firstly, their general approach to Europeans as reflected in their T.A.T. stories is, on the whole, more subservient than that of their Johannesburg counterparts. The tendency to use the word 'boss' or 'baas' (Afrikaans for 'boss') to denote a European, while fairly commonplace in the stories of the Durban group, is seldom found in the stories of the Johannesburg group. In the Durban sample we find stories like the following:

CARD E : 5

The two men meet, it's a master and his servant. The baas is telling his servant what to do. It is seen that the servant does not like the treatment of his employer by showing no respect, and speaking with his hand inside his pockets, and he is showing a bad face to his employer.

CARD E : 5

This picture shows that we must be kind to our boss. If you are interested in your job you must obey your bosses instructions . . .

CARD E : 5

A European man called his boy to come and tell why he did not go where he was supposed to. The boy explains to his boss that the trains were late . . .

CARD B : 8

This man has done wrong, he is praying that his boss should not fire him . . .

Another word often found in the Durban stories is the noun 'Bantu', to denote their racial group. This is a word which the more sophisticated Johannesburg Africans definitely avoid. For them it has a definite political connotation, being the term by which they are denoted in Government communiqués. In Durban stories we often find the term Bantu used, as in the following examples:

CARD C : 7

. . . If our forefathers would come to life again today they would be surprised at the changes they would find since the time of their departure from this world. I think one of the things they would marvel at is our locations like Kwa-Mashu, Chesterville, Glebelands etc. Because in the olden days they never thought the Bantu would one day be residents of urban areas.

CARD C : 7

In this picture we see a Bantu Location, and this location is built on a nice place . . .

These Bantu are going to work, they are waiting for a bus . . .

The word 'Bantu' (from the Zulu root 'ntu' meaning human being which, with the plural prefix 'ba', becomes 'bantu'—the men of the tribe) has little or no political significance for these people, the vast majority of whom are Zulu-speaking. To them it is a Zulu term. Their stories reflect the vernacular influence very clearly. The names of most characters introduced are Zulu names, some of which even have their derivations explained for the benefit of Europeans who may read the stories:

. . . Then came their first-born, a son. He was named Mvula (rain) . . .

. . . After marriage they had one son and a baby girl. They lived in a house which was built by Kulunga the husband before they got married.

Kulunga had a lot of hard times during his married life. The difficulties came from his wife and children. Mostly from NoKuhlupheka who followed her name which meant Trouble, and she became troublesome . . .

. . . Monna took Mosali his wife to his room and notified his boss who telephoned Mosalis boss and now the whole indaba (business) was revealed . . .

However, even though generally less sophisticated than the Johannesburg sample, the emergence of race consciousness and a feeling of racial discrimination is apparent in the Durban group. The following example gives an excellent portrayal of the Durban race set-up with its added complication of Black-Indian conflicts:

These people meet here to talk about a difficult problem concerning work. We the Bantu work hard but why is it that the Europeans do not consider us and free us from this slavery. We work we do not fight them, we live with them like brothers but instead of freeing us, they like Indians better than us Bantu, because all the better jobs are for Indians, very few Bantu are in good jobs. We pay £24. to take our children to colleges to become clerks in offices or in commercial concerns, but no we are not wanted they want Indians only. For what good do our children go to school then? When a child goes to school outside town he must have permission to come back to Durban. Are we like cattle? The country is ours, we are supposed to tell you to seek permission, but you are ill-treating us like this, you free the Indians, they don't have to seek any permission, but they are foreigners in this our Zululand.

It is better than to be treated equally as non-Europeans, not to treat Indians better than us, this will cause strife, it is bad for a man's children to quarrel, give your children equal treatment. That was what the meeting was all about.

No equivalent to the 'tsotsi' 'Wittisha' language, so often used in the stories of the Johannesburg group, was found amongst the Durban Africans. And while the 'tsotsi' are known and spoken of, they do not occupy such an important position in Durban as they do in the criminal life of Johannesburg. Durban most certainly has its criminals, but they are apparently not quite up to Johannesburg standards, or if they are, they certainly have not instilled the Durban African population with as much fear as the Johannesburg 'tsotsi' has. In fact, many a Durbanite refers, in his stories, to the Johannesburg criminal with considerable trepidation:

CARD G : 3

I then settled in the worst part of the town, that was Alexandra Township, where there was Msomi gang. This gang was not only stealing but it was deeply engaged in committing murder.

This in no way implies that Durban, unlike Johannesburg, has no criminal gangs. Gangs exist but they do not appear to exercise such a terror over the Durban African as they do in Johannesburg. Durban gangs, however, are spoken of:

CARD I : 1

And I wonder what do they think about other people who have to live like hunted rabbits because of their terrifying abominable behaviour.
If I was the Prime Minister I would send them to the Rope without investigation of their cases.

In the Durban story themes, while aggression exists and killings are done and theft is very prevalent, the general atmosphere is not charged with quite such an undercurrent of anxiety and personal insecurity as is found in the stories of the Johannesburg urban African.

Aggressive themes most certainly occur—for example:

CARD I : 1

It happened that one day the girl went out with the new boy friend and James was informed and waited there for them under the tree he is sitting under. When they approached him James halted them and fought with the man who ran away and James then came back to the girl and molested her and left her unconscious.

But such themes are associated more with individual grievances than with the results of gang warfare or organized terrorism on the Johannesburg scale.

Inter-City Comparison

As with the Johannesburg T.A.T.s, money in the Durban stories forms the primary motivation. Their sentiments are very similar to those expressed by the Johannesburg urban Africans:

CARD **D : 6**

We all like money because you cannot live without money . . .

CARD **D : 6**

Sure money is my friend, a true friend who could help me any time dead or alive . . .

CARD **D : 6**

Years back most of our people never worried themselves about money as they did not see the need of having any money. Our great grandfathers had their stocks of cattle, goats, sheep, fowls and horses, so there was no need for money. It is civilization that has brought about the position that makes money so important.

As with the Johannesburg sample, the Durban group consider education as the most socially acceptable means of obtaining more money. Education furthermore imparts status:

CARD **D : 6**

He doesn't like school. He must be silly, he wants to remain ignorant and start messing around with poor misunderstanding Riksha Boys.

A striking difference between the Durban and Johannesburg approaches, as revealed in their respective grouped responses, is the relative lack of exhibitionism in the Durban T.A.T.s, as compared with the Johannesburg themes. The Durban subjects are less sophisticated and less urbanized than the Johannesburg people, they are also more restrained and more reserved, and less exhibitionistically inclined. They are neither as vocal nor as emotionally uninhibited as their Johannesburg counterparts. While the Johannesburg urban Africans are still very tribally biased, the Durbanite is still virtually completely tribally conditioned—Zululand is, so to speak, just over the hill for most of them. This, coupled with the fact that the Durban sample is almost wholly composed of one ethnological group, the Nguni—and tribal Nguni at that—has eliminated the variety of cultural responses obtainable from a more heterogeneous society such as the Johannesburg group, and tended to preserve traditional modes of behaviour and emotional reserve with far greater strength than in a more culturally loose society.

In overview, as a broad basic comparison, one may say that while the Durban urban Africans are not generally as sophisticated as their Johannesburg counterparts, nor are they as unrestrained in the expression of their emotions as the Johannesburg urban African, the

151

most striking difference in the personality responses of these two groups is the relative lessening in the Durban sample of feelings of anxiety and insecurity, the fear of personal attack, and the under-current of terrorism imposed by the criminal element on the law-abiding section—feelings which predominate amongst the Johannes-burg population.

XII

THE PERSONALITY OF THE URBAN AFRICAN

WHEN an individual is exposed to a particular culture, a process occurs which can be defined as socialization. This socialization tends to make the individual conform to certain group standards so that he can get along amicably with that group and become an accepted member of it.

Through the process of socialization the individual acquires a social frame of reference. This frame of reference, to be socially acceptable, demands conformity to recognized prevalent social values, mores and modes of living. The social pressures of ostracism or social disgrace are brought to bear on the non-conformists.

> The task of society, in a sense, is to perpetuate that society by a continuance of values and mores of living that have been found satisfactory in the past. And to this end it will coerce and distort the individual and, if necessary, sacrifice him (W. E. Henry).

There is in every society a social mould made up of the dominant values of that particular society and, in the process of socialization, the individual gains the satisfaction of his personal needs by a process of partial conformation and partial uniquenesses. What are loosely spoken of as 'national characteristics' are nothing more than observable trends of social conformity obvious in the majority of the group's members.

In the light of this framework it is obvious that the responses elicited by projective tests are determined partly by the personality of the individual and partly by the influence on this personality of the cultural setting in which he functions. The former determinant makes for the individuality and partial uniquenesses of the test data, the latter determinant accounts for the socialization and partial conformities present amongst subjects of the same cultural group.

Urban African society is by no means an established society, yet the effects of its developing cultural pattern are already becoming

153

apparent in a number of partial conformities or trends in the personalities of its members.

Urban living, with its social peculiarities, its economic emphasis, its cultural clashes and its environmental pressures in terms of laws, regulations and various restrictions, is a type of living which, for the African, requires a number of adjustments and readjustments.

Such adjustments require alterations in traditional cultural beliefs, changes in patterns of social living and modifications in the formation of what constitutes the family unit. The urban African must adjust not only to the demands of European society but also to the requirements of urban African culture. He must evolve a way of living and thinking which is compatible with the beliefs of his tribal past and the demands of his urban present. Indeed, social adjustment for the urban African requires a compromise between three societies: the tribal society, the urban township society, and the European society.

The urban environment is one containing new values, new ideals, new social attitudes, new moral standards and new ways of life: it contains cultural concepts vastly different and often contradictory to the patterns of traditional African culture.

Under the impact of the cultural clashes in the urban areas the African is not only in the throes of adjusting to Western European society, but he is in the process of virtually evolving the fabric of a new cultural pattern from his tribal past and from the variety of socio-economic pressures and Western cultural influences to which he is exposed. In this cultural reformation, the tradition-directed society of the rural areas with its tribal cultural outlook is being supplanted by what may be called an individually-directed society with a predominating id-complex.

Rather than a society co-operating as an integrated tribal unit for the mutual benefit, security and protection of the whole—as under 'tradition-directed' group rule—we find in the urban areas a society of individuals, with individualized values and selfish attitudes, a money-conscious type of society in which the id directed 'I want, therefore I take' type of rationalization is very common.

The 'law of the jungle' has a very real application in African urban townships and locations: the fear of sudden attack, of violent unprovoked assault, or of robbery with murder is accepted by inhabitants as a constant possibility—especially at night.

The environment he lives in is definitely a hostile one: he is very often exposed to robbery and assault by his own people, and imprisonment by European and African police. He is more often than not confused, uncertain and bewildered by the numerous laws, regulations and restrictions of movement to which he is subjected.

The Personality of the Urban African

The urban African finds but little stability in the urban areas; he 'owns no home of his own' (in Alexandra Township, the only freehold urban African area, he is at the moment losing his freehold property rights); and he is very, very often in financial difficulties —difficulties which, although due primarily to his low wages, are undoubtedly accentuated by his lack of financial acumen. The urban environment gives him little personal, financial or material stability. His personality, riddled with anxieties and insecurities, turns very often to the escapism of dagga and drink, which in turn causes other social evils.

The Urban African Personality is Characterized by Strong Feelings of Anxiety and Insecurity

The money economy of the urban areas, coupled with the general low level of African wages, has resulted in the urban African becoming extremely money-conscious. Receiving African wages, but buying his requirements at European prices, his salary is seldom sufficient to cover his immediate needs. What was originally a luxury becomes in time a necessity, and to the urban African, European clothes and furniture have definitely become necessities. His range of requirements is steadily growing. And, with his growing needs, his salary is becoming more and more insufficient.

The vast majority of urban Africans live a hand-to-mouth existence.

The overall average wage in the Johannesburg area (for Bantu industrial workers) is less than £14.0.0. per month or £3.5.0. per week . . . The average for all occupations in the Johannesburg area, excluding domestic servants and workers in the gold mining industry, is £13.16.0. per month or £3.3.9. per week (Chairman's Report—Bantu Wage and Productivity Association).

Olive Gibson, in a survey on urban African cost-of-living problems as far back as the year 1954, gave the following cost-figures for the Johannesburg Non-European Affairs Department's 'scientific minimum diet'. The cost of such a diet for an average family of 2 adults and 3 children was:

Area	Total Weekly Cost	Total Monthly Cost
Alexandra	£3.12. 4¼	£15.13.6
Western Native Township .	£3. 6. 6½	£14. 8.4
Orlando . . .	£3. 3.10	£13.16.7¼

Gibson furthermore calculated the percentage increase in the total price for the five major items in this minimum diet, between the years 1950 to 1954, to be 33 per cent.

155

As these prices have increased yet more in the intervening years, one may well ask how the average urban family, earning £3.3.9. per week (1959 estimate), can exist, especially when no provision has been made in the above figures for rent, fuel, clothing, transport and tax. The solution to the problem leaves three paths open to the average family:

1. they can simply spend more than they earn and land in debt;
2. they can maintain a semblance of respectability by making drastic cuts on the purchase of food stuffs;

and/or 3. they can turn to crime to supplement their wages.

None of these solutions is particularly desirable from either the personal or social point of view, and none leads to the development of a secure, contented family unit.

African urbanization in the Union has not, as Ellen Hellmann has pointed out, been a straightforward process of the townward migration of a rural population, as in other countries where industrialization necessitated a concentration of population in specific centres or where improvements in agricultural techniques drove people off the land. In the past the Union's economy has been based on an unskilled African labour force,

> paid not a family but an individual wage, on the assumption that the worker's dependants had a plot of land in a Native reserve from which they could provide their essential needs. The creation of a permanent labour force in secondary industry dependent entirely on a cash wage and living a family life in the area of employment is a comparatively recent phenomenon.

The present-day African wage structure is a carry-over from this period of 'individual migrant wages'.

The Position has been reached Today where the Quest for more Money has become the Urban African's Basic Motivation

This constant quest for more money drives the urban African from job to job in search of yet higher wages. It is not at all unusual to find work-seekers with an employment record of seven jobs over the past two years.

This constant drive for more money certainly does not make for a very stable labour force.

The law-abiding individual sees his financial salvation, or that of his children, in terms of education. According to the Department of Bantu Education there are 46 training colleges for African school teachers in the Union. At present they turn out 2,000 teachers a year. While in the Johannesburg and Witwatersrand areas combined there are 119,374 non-European schoolchildren, the vast majority of whom are African. Over the past five years the number of African pupils in the Union of South Africa as a whole has increased from 800,000 to 1,400,000. 'The illiteracy rate among the Bantu, which according to a UNESCO report was 73 per cent in 1946, was by 1951 reduced to 69 per cent and by 1956 to 63 per cent. It can be assumed that today, three years later, it is even lower' (South African Minister of External Affairs in an address to the United Nations, 1959). But the problem remains—what frustrations are going to be built up if the urban African cannot find scope and financial reward for this education?

The individual with little social conscience turns to crime; and the social conditions within urban African society are very conducive to the promotion of crime. Illegitimacy, lack of parental guidance and control, plus the high rate of unemployment and the restriction of movement enforced by Section 10 of the Natives (Urban Areas) Consolidation Act, No. 25 of 1945, coupled with the prevalent low wages rates, have resulted in great numbers of township youths turning to crime as an easier, more remunerative and more satisfying way of life. The majority of these youthful criminals or 'tsotsis' are literate, educated boys between the ages of twelve and twenty, who live by crime alone. 'In 1950 it was estimated that Johannesburg alone had nearly 21,000 unemployed African youths of employable age' (Longmore).

The 'tsotsi' is a living example of an id-directed personality evolved from the clash between a tradition-directed society and the individualizing forces found in the social, economic, religious and political cultural ramifications of Western European life. As Raymond Firth puts it in his book, *Human Types*:

> The great technical efficiency of our (Western European) civilisation, the desires for extension of sovereignty, for economic exploitation of new natural resources, for new markets for our expanding productive system, and for the religious proselytization of those whom we conceive to be lacking in certain of the higher values, all have combined to affect, and in some cases to shatter, the framework of institutions and values which primitive peoples have built up with difficulty over long periods of time.

As a result of certain laws and restrictions that have been applied to urban Africans and which have caused widespread resentment, annoyance and frustration amongst them—such as the pass laws, the prohibition of beer brewing and the Natives (Urban Areas) Act—there has been the development of a dual standard of morality in the urban African conscience.

> There is the European law, affecting only Natives, infringement of which is not regarded as morally reprehensible. Yet, under it, scores

157

of thousands of Africans are convicted each year. Offences against the common law are regarded in a totally different light, but in an unstable society the danger that the two types of offences will not be kept separate is always present, and a gradual merging is apparently already taking place (Hellman).

Public opinion, invariably the strongest deterrent to anti-social behaviour, can hardly be expected to operate in a society whose members feel legally discriminated against. There is accordingly a feeling prevalent amongst urban Africans, that there is 'one law for Europeans and another for Africans'. This duality of reasoning has tended to colour the urban African's conception of what constitutes a crime against society. It is small wonder, therefore, that urban Africans tend to classify their 'tsotsis' as:

'Bad' 'tsotsis'—that is: those who rob and attack Africans; and 'Good' 'tsotsis'—that is: those who rob and attack Europeans.

These 'bad' 'tsotsis' are a menace in the urban townships and locations. A law unto themselves, they prey on the law-abiding population. Real killers, they stop at nothing: they murder without provocation, and live on the earnings of their robberies and assaults.

A survey of the T.A.T. protocols reveals a high trend of aggression amongst the population responses—an aggression which is best seen as a personality modification required for adjustment to a highly aggressive environment, coupled with the fact that the urban African still retains within himself a great deal of the uninhibited, uncontrolled primitive.

The urban dweller is an extreme character, one who easily explodes emotionally. His latent aggression changes with amazing rapidity to uncontrolled violence. His ego-controls are weak, his id pressures powerful.

The Urban African is a Personality with Strong Latent Aggression and Insufficient Moderation and Control

This latent aggression when directed into anti-social channels becomes positively uninhibited and openly sadistic. Urban African crime is characterized by its violent aggression and primitive bestiality. Robberies are almost invariably robberies with violence. The urban African criminal cannot moderate his aggression; if he attacks, he attacks violently. The knife, a needle-sharp tempered strand of wire, or the 'knop-kerrie' or cudgel are his favourite weapons, the head and face his favourite target.

A story concerning Shadrack Mathews, the self-appointed leader of the Msomi Gang, will serve to reveal the type of sadistic violence which characterizes the anti-social urban African personality. The following extract from *Die Vaderland* of 30 December 1959 has been corroborated by Africans who knew the set-up:

> . . . In a chair sat a member of the Spoiler Gang. His eyes were wide and frightened. His hands were tied with wire, his wrists were bleeding —so was his nose.
>
> Mathews said 'Now we will show you how we kill Spoilers. He must die, it is our law that he must die.'
>
> One of the other gang-members who was with Mathews, took out a small knife and systematically began cutting out the Spoiler Gang member's eye. The Spoiler screamed like a wounded animal and pleaded that he was innocent . . .
>
> The Msomi gangman cut out the one eye and placed it on a table. The Spoiler was bleeding and semi-conscious.
>
> After cutting out the Spoiler's eyes, a cloth was tied around his mouth to smother his moans.
>
> The Msomi then proceeded to further mutilate the Spoiler . . . Mathews looked on smiling.
>
> The Spoiler died shortly after this . . .

Violent attacks have become part of the urban African's life. African newspapers constantly report cases of violence. *The World* of 1 June 1960, for example, states: 'More than 400 victims of assaults were taken to Reef hospitals over the weekend.'

While such reports as the following are not uncommon: 'Five gangsters carrying torches and revolvers went from house to house in Edenvale Location, Germiston, after midnight, murdering, raping and robbing. They moved in a big black car—and threatened to return.'

Urban African aggression has made violence part of urban African life.

The urban environment with its loose morals, its many 'shebeens', and its aggressive atmosphere, has tended to colour the male-female relationship of the urban areas. Morals are very lax, sexual expressions uninhibited and illegitimacy rife.

The forces of urbanism are such that home life is continually threatened. Money has proved a stimulus for individualisation, for the younger generation today may become financially independent of their relatives. This leads to individuality in the sexual sphere, and young men and women no longer depend on the choice made by their parents. They choose for themselves, but in so doing they are exposed to all kinds of impulses (Longmore).

The relation between the sexes is a loose relationship. Family life has suffered considerably as a result.

Figures obtained from the Medical Officer of Health for the

Johannesburg area reveal the extent of the subsequent moral degeneration. The recorded illegitimacy rate for the year ending 1958 was 38·92 per cent. These figures record neither private abortions nor 'hidden' births.

Male-Female Relations amongst the Younger People of the Urban Areas are an Aggressive, Morally Lax Association, Characterized by Uninhibited Primitivism and Sexual Licentiousness

Urbanization, while it has modified tribalism, has by no means submerged the tribal influence. The urban African even today is very tribally biased. Complete detribalization, while it may exist, is definitely the exception rather than the rule. The typical urban African is an individual who, while he may have dropped a great many of the customs and beliefs which his forefathers held dear, has, nevertheless, retained his tribal affiliation, plus a goodly number of tribal beliefs. These beliefs he has modified to fit into the requirements of urban society—'lobola', for example, is paid in money and not in cattle—but he is definitely not completely emancipated from tribal influence.

The urban African sees himself as a member of a particular tribe and he recognizes his fellows according to their tribe. He has adopted European dress and many of the white man's customs, but he has retained many of the beliefs, cultural mores and practices, peculiar to his particular tribe.

The Urban African is still Very Tribally Biased

The survival of tribal belief has ensured the importance in the urban areas of African magic, and the witchdoctor, in his various forms, is a respected and valued member of urban society. Witchcraft and sorcery are powerful urban institutions. The witchdoctor is consulted regularly by many Africans, who are dissatisfied with the results of European medicine or legal judgments.

Urbanization has had remarkably little effect upon the practice of witchcraft; witchdoctors flourish in the urban areas.

In fact certain aspects of European culture have been readily accepted because conformation for their use existed in traditional African magical beliefs. European patent medicines have a wide sale because they are new and powerful magic to put to traditional ends. European magical beliefs . . . are readily absorbed because they fit in with old beliefs. Sunday observance was quickly taken over because the idea of it being taboo to work on certain days was part of the old culture (Monica Hunter).

The Personality of the Urban African

The 'nyanga' (the herbalist) and the 'asangoma' (who diagnoses by divine inspiration) are still powerful and oft-consulted figures in the urban townships. Their powers are so revered that some witch-doctors are especially 'imported' into the urban areas to deal with specific cases which have eluded the skills of local practitioners. Contrary to popular belief, the influence of witchdoctors has not diminished under urban conditions or with association with European culture; in fact, their magic has expanded and takes new forms to cope with situations, difficulties and experiences arising from contact with Western European culture. This trend appears to be fairly widespread. Marwick, referring to the east-central Bantu of Rhodesia and Nyasaland, states in an article on 'The Continuance of Witchcraft':

> An immediate effect of contact with western influence is not a decrease but an increase in the African's pre-occupation with beliefs in magic, witchcraft and sorcery . . . the proportion of people accepting this belief is high among both educated and uneducated Africans.

The prevalence with which African witchcraft beliefs and practices adjust themselves to the European situation was realized as long ago as 1927, when the Native Administration Act of that year prohibited the advertising of 'any native medicine alleged to contain or to be derived from the fat or entrails of a human being, animal, insect, reptile or any other thing, or a super-natural, legendary or mythical being'.

The only marked influence that urban conditions have had upon witchcraft practices in the townships has been the combination of the functions of the 'nyanga' and 'asangoma' by local practitioners. Unlike tribal society where the 'nyanga' and the 'asangoma' are clearly differentiated functions, carried out by different specialists, urban commercialization has caused a fusing of these duties. In tribal society the 'asangomas' (the inspired ones) diagnose and then send the patient to a 'nyanga' (a herbalist) in much the same fashion as Europeans take a medical doctor's prescription to the pharmacist. In the urban areas, however, the 'nyanga' has tended to usurp the functions of the 'asangoma'; he both diagnoses and prescribes.

In Alexandra Township alone, with its estimated population of 100,000, I have it on very good authority that there are well over 1,000 full-time and part-time 'nyangas'.

The Influence of Witchcraft is still a Powerful Determining Factor in the Life of the Urban African

Magic plays an extremely important part in the ritual life of the tribal Bantu. But as Eiselen and Schapera have stated:

There is also a well-defined belief in certain super-natural beings able to influence for good or for evil the destinies of the living. Foremost among these are the spirits of dead ancestors, round whom there has developed an elaborate system of worship . . . It should be noted that magic and religion are closely inter-related in Bantu life.

It has been truly stated that all men must have some kind of religion, yet religion in the Western world is often erroneously interpreted as being synonymous only with Christianity.

There is a tendency, a product of the egotism in all of us, to mock the unfamiliar in other men's faith and worship. Such words as 'heathen', 'idolatry', 'superstition', are used more often in derision than in their legitimate meanings. They are words we hurl at others; seldom do we apply them to ourselves (Hutchinson).

Man is a religious being. From the time he became human he has shown an irresistible urge to worship. The Bantu are a very religious people, and it is surely too much to expect of such a people that they completely change their centuries-old religious traditions in a mere forty or so years of urbanization. While missions have operated amongst the Bantu for a considerably longer period, it is only comparatively recently that Black has met White in any great numbers, it is only recently that real cultural contact has taken place in the urban areas. In this cultural clash the European is often inclined to underestimate the continuing strength of the Bantu's deeply rooted cultural traditions.

An analysis of the fantasy productions of some 2,500 urban dwellers, illustrated by typical examples from their actual stories, has revealed:

1. The presence of strong tribal influences and biases amongst these people;
2. the existence of strong beliefs in witchcraft and the power of magic;
3. the existence of a religious bewilderment amongst urban Africans when considering the 'new' religion of Christianity.

The religious outcome of the clash of Christianity and Bantu religious beliefs has been—as one may well expect on the basis of the above conclusions—a cultural religious modification, a modification shown in the Johannesburg urban areas by the fact that some 2,254 non-recognized religious sects have emerged to date, and in the Durban urban areas by the fact that 45 per cent of the African population belongs to minor sects, many of which combine Christian observance with elements of African belief and ritual.

The Personality of the Urban African

The Religious Super-ego of the Urban African is still Very Tribally Biased

This tendency towards the formation of Bantu ritual-type 'Christianity' is not confined to the urban areas only. Breutz, in a very detailed study of *The Tribes of Mafeking District*, writes:

> The majority of the baRalong are Christians as they came under the influence of European missionaries at an early date. A small proportion of the Christians are active church members, but very few understand Christianity. The majority are only nominally Christians who have been baptized but have little knowledge of fundamental Christian principles. These nominal Christians generally accept Christian rules of conduct and forms of ritual (marriage, burial) and the wearing of European clothes, but all these practices are mixed with traditional Tswana customs and conduct.

Such African modifications of Christianity are by no means isolated to the Union of South Africa. Christensen, in an article on 'The Adaptive Functions of Fanti Priesthood'—a study, undertaken in 1951, of the adaptation of a West African religion to Christianity, says:

> Generally speaking, Christianity has resulted in a weakening of the autochthonous religion, but Christianity has only partially succeeded in imposing its own code of ethics and behaviour . . . Many who claim to be Christian rarely if ever attend church services, and continue to practise tribal ways.

And like the numerous non-recognized religions of the Johannesburg urban areas, Christensen mentions the growth of large numbers of new cults in Ghana, which he attributes in part to 'an attempt to assuage the anxieties arising from rapid social change'. Such cults have spread rapidly over the southern half of Ghana since 1930, and present a complex combination of African, Christian and Moslem elements. Like their South African counterparts, the patronage of the new West African cults is, according to Christensen, greatest in the larger centres with a higher degree of contact with European culture, rather than in the more remote sections. ·

Similar findings to those of Christensen's were made by Messenger in his studies in 1952 on the Anang Ibibio of the Calabar Province in south-eastern Nigeria. Discussing the religious acculturation of the peoples, he writes:

> Most young people, although accepting Christian dogma in most areas, maintain traditional beliefs concerning malevolent forces despite missionaries' efforts to discount their reality. No matter how Europeanised a person may be, he usually is able to recount his numerous experiences with ghosts and can recite the Anang rationals for their existence . . .

The Personality of the Urban African

. . . Techniques of magic are widely employed by young persons to attain scholastic success, to win a girl's hand, to gain a desired position, to harm a rival, and for many other purposes. The tenacity of religious belief in this area is a constant source of irritation and frustration to the missionaries and administrators alike.

With this widespread tendency to introduce African religious practices, customs and beliefs into Christianity, one may well wonder why the African has not rejected Christianity completely and returned to his tribal deities? An answer, given by Melville Herskovits, as a result of West African studies, seems to apply equally well to all Africa. He says: 'When one group conquered another, the superior power of the gods of the conquerors was self-evident, and it was thus to the advantage of the conquered to appease them.'

The majority of Africans in the continent of Africa appease the Christian God of their conquerors, the white men, but they are doing so in an increasingly traditional fashion. With the increase of political independence in the African states, with the decrease of European domination in Africa, with the 'conquered' now becoming the 'conquerors', it will be interesting to see which direction Christianity will take in Africa. Will it become conquered by the gods of independent Africa?

Urban African attitudes are greatly influenced by the multi-racial contacts made in the urban areas. Association with the white man has resulted in the formulation of certain attitudes towards the European race. When black meets white in South Africa, the vast majority of contacts are within the work sphere, in industry, or in a master-servant relationship in the European home. The nature of these contacts, coupled with the urban African's predominating drive for more money, highlights in his mind the disparity between African wages and the wages paid to the European group. This line of thought forms the basis of the urban African's attitude towards the European group, namely, a feeling of being discriminated against.

The crux of African-European racial antagonism in the urban areas is centred on the restrictions placed by the Europeans in the paths of the urban Africans who, in their constant quest for satisfaction in their desire for more money, become frustrated, annoyed and antagonistic towards the Europeans as a group.

The Industrial Colour-bar which thwarts the Urban African in his Quest for more Money has become one of the main Bones of Racial Contention amongst the Urban Africans

Legal statutes exist to enforce the industrial colour-bar in South Africa, but as Franklin has pointed out in his *Economics in South Africa*:

The Personality of the Urban African

. . . perhaps the most important of all elements making up the colour bar is the purely conventional element. Certain jobs are by convention reserved for Europeans. The pressure upon employers to conform to these conventions comes not only from the European employees, but from virtually the whole of white society.

The urban African aggression associated with the frustrations imposed by the industrial colour-bar is usually dissipated in verbal outbursts against some distant body such as the Government. Every so often, however, mass emotional explosions do occur when aggression, usually directed against individual upholders of the law, bursts into violence and killing. Such mass reactions are very often associated with matters relating directly to the urban African's primary motivation—the drive for more money.

This is well shown in the uncontrolled African mass fury which has so often characterized police beer raids, in which a number of police have lost their lives. The instigators of these riots are, more often than not, the persons who stand to lose most by the raids, namely, the 'shebeen queens'—the women who brew and sell illicit liquor. Support is given to them by many of the local residents who become incensed by the raids, not only because of their feelings of antagonism towards the police but because the concoctions made by the 'shebeen queens' are a very real source of pleasure to them. This, coupled with the fact that many of the 'shebeen' patrons are in any case very drunk, produces a combination of forces which readily merge into a savage fury of murder and killing.

The American influence is very strong in the urban areas. The words and phrases incorporated into the vernacular of the urban Africans indicates this. This influence is especially marked in the 'tsotsi', who models himself almost wholly on tales of American gangsterism. The gang organization, methods and leadership hierarchy of the township and location gangs, shows this American influence very clearly. Shadrack Mathews, the leader of the Msomi Gang, for example, dressed American style, rode around in new American cars, had a personal bodyguard—one 'Ginger' Masheane —and a personal chauffeur. A black replica of 'Scarface' Al Capone.

The T.A.T. fantasies of urban Africans are full of Americanisms. In real life we find that traditional African nicknames have been changed by this influence—names, for example, like 'California' Serote, 'Baby Face' Sebidi, 'Kalamazoo' Kumalo and 'Killer' Mcwabein. African entertainment groups have come to adopt names of their American counterparts, names like 'The Boston Boys', 'The Haarlem Swingsters', 'The Jazz Maniacs' and the 'Manhattan Brothers'. In the sporting field, too, as America has her 'Babe'

Ruths and 'Rocky' Marcianos, so the urban townships have their 'Black Hawk' Hlubis, their 'School Boy' Nhlapos and their 'Iron Man' Mavusos.

The Urban African Personality shows Very Strong American Influence

The African peoples of the urban areas are drawn from members of all Bantu groups, and as a consequence most of them speak a number of Bantu languages, in addition to English and Afrikaans. Their familiarity with American films, advertising media, comics and literature has added a goodly portion of American slang to their vocabulary.

The 'tsotsis', the young criminal delinquents growing up in the townships, have developed a language of their own, a dialect born of a verbal mixture of the tongues of the Nguni, the Sotho and Shangana-Tonga groups, plus Afrikaans and English and a great many Americanisms.

This verbal conglomeration has also produced its own unique words and phrases, language elements whose derivations it is impossible to trace. This is 'Wittisha'—the language of the 'tsotsi'.

The urban Africans have assimilated 'Wittisha' words and phrases into their everyday speech. Today the vast majority of township youths, and very many of their elders, speak neither pure Zulu nor Sesotho, but a vernacular liberally sprinkled with 'Wittisha' words and phrases.

A Great many 'Wittisha' Words and Phrases have become incorporated into the Everyday Speech of the Urban African Population

This language is growing, for its main adherents are daily increasing their numbers.

> Tsotsism is spreading in a community which is socially ripe for it, where juvenile delinquency has become inevitable. It may be claimed that the tsotsi gang has come to stay and to spread. Already it embraces the whole of the Witwatersrand and Pretoria native areas. The fact that the gangs from one city operate in other cities has strongly stimulated the spread of the idea of tsotsism (Longmore).

The urban African loves to show off and attract attention. His form of exhibitionism is remarkably naïve and unsophisticated and tends to be immature in its conception and execution.

The urban African does not like half-measures—he is a character of extremes. When he engages in exhibitionism for effect—which he often does—his low level of inhibitions, and his relative lack of moderation, turn him into a blatantly immature exhibitionist.

The Personality of the Urban African

In the townships it is no unusual sight to see grown men dressed in complete cowboy uniforms; while the carrying of empty brief cases, for 'intellectual effect', is a universal township phenomenon.

This exhibitionistic streak, coupled with a lack of inhibitions, is undoubtedly a major contributory factor to making urban African T.A.T. fantasy productions such interesting reading.

This exhibitionistic element is obvious in urban African humour. The urban African loves to enact and relate comic stories. He appreciates most, jokes of the comic variety, farcical stories related with much gesticulation and action.

The Urban African Personality shows a Definite Exhibitionistic Trend

As a group the urban Africans are anti-Government, they definitely feel discriminated against and are generally suspicious of Europeans. They are outspokenly critical of urban policy—a criticism which tends generally to grow with the individual's educational advance—but they are, nevertheless, genuinely appreciative of the better environmental conditions prevailing in the new townships.

From our observations it would appear that the more urbanized and sophisticated the African community becomes, the more political consciousness they develop—this in itself is neither surprising nor unexpected. What is interesting, however, is that such urbanized communities seem to develop a 'being-discriminated-against' type of complex, with the result that their general perception has become so biased that in many instances they apperceive well-meaning European motives in a totally wrong light.

An excellent illustration of this 'being-discriminated-against' type of complex is found in the persistent rumours circulating the townships regarding the health services and clinics which have been established for the benefit of the inhabitants. Rumour has it that the medicines issued to the Africans are made from inferior ingredients. The Europeans, it is said, are receiving the best mixtures, while the African is getting poorer quality stuff.

The Johannesburg urban African has become very sensitive about his status. In Durban the less-sophisticated Africans spoke freely of 'the boss and his boy', in Johannesburg the same relationship was referred to as 'the employer and employee'. In Durban the term 'Bantu' was commonly used, in Johannesburg it was completely supplanted by the term African. In Durban, where the African is less certain of himself in 'urban society', he is relatively reserved and retiring; in Johannesburg, fewer inhibitions prevail and exhibitionism for effect is standard practice. In general, in Durban the black-white relationship is characterized by African obedience of a relatively

167

subservient master-servant relationship; in Johannesburg black-white race relations were critically viewed by a very 'discrimination-conscious' African population.

Urbanization and its Attendant Effects has tended to increase the African's Feeling of Being Discriminated Against

In the urban areas, with their many racial groups, the African has developed certain attitudes towards the question of race. These are characterized as follows: their attitude towards the Europeans as a group is one of antagonism born of frustration due to discriminatory practices (this frustration is primarily centred on the effects of the industrial colour-bar); to other African tribes their attitude is one of suspicion and a feeling of difference due to differences in tribal culture, upbringing and history. It must be stressed, however, that this feeling of tribal difference is tending to fade in the urban areas and, while it is still very apparent, it is by no means as established and dominant as it is in rural African society. As Ellen Hellmann has pointed out:

> Intermarriage is certainly tending to weaken the bonds of exclusive tribalism, and there is no doubt that urban residence is aiding in the elimination of intertribal mistrust and suspicion. But national consciousness is as yet a tender growth requiring careful nurture.

The urban African is not, nor will he ever be, completely europeanized—in the sense that he will become a white man with a black skin.

The urban Africans are undoubtedly the most articulate section of the whole African population. They are the section that will, as time progresses, increasingly provide the leadership for their people. As a group, their strongest motivating force is economic necessity, their anchor is tribal custom, and their ideal is the development of an Afro-European way of life.

Traditional Bantu culture is adjusting to the urban situation, but it is by no means undergoing a complete collapse. The communal personality components which have emerged in this modification include elements foreign to traditional culture-elements which have resulted as a consequence of the intermingling of the three important formative influences on the life of the urban African: tribal society, the urban township environment and Western European culture.

XIII

CONCLUSIONS

THE concept of social attitudes has assumed a fundamental position in the description and explanation of human behaviour. Attitudes are psychologically described as having conative, cognative and affective aspects—that is, an attitude is dynamic, purposive, and emotional in character. The presence of an attitude means that an individual is set to react in a definite, meaningful manner towards an object which, on account of the individual's previous experience with it, has an emotional value. An attitude is in fact a residuum of experience which conditions and controls activity.

In the development of attitudes, the cultural background and upbringing of the person plays a most important formative rôle. In studying the urban African we have seen the effects of the township environment upon his personality; we have noted also the strong tribal influences on his attitudinal formations. Traditional African society is fundamentally an established society, a society well-set in its cultural patterning, a society with traditionally-directed attitudes, organized and established over generations. The influence and continuing strength of these deeply rooted African cultural traditions and attitudes are often underestimated when considering the impact of the Western world on Africa.

In the tremendous changes taking place in Africa today, direction is being given by Western culture as well as by traditional African patterns of attitudes and mores. And while many tribal sanctions have become inoperative due to the clash of white and black cultures in the urban areas, the complete europeanization of the African personality and the absolute westernization of his attitudes will never occur. The urban African is, at this very moment, not only in the throes of adjusting to Western European society, but he is also in the process of virtually evolving his own cultural pattern from his attitudes to European society, coupled with aspects of his tribal past and elements of his traditional culture.

It is in the Johannesburg urban areas that this new African

personality is emerging most clearly, for it is here that the greatest cultural clash and the resulting marked cultural changes are taking place. It is in the urban areas that the concept of African advance finds its greatest impetus; it is here that what has so often been called the 'new Africa' is taking shape. The urban areas are the African political melting-pots of the Union, and the type of personality emerging from this cultural cauldron is of political and economic interest, as well as being of psychological and sociological significance.

We have observed the close tie-up between the personality and its social context—in certain cases an almost direct association. So much so that, if we could manipulate certain sociological factors, we could expect, in time, a resultant modification in the group personality structure.

We may argue, for example, that if some drastic steps were taken, with the full co-operation of the urban dwellers, to curb the lawless criminal element in the townships; that if relations between the police and the urban African were improved by a greater stress on courtesy, helpfulness and understanding on the part of the police; that if a deeper appreciation of police problems were brought about amongst the urban dwellers by means of a public relations pro-gramme; such sociological modifications would cause resultant modi-fications in the undercurrent of anxiety and insecurity within the African personality.

This is no Utopian ideal nor is it a hair-brained impracticable scheme—it is an essentially feasible, workable idea, following logic-ally on the recent police instructions from the Minister of Justice to employ more understanding in the application of the law regard-ing technical contraventions of the pass-laws.

Training courses for European police and, equally important, for African police (who, in accordance with governmental policy, are slowly taking control of African township stations) in such subjects as African criminology and, strange as it may seem, in human rela-tions, would not be out of place. Such human relations training, with the stress on African culture and personality, would do much to alleviate the unnecessary hurts which are so often caused by applying the pass regulations without sufficient understanding of the human problems involved, but rather in a spirit of the 'letter of the law'.

The complete elimination of the 'pass system' which has been suggested by various bodies is a problem fraught with difficulties. To summarily sweep aside such a system may satisfy many a moral conscience, but only at the expense of the social chaos which would result. As it is a problem which concerns both the Africans as well as the Europeans, joint consultation between the two parties con-cerned in this problem is surely an essential prerequisite to the making of any future decision or policy regarding it. It is a sad fact that the Europeans in the Union tend to completely disregard the African viewpoint in such questions—a state of affairs which results not so much from European bias as from European ignorance.

A programme of European re-education is required if we are to have an alteration in traditional attitudes and are to break down the European barrier of ignorance about the African. Bantu language courses should be introduced as compulsory subjects in all European schools, while the present South African history syllabus, which deals largely with 'Kaffir Wars', should be altered to include a greater stress on African custom and history. The system recently introduced into the Civil Service, whereby staff are given a bonus on passing a proficiency test in one of the main Bantu languages, should be expanded to all spheres of South African commerce and industry. The newspapers and the radio can give impetus to such a campaign by the introduction of a Bantu language training course as a regular daily feature. The possibility of obtaining an organization to sponsor such a language feature may well be investigated by the commercial radio service 'Springbok Radio'.

Regarding the problem of African wages, one can do no better than quote what Franklin has to say in the opening paragraph of his *Economics in South Africa:*

> The legend that South Africa is a rich country possesses remarkable powers of survival. It is true that the Union possesses exceptionally rich mineral deposits. It is also true that industrial development has proceeded extremely rapidly in recent years and that the national income has increased by leaps and bounds. Yet, if the test of the wealth of a country is the average standard of living of its people, no legend is less true. Notwithstanding the prosperity of most of the white population, the great mass of the people of this country live in conditions of degrading poverty.

It is considered that urban Africans should be paid higher wages, but to reap the greatest benefit from such increases—from both the African's point of view and that of his employers—the application of such wage increases will have to be approached on a far broader basis than has hitherto been the case.

An increase in the minimum wage is very necessary to bring the income of the urban African labourer up to a level where he can obtain the basic necessities for his family. But any general raising of wages for the urban African community as a whole should be accompanied by a widespread campaign for teaching the principles of diet and family budgeting to help the African to spend his money more wisely.

Furthermore, industrialists would be well advised to pay considerably more attention to the establishment of systematic wage progression scales for their urban African workers than they are wont to do. The urban African money drive will be utilized to the best possible advantage if it has the encouragement of a wider wage progression scale, rather than simply a general increase in wages 'up to the breadline', with little prospect of achieving *more* money after that: and *more* is the operative word in this instance.

Wage progression scales will naturally have to be systematically established; while such a programme, to be fully successful, will have to be approached on a national scale, with full governmental backing and support. The radio would be one ideal public-relations medium for the dissemination of dietary and budgetary education.

An increase not only in wage progression scales but also an increase in the range of jobs available to educated Africans (UNESCO reports that the Union has one of the highest literacy rates in Africa —63 per cent in 1956) would do much to alleviate the frustrating effects of the industrial colour-bar—effects which are so damning to the maintenance of good race relations.

The educated African must be given an outlet. He has become educated to increase his earning potential and, if he cannot do so, he will turn either to crime (many of the 'tsotsis' are well-educated youths) or become disgruntled, frustrated and an agitator.

The urban African tends towards immature attitudes and an exhibitionistic approach, but such functions in no way imply that he will not respond to understanding and tactful handling. He has still much to learn, especially in the spheres of emotional moderation and control. His alterations in emotional states are frightening in their suddenness, his ideas are rather egoistically biased, and education tends to make him feel disproportionately superior—but he is learning.

The problem which the Europeans in South Africa must face, is what to do with those Africans whose learning has given them ambitions beyond the industrial colour-bar. Ambitions need outlets if their latent energies are not to be diverted by continual frustration into anti-social activities.

The Europeans, like the urban Africans, are living not in a traditional society but in what is essentially an adaptive society, and life in an adaptive society requires flexibility of both attitude and approach. What Franklin has called the 'conventional element' in the maintenance of the industrial colour-bar will have to be superseded by a more flexible approach. Whether this relaxation of the industrial colour-bar will find its solution in a process of separate development for Africans, or by integrating them wholly into the urban industrial set-up, only time can tell. Either way, the Europeans will have to show more attitudinal flexibility towards the educated African as such and to the urban African in general.

This study of the urban African personality has revealed the strength of tribal customs, it has stressed the important influence of his tribal past upon the urban African's present beliefs and adjustments. It has emphasized the truth of the statement of Bascom and Herskovits that, 'the rapidity with which the impact of the Western world is taking effect in Africa is so obvious that the continuing strength of Africa's own deeply rooted cultural traditions is often underestimated'.

In Africa as a whole, tribalism is the predominating force, and while nationalistic movements tend to gain prominence in the European Press, possibly because of their news value, the tribe is still the basic unit in African society. Sir Andrew Cohen, formerly Governor of Uganda, delivering the Harris Lectures at Northwestern University in 1958, considered the position as follows: 'In the part of Africa I know best, nationalism so far is less powerful than tribalism, and this is natural, since it is a recent growth, whereas tribalism is deeply rooted in custom and tradition.' In the Gold Coast tribalism caused difficulties between the Central Government and the Ashanti tribe soon after the ministerial system was set up, difficulties which have persisted ever since. Tribal affiliations have dominated Nigerian politics for years and we have recently witnessed the results of tribal frictions in the emergent independent Congo states. Only recently, too, the world was shocked by the brutal and perverted Mau Mau tribal reversions of the Kikuyu tribe in Kenya. While in Tanganyika the problem of tribal associations and tribal administration is one of the fundamental problems which the envisaged independent central government of this territory will have to face. In South Africa, faction fights are common, especially between the various tribes and sub-tribes of the Nguni-speaking peoples of the Union. The tribal frictions which occur in the urban areas of Johannesburg are consequently neither unique nor particularly unexpected.

The nationalist in Africa is, as often as not, initially regarded by the traditional society with suspicion and sometimes even hostility —a suspicion which he allays and a hostility which he appeases, by stressing African independence from European domination, by appealing to the stereotypical concept of 'freedom'. As Cohen has said of the nationalistic movements in both West and East Africa: 'nationalistic movements are racial in the sense that they are movements by Africans for independence from European control', but, he adds, ultimately, 'while no one would deny the importance of racial problems, it may turn out that problems of adjustment between the tribe and the nation are even more important'. An importance which applies equally well to the vast majority of emergent African states.

In the political field it would appear that the ultimate difficulty in Africa will be to reconcile the past with the present, to reconcile tribalism with nationalism. The success of this transition, the ability to bridge this cultural gap and, to a very large extent, the establishment of democratic rule in Africa, will depend ultimately on the ability of Africans to reconcile these two opposing views. In such a process the nationalist is an important link. A human link that can pave the way to democratic national unity on the one hand, or that can, by dictatorial misrule, promote tribal sectionarism and national disunity on the other. By virtue of its tribal structure African society —and this applies especially to the strongly tribal central African states presently gaining independence—will tend to react to an African dictatorship by reverting to the most stable and secure social unit it knows—the tribe. When they have gained their independence, when the cry of 'freedom' is but a hollow echo of the past, when the domination of the white man is gone, when the nationalist has lost his main unifying message, then his real problem will begin: the problem of how to unite and mould into one nation peoples separated from one another by the strong bonds of tribal tradition and custom. As Sir Andrew Cohen has stated of the nationalist:

> He feels emotionally that with independence he and his fellows will be able to bridge this gap, but he knows in his mind that this will be a hard, long, and difficult task and that help from outside experts of all kinds will be needed for a very long time even after independence.

His is a function of the utmost importance to the future of Africa, a function in which a solid background and training in the principles of democratic government are essential, if it is hoped to perpetuate democracy in Africa, to develop a national unity in the various African states and to break down the bonds of tribalism. It seems a strange contradiction in present-day Africa that the colonial governments, who have spent millions of pounds giving the native peoples academic, technical and professional skills, have spent virtually nothing on a training programme organized to impart the human relations skills so basic to the establishment of democratic institutions.

> Neither the building up of the institutions of modern countries, nor the increasing of national wealth, nor even the growth of knowledge will achieve effective results without the development of the human potential in Africa. The most important part of building a nation is the production of leaders . . . (Sir Andrew Cohen).

In the emergent Africa, the need for leaders is great, the need for leaders trained in the fundamentals of democratic government, in the principles of co-operation, is essential if these new states are to function as national unities and not disintegrate into tribal sectionarism.

Present-day African leaders have come, for the most, from the urbanized class. Such urbanization, however, has tended to promote a feeling of rabid nationalism in these people.

In South Africa, the country in Africa with the largest European minority and possibly the largest urban African population, the position is rapidly being reached where the urban Africans are becoming almost obsessed with feelings of being discriminated against. Feelings which are hardly conducive to the promotion of racial harmony, let alone to the appreciation of democratic principles. For democracy, as such, is as much a way of thinking as it is a way of life.

In this book we have presented an overview of contemporary urban African life and thought, as it has developed in the vast African townships which sprawl along the line of the Witwatersrand gold-bearing reef. It is a type of life and thought of which the average man, both in South Africa and overseas, knows very little. Yet it is a way of living, and of thinking, which will exert an increasingly strong pressure on the future of South Africa and, it is ventured, on the future development and promotion of the democratic ideal in Africa as a whole.

SELECTED BIBLIOGRAPHY

1. HAILEY, LORD *An African Survey.* Revised 1956. Oxford University Press, London, 1957.
2. SELIGMAN, C. G. *Races of Africa.* Third Edition. Oxford University Press, London, 1957.
3. BASCOM, W. R. and HERSKOVITS, M. J. *Continuity and Change in African Cultures.* The University of Chicago Press, 1959.
4. FRANKLIN, N. N. *Economics in South Africa.* Second Edition. Oxford University Press, 1954.
5. MALINOWSKI, B. *Sex and Repression in Savage Society.* Routledge and Kegan Paul Ltd., London, 1927.
6. LINTON, R. *The Cultural Background of Personality.* Routledge and Kegan Paul Ltd., London, 1947.
7. BREUTZ, P. L. *The Tribes of Mafeking District.* The Government Printer, Pretoria, South Africa, 1956.
8. KRIGE, E. J. *The Social System of the Zulus.* Shuter and Shooter, Pietermaritzburg, South Africa, 1957.
9. ASHTON, H. *The Basuto.* Oxford University Press, London, 1952.
10. KUPER, H. *The Swazi.* International African Institute, London, 1952.
11. SCHAPERA, I. *The Bantu-Speaking Tribes of South Africa.* Routledge and Kegan Paul, London, 1937.
12. PHILLIPS, H. *Survey of African Marriage and Family Life.* Oxford University Press, London, 1953.
13. LONGMORE, L. *The Dispossessed.* Jonathan Cape, London, 1959.
14. CAROTHERS, J. C. *The African Mind in Health and Disease.* World Health Organisation, Geneva, 1953.
15. KUPER, L., WATTS, H. and DAVIES, R. *Durban—A Study in Racial Ecology.* Jonathan Cape, London, 1958.
16. MASON, P. *An Essay on Racial Tension.* Royal Institute of International Affairs, London and New York, 1954.
17. PARRINDER, E. G. *African Traditional Religion.* Hutchinson's University Library, London, 1954.
18. LIFE EDITORIAL STAFF. *The World's Great Religions.* Collins, London, 1959.
19. BRAM, J. *Language and Society.* Doubleday and Company, Inc., New York, 1955.
20. BELLAK, L. *The Thematic Apperception Test and the Children's Apperception Test in Clinical Use.* Grune and Stratton, New York, 1954.
21. TOMKINS, S. S. *The Thematic Apperception Test.* Grune and Stratton, New York, 1955.

Selected Bibliography

22. STEIN, M. I. *The Thematic Apperception Test.* Addison-Wesley Publishing Company, Inc., Cambridge 42, Mass., 1955.
23. BELL, J. E. *Projective Techniques.* Longmans, Green and Co., New York, 1948.
24. ANDERSON, H. H. and ANDERSON, G. I. *Projective Techniques.* Prentice-Hall, Inc., New York, 1951.
25. HARVARD PSYCHOLOGICAL CLINIC. *Explorations in Personality.* Oxford University Press, 1953.
26. WITKIN, H. A. *Personality Through Perception.* Harper and Brothers, New York, 1954.
27. BRUNER, J. S. and KRECH, D. *Perception and Personality.* Duke University Press, North Carolina, 1950.
28. TAGIURI, R. and PETRULLO, L. *Person Perception and Interpersonal Behaviour.* Stanford University Press, California, 1958.
29. ROUCEK, J. S. and WARREN, R. L. *Sociology—an Introduction.* Littlefield, Adams & Co., Iowa, 1957.
30. ALLPORT, G. W. *Personality—A Psychological Interpretation.* Constable and Company Ltd., London, 1949.
31. RUTHERFORD, P. *Darkness and Light—An Anthology of African Writing.* Faith Press, London, 1958.
32. MKELE, N. 'The African as a Buyer', *The Southern African Financial Mail*, 22 January 1960, Volume II, No. 2.

INDEX

178

Index

The International Library of
Sociology
and Social Reconstruction

Edited by W. J. H. SPROTT
Founded by KARL MANNHEIM

ROUTLEDGE & KEGAN PAUL
BROADWAY HOUSE, CARTER LANE, LONDON, E.C.4

CONTENTS

SOCIOLOGY OF EDUCATION

Mission of the University
JOSÉ ORTEGA Y GASSET. Translated and introduced by Howard
Lee Nostrand   *Second Impression.* 12*s.* 6*d.*

Total Education
A Plea for Synthesis
M. L. JACKS, *Director of the Institute of Education, Oxford*   16*s.*

The Social Psychology of Education
An Introduction and Guide to its Study
C. M. FLEMING, *Reader in Education, Institute of Education, London* 11*s.*

Education and Society in Modern Germany
R. H. SAMUEL, *Professor of Germanic Languages, Melbourne,* and
R. HINTON THOMAS, *Lecturer in German, Birmingham*   16*s.*

The Museum
Its History and Its Tasks in Education
ALMA S. WITTLIN   *Illustrated.* 28*s.*

The Educational Thought and Influence of Matthew Arnold
W. F. CONNELL, *Senior Lecturer in Education, Sydney.*   With an Introduction by Sir Fred Clarke   23*s.*

Comparative Education
A Study of Educational Factors and Traditions
NICHOLAS HANS, *Institute of Education, London*   23*s.*

New Trends in Education in the 18th Century
NICHOLAS HANS   25*s.*

From School to University
A Study, with special reference to University Entrance
R. R. DALE, *Lecturer in Education, University College, Swansea*   21*s.*

Adult Education
A Comparative Study
ROBERT PEERS   35*s.*

Education and Society
An Introduction to the Sociology of Education
A. K. C. OTTAWAY, *Lecturer in Education, Leeds.*   With an Introduc-
tion by W. O. Lester Smith   *Third Impression.* 18*s.*

Parity and Prestige in English Secondary Education
OLIVE BANKS, *Lecturer in Sociology, Liverpool* 25s.

Helvetius
His Life and Place in the History of Educational Thought
IAN CUMMING, *Senior Lecturer in Education, Auckland* 25s.

Adolescence
Its Social Psychology: With an Introduction to recent findings from the fields of Anthropology, Physiology, Medicine, Psychometrics and Sociometry
C. M. FLEMING *Fifth Impression.* 18s.

Studies in the Social Psychology of Adolescence
J. E. RICHARDSON, J. F. FORRESTER, J. K. SHUKLA and P. J. HIGGINBOTHAM
Edited by C. M. FLEMING 23s.

From Generation to Generation
Age Groups and Social Structure
S. N. EISENSTADT, *Head of the Department of Sociology, Hebrew University, Jerusalem* 42s.

The Social Purposes of Education
K. G. COLLIER 21s.

SOCIOLOGY OF RELIGION
The Economic Order and Religion
FRANK KNIGHT, *Professor of Social Science, Chicago,* and THORNTON W. MERRIAM 18s.

Religious Behaviour
MICHAEL ARGYLE, *Lecturer in Social Psychology, Oxford* 25s.

Islam and the Integration of Society
W. MONTGOMERY WATT, *Reader in Arabic, University of Edinburgh* 32s.

SOCIOLOGY OF ART AND LITERATURE
Chekhov and His Russia: A Sociological Study
W. H. BRUFORD, *Schröder Professor of German, Cambridge* 18s.

The Sociology of Literary Taste
LEVIN L. SCHÜCKING *Third Impression.* 9s. 6d.

Men of Letters and the English Public in the 18th Century,
1660–1744, Dryden, Addison, Pope
ALEXANDRE BELJAME, Edited with an Introduction and Notes by
Bonamy Dobrée. Translated by E. O. Lorimer   28s.

SOCIOLOGICAL APPROACH TO THE STUDY OF HISTORY

The Aftermath of the Napoleonic Wars
The Concert of Europe—An Experiment
H. G. SCHENK, *Lecturer in Political Economics, Fellow of Exeter College,*
Oxford   *Illustrated.* 18s.

Military Organization and Society
STANISLAW ANDRZEJEWSKI. Foreword by A. Radcliffe-Brown 21s.

Population Theories and the Economic Interpretation
SYDNEY COONTZ, *Assistant Professor in Forest Economics, State*
University of New York, Syracuse   25s.

Social Change in the Industrial Revolution
An Application of Theory to the Lancashire Cotton Industry, 1770–1840
NEIL J. SMELSER, *University of California, Berkeley*   40s.

SOCIOLOGY OF LAW

Sociology of Law
GEORGES GURVITCH, *Professor of Sociology, Sorbonne.* With an
Introduction by Roscoe Pound   *Second Impression.* 21s.

The Institutions of Private Law and their Social Functions
KARL RENNER. Edited with an Introduction and Notes by O. Kahn-
Freund   28s.

Legal Aid
ROBERT EGERTON. With an Introduction by A. L. Goodhart
                                          Second Impression. 12s. 6d.

CRIMINOLOGY

Criminal Justice and Social Reconstruction
HERMANN MANNHEIM   *Second Impression.* 20s.

Social Policies for Old Age
B. E. SHENFIELD, *Lecturer in Social Studies, University of Birmingham*   25s.

Voluntary Societies and Social Policy
MADELINE ROOFF, *Lecturer in Social Policy and Social Administration at Bedford College, London*   35s.

Children in Care
The Development of the Service for the Deprived Child
JEAN S. HEYWOOD   25s.

In Place of Parents
A Study of Foster Care
GORDON TRASLER, *Lecturer in Social Psychology, University of Southampton*   25s.

SOCIOLOGY AND POLITICS

Social-Economic Movements
An Historical and Comparative Survey of Socialism, Communism, Co-operation, Utopianism; and Other Systems of Reform and Reconstruction
H. W. LAIDLER   *Illustrated.*   45s.

Dictatorship and Political Police
The Technique of Control by Fear
E. K. BRAMSTEDT   20s.

Nationality in History and Politics
A Psychology and Sociology of National Sentiment and Nationalism
FRIEDRICH HERTZ   *Fourth Impression.*   32s.

The Logic of Liberty: Reflections and Rejoinders
MICHAEL POLANYI, F.R.S.,   18s.

The Analysis of Political Systems
DOUGLAS V. VERNEY, *Lecturer in Government, University of Liverpool*   28s.

The Political Element in the Development of Economic Theory
GUNNAR MYRDAL. Translated by Paul Streeten   25s.

6

Higher Civil Servants in Britain
From 1870 to the Present Day
R. K. KELSALL, *Head of the School of Social Studies, Sheffield* 25s.

Democracy and Dictatorship
Their Psychology and Patterns of Life
Z. BARBU, *Lecturer in Social Psychology, Glasgow* 28s.

How People Vote
A Study of Electoral Behaviour in Greenwich
MARK BENNEY, A. P. GRAY, and R. H. PEAR 25s.

Economy and Society
A Study in the Integration of Economic and Social Theory
TALCOTT PARSONS, *Chairman of the Department of Social Relations, Harvard*, and NEIL J. SMELSER *Second Impression.* 35s.

The Functions of Social Conflict
LEWIS COSER, *Associate Professor of Sociology, California* 18s.

The American Science of Politics
BERNARD CRICK 28s.

The Politics of Mass Society
WILLIAM KORNHAUSER 25s.

FOREIGN AFFAIRS, THEIR SOCIAL, POLITICAL & ECONOMIC FOUNDATIONS

Patterns of Peacemaking
DAVID THOMSON, *Research Fellow, Sidney Sussex College, Cambridge*, E. MEYER and ASA BRIGGS, *Professor of History, Leeds* 25s.

French Canada in Transition
EVERETT C. HUGHES, *Professor of Sociology, Chicago* 16s.

State and Economics in the Middle East
A Society in Transition
A. BONNÉ, *Professor of Economics. Director, Economic Research Institute, Hebrew University, Jerusalem* *Second Edition (Revised).* 40s.

The Economic Development of the Middle East
An Outline of Planned Reconstruction
A. BONNÉ *Third Impression.* 16s.

Studies in Economic Development
With special reference to conditions in the Underdeveloped Areas in Western Asia and India
ALFRED BONNÉ   32s.

Peasant Renaissance in Yugoslavia, 1900-1950
A Study of the Development of Yugoslav Peasant Society as Affected by Education
RUTH TROUTON   28s.

Transitional Economic Systems
The Polish-Czech Example
DOROTHY W. DOUGLAS   25s.

Political Thought in France from the Revolution to the Fifth Republic
J. P. MAYER   14s.

Central European Democracy and its Background
Economic and Political Group Organization
RUDOLF SCHLESINGER   30s.

ECONOMIC PLANNING
Private Corporations and their Control
A. B. LEVY   Two Volumes. 70s. the set

The Shops of Britain
A Study of Retail Distribution
HERMANN LEVY   Second Impression. 21s.

SOCIOLOGY OF THE FAMILY AND
ALLIED TOPICS
The Family and Democratic Society
J. K. FOLSOM, *Professor of Economics, Vassar College*   35s.

Nation and Family
The Swedish Experiment in Democratic Family and Population Policy
ALVA MYRDAL, *Swedish Ambassador to India*   28s.

The Deprived and the Privileged
Personality Development in English Society
B. M. SPINLEY, *Educational Psychologist, Sheffield Child Guidance Clinic* 20s.

Prosperity and Parenthood
J. A. BANKS, *Lecturer in Sociology, Liverpool*   21s.

Family, Socialization and Interaction Process
TALCOTT PARSONS and ROBERT F. BALES   30s

The Home and Social Status
DENNIS CHAPMAN, *Senior Lecturer in Social Science, Liverpool*
           119 *tables, diagrams and plates,* 35s.

Women's Two Roles: Home and Work
ALVA MYRDAL and VIOLA KLEIN   25s.

The People of Ship Street
MADELEINE KERR   23s.

TOWN AND COUNTRY PLANNING
HUMAN ECOLOGY

The Social Background of a Plan: A Study of Middlesbrough
Edited by RUTH GLASS. With Maps and Plans   42s.

City, Region and Regionalism
A Geographical Contribution to Human Ecology
ROBERT E. DICKINSON. With Maps and Plans   25s.

The West European City: A Study in Urban Geography
ROBERT E. DICKINSON. With Maps and Plans   42s.

Revolution of Environment
E. A. GUTKIND   *Illustrated.* 32s.

The Journey to Work
Its Significance for Industrial and Community Life
K. LIEPMANN, *Research Fellow in Economics, Bristol.* With a Foreword
by Sir Alexander Carr-Saunders   *Second Impression* 16s.

Stevenage: A Sociological Study of a New Town
HAROLD ORLANS   30s.

The Genesis of Modern British Town Planning
A Study in Economic and Social History of the Nineteenth and Twentieth
Centuries
W. ASHWORTH, *Professor of History, London School of Economics*   21s.

SOCIOLOGY AND PSYCHOLOGY OF THE PRESENT CRISIS

Diagnosis of Our Time
Wartime Essays of a Sociologist
KARL MANNHEIM   *Sixth Impression.* 18s.

Farewell to European History or the Conquest of Nihilism
ALFRED WEBER   18s.

The Fear of Freedom
ERICH FROMM   *Seventh Impression.* 21s.

The Sane Society
ERICH FROMM   28s.

Freedom, Power, and Democratic Planning
KARL MANNHEIM. Edited by Hans Gerth and E. K. Bramstedt 28s.

Essays on Sociology and Social Psychology
KARL MANNHEIM. Edited by Paul Kecskemeti   30s.

Essays on the Sociology of Culture
KARL MANNHEIM. Edited by Ernest Manheim and Paul
Kecskemeti   28s.

SOCIAL PSYCHOLOGY AND PSYCHO-ANALYSIS

Psychology and the Social Pattern
JULIAN BLACKBURN, *Associate Professor of Psychology, McGill University, Canada*   *Fifth Impression.* 14s.

The Framework of Human Behaviour
JULIAN BLACKBURN   *Second Impression.* 15s.

A Handbook of Social Psychology
KIMBALL YOUNG, *Professor of Sociology, North-western University*
                                 Revised edition. 35s.

Solitude and Privacy
A Study of Social Isolation, Its Causes and Therapy
PAUL HALMOS, *Lecturer in Psychology, University College of N. Staffs.* 21s.

The Human Group
GEORGE C. HOMANS, *Associate Professor of Sociology, Harvard* 28s.

Sigmund Freud: An Introduction

A Presentation of his Theories and a Discussion of the Relationship between Psycho-analysis and Sociology
WALTER HOLLITSCHER   *Second Impression.*   12s.

The Social Problems of an Industrial Civilization

ELTON MAYO   *Second Impression.*   15s.

Oppression

A Study in Social and Criminal Psychology
TADEUSZ GRYGIER. Foreword by Hermann Mannheim   28s.

Mental Health and Mental Disorder

A Sociological Approach
Edited by ARNOLD M. ROSE, *University of Minnesota*   40s.

Disaster

A Psychological Essay
MARTHA WOLFENSTEIN   23s.

APPROACHES TO THE PROBLEM OF PERSONALITY

The Cultural Background of Personality

RALPH LINTON, *Prof. of Anthropology, Yale.*   *Fourth Impression.*   14s.

The Feminine Character: History of an Ideology

VIOLA KLEIN. With an Introduction by Karl Mannheim   16s.

A History of Autobiography in Antiquity

GEORG MISCH, *Professor of Philosophy, Göttingen*, Translated by E. W. Dickes.   *Two volumes.*   45s. *the set*

Personality and Problems of Adjustment

KIMBALL YOUNG   *Second Edition (Revised).*   40s.

Towards a Measure of Man

The Frontiers of Normal Adjustment
PAUL HALMOS   28s.

Problems of Historical Psychology

ZEVEDEI BARBU   25s.

PHILOSOPHICAL AND SOCIAL FOUNDATIONS OF THOUGHT

The Ideal Foundations of Economic Thought

Three Essays on the Philosophy of Economics
WERNER STARK, *Reader in Economics, Manchester*
                                        Third Impression.   16s.

The History of Economics in its Relation to Social
Development
WERNER STARK   *Fourth Impression.* 12s.

America: Ideal and Reality
The United States of 1776 in Contemporary European Philosophy
WERNER STARK   12s.

Society and Nature: A Sociological Inquiry
HANS KELSEN, *Department of Political Science, California*   25s.

Marx: His Time and Ours
R. SCHLESINGER   *Second Impression.* 32s.

The Philosophy of Wilhelm Dilthey
H. A. HODGES, *Professor of Philosophy, Reading*   30s.

Essays on the Sociology of Knowledge
KARL MANNHEIM   35s.

The Sociology of Knowledge
WERNER STARK   36s.

Montesquieu
Pioneer in the Sociology of Knowledge
WERNER STARK   25s.

The Nature and Types of Sociological Theory
DON MARTINDALE, *University of Minnesota*   *In preparation*

GENERAL SOCIOLOGY

A Handbook of Sociology
W. F. OGBURN, and M. F. NIMKOFF   *Fourth Edition (Revised).* 35s.

Social Organization
ROBERT H. LOWIE, *late Professor of Anthropology, Chicago*   35s.

Professional Ethics and Civic Morals
EMILE DURKHEIM. Translated by Cornelia Brookfield   30s.

Systematic Sociology
KARL MANNHEIM
Edited by W. A. C. STEWART and J. S. EROS   24s.

15

Value in Social Theory
GUNNAR MYRDAL   32*s*.

The Logic of Social Enquiry
QUENTIN GIBSON, *Senior Lecturer in Philosophy, Canberra University College*   24*s*.

Sociology: A Systematic Introduction
HARRY M. JOHNSON   42*s*.

FOREIGN CLASSICS OF SOCIOLOGY

Wilhelm Dilthey: An Introduction
A comprehensive account of his sociological and philosophical work, with translations of selected passages.
H. A. HODGES   *Second Impression.* 14*s*.

From Max Weber: Essays in Sociology
Translated, Edited and with an Introduction by H. H. GERTH and C. W. MILLS   *Third Impression.* 28*s*.

Suicide: A Study in Sociology
EMILE DURKHEIM. Translated by J. A. Spaulding and George Simpson   28*s*.

Community and Association
FERDINAND TONNIES. Edited and supplemented by Charles P. Loomis   25*s*.

Socialism and Saint-Simon
EMILE DURKHEIM, *Preface by Marcel Mauss*   28*s*.

DOCUMENTARY

Changing Attitudes in Soviet Russia
Documents and Readings. Edited with an Introduction by
RUDOLF SCHLESINGER
Volume 1: *The Family in the U.S.S.R.*   30*s*.
Volume 2: *The Nationalities Problem and Soviet Administration*   30*s*.

Psychology in the Soviet Union
BRIAN SIMON, *Lecturer in Education, University College, Leicester* 32*s*.

Soviet Youth: Some Achievements and Problems
Excerpts from the Soviet Press
Edited and translated by DOROTHEA L. MEEK   28*s*.

All prices are net and subject to alteration without notice